GLOBALIZATION, GENDER, AND RELIGION

THE POLITICS OF WOMEN'S RIGHTS IN CATHOLIC AND MUSLIM CONTEXTS

EDITED BY
JANE H. BAYES
AND NAYEREH TOHIDI

GLOBALIZATION, GENDER, AND RELIGION

First published 2001 by
PALGRAVE
175 Fifth Avenue, New York, N.Y.10010 and
Houndmills, Basingstoke, Hampshire RG21 6XS.
Companies and representatives throughout the world

PALGRAVE is the new global publishing imprint of St. Martin's Press
LLC Scholarly and Reference Division and Palgrave Publishers Ltd
(formerly Macmillan Press Ltd).

ISBN 0-312-22812-0 hardback
ISBN 0-312-29369-0 paperback

Library of Congress Cataloging-in-Publication Data
    Globalization, gender, and religion: the politics of implementing
women's rights in Catholic and Muslim contexts / edited by Jane H. Bayes
and Nayereh Tohidi.
        p.   cm.
    Includes bibliographical references and index.
    ISBN 0-312-22812-0—ISBN 0-312-29369-0 (pbk.)
    1. Women's rights—Cross cultural studies.   2. Women in the
Catholic Church.   3. Women in Islam.   4. Globalization.   I. Bayes,
Jane H., 1939–   II. Tohidi, Nayereh Esfahlani, 1951–

HQ1236.G54   2001
305.42—dc21

                                                                    2001031735

A catalogue record for this book is available from the British Library.

Design by Letra Libre, Inc.

First edition: November 2001
10 9 8 7 6 5 4 3 2 1

Printed in the United States of America.

CONTENTS

ACKNOWLEDGMENTS

The impetus for this book came from the United Nations Fourth World Conference on Women held in Beijing, China in 1995. Five of our contributors attended the 1995 Beijing conference, two as members of their official government delegations, (Najma Chowdhury and Laura Guzmán Stein), and three as non-governmental organization (NGO) delegates (Ayşe Güneş-Ayata, Nayereh Tohidi, and Jane Bayes). Our first international gathering to discuss this project occurred in Seoul, Korea at the International Political Science Association meetings in July 1997. A second meeting occurred at the Middle-East Technical University in Ankara, Turkey in 1998. For financial and other support in making these meetings possible, we are grateful to the International Political Science Association, the Middle East Technical University, Ankara, and the College of Social and Behavioral Sciences and the College of the Humanities at California State University, Northridge.

Many have contributed to this project other than those named. Shahla Sherkat joined us for our meetings in Turkey where she shared with us her experiences as founder and editor of the Iranian women's magazine, *Zanan*. As a Muslim feminist lawyer and advocate of human rights in Iran, Shirin Ebadi graciously responded to our queries about a number of legal and intellectual issues concerning the women's rights movement under the Islamic Republic of Iran. Eloise Buker of Denison College, Mary Hawkesworth of Rutgers University, and Rita Mae Kelly of the University of Texas read, critiqued, and made helpful suggestions for early versions of parts of the introductory chapters. The editors are most grateful to Linda Moody of Mills College, Elizabeth Say of California State University, Northridge, and Eloise Buker for their helpful comments, opinions, and suggestions on the later version of the two introductory chapters. To Nikki Keddie, we offer our special thanks for her careful and thoughtful reading of the manuscript and for her particularly insightful suggestions. Alana Powell, a graduate student at CSUN, was of invaluable service in helping to edit the manuscript as was Mahnaz Towhidi in helping with the translation of chapter 8 from Persian into English. This manuscript has also benefited from the feedback and comments we have received from our students who read some of the chapters before its final publication.

During the course of this project, one of our authors, Merhanguiz Kar, has been arrested, jailed, and charged with treason by the Iranian regime for her critique of the discriminatory laws against women and the violation of women's human rights under the Islamic Republic of Iran. She is currently released on bail and awaiting another trial in Iran. It is to her, her courage, her resilience, and her enormous contributions to the democracy movement in her own country, and to all the other brave and dedicated women in different parts of the world who are in the forefront of the struggle for women's human rights and empowerment, that we dedicate this book.

LIST OF ACRONYMS

AIM	Action, Information, Motivation
AVAW	Spanish central state policies against violence against women
AWGA	Association of Women's Global Alliance
CEDAW	Convention for the Elimination of All Forms of Discrimination Against Women
CFFC	Catholics for a Free Choice
CIDA	Canadian International Development Agency
Col.	Colorado
CONAPO	National Committee on Population
Conn.	Connecticut
CSW	United Nations Commission on the Legal and Social Status of Women
DANIDA	Danish International Development Assistance
DGPSW	Department General for the Problems and Status of Women
DSCSD	United Nations Department for Policy Coordination and Sustainable Development
EU	European Union
FGM	Female Genital Mutilation
FWCW	the United Nations Fourth World Conference on Women held in Beijing, China in 1995
HCCR	High Council of Cultural Revolution
ICA	Irish Countrywomen's Association
IPPF	International Family Planning Federation
IWO	Iranian Women's Organization
NGO	non-governmental organization
Mass.	Massachussets
MEC	Ministry of Education and Culture
NGOPC	Bangladesh National Preparatory Committee Toward Beijing

N.J.	New Jersey
N.Y.	New York
NWCI	National Women's Council of Ireland
PFA	Platform for Action at the United Nations Fourth World Congress on Women in Beijing in 1995
PIOMH	Plan for Gender Equity Among Men and Women
PLAGE	Policy Leadership and Advocacy for Gender Equality
PLAU	Policy Leadership and Advocacy Unit
PREPCOM	United Nations Preparatory Committee for Fourth World Conference on Women
SNAT	Sectoral Needs Assessment Team
SNJM	Sisters of the Holy Names of Jesus and Mary
UK	United Kingdom
UN	United Nations
UNFPA	United Nations Fund for Population Activities
UNICEF	United Nations Children's Fund
USAID	United States Agency for International Development
USCC	United States Catholic Conference
WID	Women in International Development

CHAPTER 1

INTRODUCTION

Jane H. Bayes and Nayereh Tohidi

Conflict in Beijing

Unlike the previous world conferences on women, the 1995 United Nations Fourth World Conference on Women in Beijing, held in the post–Cold War context, was not characterized by intense ideological disputes over grand theories or between the left and right. This was a more action-oriented conference, with practical solutions and pragmatic compromises overriding theory and ideology. The final document of the conference, the Platform for Action, reflects this orientation. Yet, during the preparatory sessions as well as at this historic conference itself, two important trends that reflected certain old international divisions of political, cultural (especially religious), and economic nature became more prominent. The first was related to a new transnational and cross-cultural conservative and religious alliance against equal rights for women, and the second concerned the growing implications of globalization for women and gender politics.

The first trend was the display of a major split among the delegates around issues of sexuality and sexual orientation, women's control of their bodies—including abortion rights—as well as over questions of equity versus equality and sex versus gender. The intensity of this controversy surprised many at the conference and many in the global women's movement. That an alliance of some Catholic and some Muslim delegations led by the Vatican (the Holy See) were united as a bloc in lobbying for a unified position on these issues was the news of the conference (Moghadam 1995; Woodman 1995; Tohidi 1996; Afkhami & Friedl 1997).[1]

As participants in the Beijing conference, we were intrigued by these new trends and have been exploring their historic, sociological, cultural, and political roots and dimensions. Why should some Catholics unite with some Muslims against equal rights for women? Why do some groups of men and especially women keep emphasizing male-female differences rather than similarities? Why do these men and women continue to advocate male supremacy rather than gender egalitarianism and why do they oppose equal rights for men and women? These questions led us to some even broader issues. To what extent are equal rights for women tied to issues of modernization, democratization, westernization, and globalization? In the inevitable conflicts that arise between the old and the new in the processes of industrialization and modernization, why is it that women and their status, especially their sexuality, become such a focus of attention? Why is it that politics in Catholic and Muslim contexts are so often played out on women's bodies?

A related question that emerged from the Beijing conference concerned how religious Catholic and Muslim women who believe in women's equal rights were coping with the contradictions between their own beliefs in women's equal rights and the official positions of their religious authorities. More specifically, we were interested in the spectrum of opinion and the variety of strategies that women have adopted with regard to this contradiction in a variety of contexts. The broader question here concerns the interplay between the processes of change in religion and in patterns of gender relationships. What variety of strategies do women adopt when traditional patterns of gender relations are challenged by new economic arrangements or by exposure to new ideas and cultural practices? This book is an outcome of our search for a better comprehension of these questions and for better strategizing for the global women's movement in regard to the recent religio-political trends.

THE CONSERVATIVE MUSLIM-CATHOLIC RELIGIOUS ALLIANCE AGAINST WOMEN'S RIGHTS

The Beijing Platform for Action identified twelve critical areas, including equality, poverty, education, health, reproductive and sexual health, violence, armed conflicts, economic participation, and human rights. The traditional practices of female genital cutting, forced marriage, and honor killings also were addressed for the first time in an international consensus document, with the draft text calling for laws to eradicate such human rights violations (Rumsey 2000). The Beijing Platform for Action has been considered an internationally accepted blueprint for achieving women's equality, development, and peace, hence a significant and major human rights accomplishment for women.

But, as mentioned above, the alliance of conservative Catholic and Muslim delegations around issues related to sexuality and the definition of women's rights has been an important force challenging the implementation of the Beijing commitments. Pope John Paul II was the initial architect of this coalition, an architect who understood the similarities between conservative Catholics and conservative Muslims and sought to unite the two groups. This organizing effort began in response to the Clinton-Gore U.S. presidential campaign in 1992, in which the Pope perceived Clinton and Gore as campaigning for federal funding for abortion on demand at any time during pregnancy, for federal funding for greater family planning efforts in poor countries in exchange for foreign aid, and against population growth anywhere in the world. When Clinton signed five executive orders dealing with this topic on the day of his inauguration, January 23, 1993, the Vatican responded with a carefully planned mobilization of the global organization of the Catholic Church to oppose the Clinton administration, the United Nations Fund for Population Activities (UNFPA), and various international NGOs such as the International Planned Parenthood Association and their population control initiatives which were to be presented for approval at the United Nations Conference on Population and Development in Cairo in 1993. The Pope also sent emissaries to Muslim countries to garner their support against abortion on demand as a universal human right and against the definition of sexual expression not connected to marriage or procreation, as an individual right under international law (Weigel 1999, 715; Szulc 1995, 468–69). In addition to making a moral plea against what the Pope perceived as anti-marriage, anti-family, anti-procreation, and pro-death initiatives, the Pope also made an anti-imperialist, anti-western individualism argument to build his conservative alliance, characterizing the Cairo initiatives as serious imperialistic threats designed to impose population control measures and western morality on poor countries in exchange for foreign aid. In Beijing, the coalition of Catholic countries that joined the Vatican included Guatemala, Honduras, Ecuador, Peru, Bolivia, and the Philippines. These were joined by the Muslim countries of Iran, Sudan, Libya, Egypt, and Kuwait. In 1995, the Catholics and Muslims established a Catholic-Islamic commission for the purpose of fostering interfaith dialogue, a commission that continues to operate in 2001. During the 1995 – 2000 period, other Catholic Muslim cooperative efforts occurred. In 1997, the Pontifical Council on the Family met with the Supreme Council on Islamic Affairs in Rome to unite to protect families (www.al-bushra.org/mos-chr/catholic.htm). In 2000 at the Beijing Plus Five Conference in New York, the conservative religious alliance continued its opposition to the initiatives involving sexuality, abortion, and for some, even the issue of women's rights as human rights, (arguing instead for "human dignity") although the group had lost many of its Catholic supporters and shrunk to a hard core coalition of the Holy See, Iran, Algeria, Nicaragua, Syria, Libya, Morocco, Sudan, and Pakistan (Amnesty International Index 2000). In a direct joint attack on globalization, the Catholic-Islamic Linkage Commission on July 13, 2001 issued a statement on globalization that noted the benefits of globalization but warned of its dangers, signaling a continuing interest and cooperation between the leaders of the two faiths (Zenit 2001: www.zenit.org/english).

This does not mean that all Catholics and all Muslims agree with the conservative leaders of their religions. A number of Muslim NGOs, including Al-Khoei Foundation, the international Islamic institution based in London and New York, opposed the stance of the Vatican and its Muslim allies in 1995 and again in 2000. The progressive Muslims said that while some of the issues raised by the conservative alliance were legitimate, these should not obscure the overall framework and fundamental basis of the Beijing document—the promotion of a clearly secular vision of women's rights. They emphasized that the need to respect cultural differences should not preclude universal adherence to fundamental human rights as embodied in the UN Charter (Rumsey 2000).

What theoretical and practical inferences can be drawn from these recent alliances made on the basis of supra-national and supra-confessional lines in support of or in opposition to women's rights as human rights? First, let us note which issues and what interests have brought conservative religious Muslim and Catholic groups together. The main areas of consensus among conservative Catholics and Muslims have been specifically over the divinely ordained and biologically determined different yet complementary masculine and feminine roles; the definition of the institution of the family; the primacy of women's role as mothers; confinement of sexuality to marriage (heterosexual marriage only); opposition to abortion; the central role of religion in society; emphasis on religious values; opposition to pornography and degrading images of women in the media; and opposition to the individualism of western culture which would give women's individual rights priority over women's communal family and religious duties. (Moghadam 1995; Tohidi 1996). While the Pope was the first to organize Catholics and Muslims around these shared beliefs he was not alone in his creative leadership. One illustrative instance of collaboration between the Catholic and Islamist delegations during the NGO Forum '95 in Beijing was the workshop on "The Life and Status of the Virgin Mary" organized by an Islamist delegation from the Islamic Republic of Iran. The underlying proposition of this workshop was reflected in the following words:

Social scientists are now seriously questioning the moral relevancy of the models presented in mass media. As a common model shared between the two major religions of the world we aim to address the question of whether Mary the mother of Christ can serve as a symbolic model for women and perhaps men. . . . At the threshold of the twenty-first century, faith, chastity, sincerity, purity, moral and social commitment and spiritual elevation are all attributes of [Mary] a flawless personality that deserves to be considered as a model for the bewildered human race. (Gorji and Ebtekar 1995)

This was an interesting attempt on the part of the Iranian Islamists to expand their conservative gender agenda globally across national, cultural, and confessional lines. While at national level in Iran and amongst Shià Muslims, Islamists have promoted Fatima (the daughter of the Prophet and the wife of the First Imam, Ali), internationally they are willing to adopt a non-Muslim but conservative role model for women in order to bridge sectarian gaps.

The disagreements among delegates over specific aspects of the Beijing Platform for Action appears to be related to basic differences between modern versus premodern (as explained in chapter 2 of this book) or traditional political and gender regimes. The struggle is between those who define gender roles and sexuality on a fixed hierarchical order often sanctioned by religious doctrinal necessity as predetermined by divine and/or natural order, and those who view these as matters of social-historical construction and individual choice. One side believes in the rule of law—a law that is fixed, can be interpreted by religious or traditional authorities only, and then obeyed by the believers. The other side believes in a law that can be constructed and reconstructed by social change, human agency, and the choices of citizens. These differences have their roots in different historical eras and are a part of an ongoing historical struggle associated with the emergence of modernity and industrialization, and the spread of modernity by globalization since the seventeenth and eighteenth centuries.

GLOBALIZED GENDER-BASED ALLIANCES

As manifested during the Beijing conferences, tremendous diversity and heterogeneity exist in the cultural, religious, and civilizational components of each side of this gender-based division. The alliance in support of equal rights includes most South American, Western, African, and many Asians of Christian, Muslim, and other religions, cultures, or civilizations. The alliance against equal rights, too, includes Christians and Muslims of various nations and civilizations. The cultural and religious heterogeneity of this alliance challenges the controversial thesis of the "clash of civilizations" formulated by Samuel Huntington (1993), according to which the principal source of conflict in the post–Cold War world order is a cultural division between the Confucian-Islamic and Christian western civilizations. An important division, however, seems to be between those forces supporting democracy, pluralism, and universal human rights, and those supporting a political order based on religious authoritarianism, be it Islamic or Christian, a division that has a not-so-subtle gendered nature. The contestation over a visible and articulated subordinate status for women has in many situations become the arena of conflict symbolizing much larger cultural, political, and ontological differences. Gender ideology has consequently become a significant basis on which to draw the lines of demarcation for global alliance or conflict. A broad supra-national alignment for equal rights for women has emerged in the last fifty years as symbolized by the United Nations conferences in Vienna on human rights in 1993, in Cairo on population in 1994, and in Beijing on women in 1995, to form the basis of an emerging supra-national global feminism. In reaction, a supra-national, supra-religious alliance has emerged beginning in Cairo in an attempt to maintain and reinforce a hierarchical sex/gender regime based on male supremacy and justified by religious beliefs.

The real picture is, of course, more complicated and nuanced than this simple dichotomy may suggest. Other factors, especially nationality, economic and class interests, racial, ethnic, and religious differences, cultural and political rivalries all interplay and intersect with gender ideology and gender system.

THE THEMES AND ORGANIZATION OF THIS BOOK

To organize our exploration of these issues, this book will in the next chapter review three complex topics: (1) how the Catholic and Muslim religions recognize women; (2) Catholic and Muslim responses to the globalization of modernity; and (3) the centrality of religion and spirituality to social change for women and women's agency in transforming religious ideas and institutions. Our argument is that the conflict in Beijing in 1995, and the similar conflict in Cairo and Vienna in preceding years, offer a lens through which to examine some important aspects of social change, especially with regard to women, religion, and gender relations. Rather than finding the Catholic and Muslim religions and civilizations diametrically opposed to and different from one another, we find that with regard to their recognition of women and also with regard to many aspects of their world views, the Catholic and Muslim religions are quite similar. Although the histories of Muslim and Catholic religions and peoples are very different, we also find some similarities across time and across cultures in the way that Catholic and Muslim conservatives and fundamentalists have responded to modernity, especially as this response affects women. Finally, this book attempts to show how women in the late twentieth century in Muslim and Catholic contexts are negotiating modernity in eight separate contexts: four Catholic and four Muslim.

A main concern of this book is that thanks in part to globalization, women's movements for equal rights and feminists from different parts of the world have brought their forces together through international and global forums like the UN conferences and growing transnational NGO networking. At the same time, the various conservative religious forces have formed united blocks against the implementation of equal rights. The world religions of Catholicism and Islam are among such powerful ideological, sociopolitical as well as spiritual forces. They carry with them influential strictures regarding the proper role of women and the proper relationship between women and men. They play a crucial role in the organization and reinforcement of particular gender relationships in many of the social institutions (families, mosques, churches, schools, and, in most instances, states, courts, bureaucracies, and legislatures) in many countries. Women, whether feminist or not, face neopatriarchal conservative forces that operate through religious states or new religiopolitical movements known as communalism, fundamentalism, and Islamism. They also experience changes in women's roles, opportunities, and self-perceptions, especially in the realm of education, professional occupations, and feminist consciousness, all of which have accelerated in the era of globalization.

Globalization in the form of increased trade, cross-national investment, global organization of production, and increasing speed of communication and transportation has brought modernization (including industrialization, global capitalism, modern education, and changes in the family structure and functions) to many Catholic and Muslim contexts. Modernization brings with it new ideas about gender roles and gender relationships and how women are to be recognized in the society as well as how women perceive themselves. This is not to say that notions of equality originated in or are confined to modernity. At the time of their origins, both the Catholic and Muslim religions included (and continue to include) notions of equality that recognize all people as equal before God or Allah. Neither do we intend to assert that all that is modern or secular is egalitarian. Modernity has been associated with its share of authoritarian and totalitarian governments. In "modern" societies, gender equality continues to be highly disputed in definition and, at most, is a goal rather than an actuality. In spite of these caveats, the phenomenon of capitalist globalization, beginning in the sixteenth century with European imperialism and its transformation and acceleration in the last third of the twentieth century, has disrupted traditional societies, feminized the labor force in a global way, encouraged migration, and brought new ideas about changing gender relationships to men and women all over the world. Of course, these changes do not come easily or automatically. Both religious and non-religious women in their own contextual and historical circumstances struggle to integrate the old with the new, the traditional with the modern. They make choices and pursue political strategies. This book attempts to tell this story in nine different chapters. Chapter 2 offers a broad analysis and theoretical treatment of the ways women redefine religion and negotiate modernity in the present globalized context. Following chapter 2 are eight country chapters written by feminists who live and work in either a Catholic or Muslim context in one of these eight countries. Each of these authors is native to the region about which she writes. Although each is attempting to present the views of a variety of religious and non-religious women from their region in their chapters, they each have positions in the controversies they describe. As a group, they represent a variety of positions, ranging from those who are secular, non-religious, and in favor of the Beijing Platform for Action, to those attempting to negotiate modernity and the Platform for Action as religious believers.

For example, our author from Egypt, Heba Raouf Ezzat, is a supporter of the Muslim Brotherhood, a group that many would consider "Islamist" or "fundamentalist." We feel privileged to have the chance to present the voice of this prominent Islamic woman activist. Secular feminists have been writing and reading *about* Islamic or Islamist women. Rarely, however, do we hear or read their own direct voices articulated in academic feminist literature. Our author from Iran, Mehranguiz Kar, is a prominent secular activist lawyer who believes in reform. She was recently imprisoned and charged with treason for criticizing the male-bias of the *sharià* and the family law under the Islamic Republic of Iran. Following an international campaign on her behalf, she was released on bail and is waiting another trial for a number of charges, among them her denial "that Islam has mandated the veil (*chador*) as a necessary requirement." Others are practicing Muslims and Catholics who favor the Platform for Action but who face many day-to-day contradictions and political conflicts that they must negotiate and resolve in a variety of ways.

Susan M. DiGaeta Maloney describes in chapter 3 how Catholic women in the United States are attempting to implement the Beijing Platform for Action in the United States. She first describes the Catholic Church both as a church and as a political state to illustrate the roles that women have in the church and the conflicts that Catholic women have with the church's patriarchal structure and the opportunities that the broad reach of the institution offer women in their efforts to implement the Platform for

Action. Next, she attempts to describe and analyze the spectrum of political actions that Catholic women have undertaken in their attempts to implement the Platform for Action. These actions include those of the traditionalists, the reformers, and the reconstructionalists. She also discusses how some individuals are making their own theological interpretations to reconcile Catholicism with women's equal rights within the Catholic framework. The third and fourth sections of chapter 3 explore some of the various ways that Catholic women are interpreting and attempting to reconcile the ideas of feminism and Catholicism, recognizing that part of the political strategy of the traditionalists has been to redefine the term "feminism" more to their own liking. Arguing that "symbolic representation of the sacred is at the heart of all religions," Maloney identifies and explains the ways that groups and individual feminist theologians are emphasizing certain aspects of traditional thought and ignoring other aspects, reinterpreting symbols, and drawing on elements of Christian thought to unmask and delegitimize the sexism in Catholic theology.

In chapter 4, Galligan and Ryan tell the story of women's rights in Ireland, a country whose population is predominantly Catholic and where the state has had a close relationship with the Roman Catholic Church. Irish society has undergone dramatic changes in the last thirty years, changes that correlate with major changes in the country's economy as foreign firms have engaged in foreign direct investment to take advantage of Ireland's relatively well educated labor force. As the Irish economy has become more linked with the global economy, not only have women become more educated and more involved in the waged economy but relations have changed between the society and the Roman Catholic Church as well as between the church and the state. As ideas about modernity challenge more traditional values, the traditional role of women has become a site for this contestation.

The international women's movement, buttressed by the Beijing Platform for Action, has been important in giving impetus and support to local Irish women interested in obtaining a change in the old order. Increasingly, political issues such as abortion, contraception, and divorce have come to define voting coalitions and political party support. Galligan and Ryan explain the importance of the National Women's Council of Ireland, an umbrella coalition of NGOs, in bringing together a spectrum of women's groups to write reports and lobby for women's rights initiatives. They also note the increased community participation of many women who do not necessarily consider themselves a part of the women's movement. Within this environment of a liberalizing society, the church has also been forced to recognize some of its sexist and patriarchal practices. As with Catholics interested in women's rights in the United States, reaction to modernization has been varied. Some women leave the church to become secular feminists; some Christian feminists attempt to reclaim Christian texts that advocate justice, human rights, the elimination of poverty and violence; and still others see no contradiction in being radical both in their feminism and in their Christianity. The conflict between church traditionalists, the state, and women's organizations on women's rights issues continues with the women's organizations and the state struggling against the church and, more recently, organized conservative groups in the society.

Celia Valiente writes about the situation in Spain in chapter 5. Spain is another homogeneous Catholic country, one that from 1936 to 1975 was ruled by an authoritarian regime backed by the Catholic Church. Spain, like Ireland, has undergone enormous changes in its economy since 1970 as industrialization and the desire to integrate with the European Union has influenced its politics. Both Spain and Ireland are similar in that both failed to "modernize" with regard to the science, technology, economic production, and trade that characterized other northern European countries in the nineteenth century. Instead, the country remained largely agricultural until the 1970s. Spain relied on conquest and dominion for its wealth more than on manufacturing and trade. Spain has had a history of struggle between liberal republican political forces and those associated with a traditionalist, Catholic *ancien regime* kind of political order. The similarities between the struggles between the forces of modernity and liberalism against Catholicism in Spain between 1850 and 1970 and the current struggles between modernity and liberalism versus Islamism in Islamic countries are striking. This topic is discussed further in chapter 2 under the heading of Globalization, Modernization, and Religion.

In her chapter on women's rights in Spain, Valiente describes a society that has changed rapidly in the twentieth century from being a society of Catholic believers, or at least regular churchgoers, to a much more secular society in a short time period. She also describes the gradual transition of Spain's economy and society as it opened itself to international markets and managed to move from a dictatorship to a constitutional democracy in the 1970s. As the economy liberalized, so, too, did the laws and the society. Unlike Ireland, popular resistance to the liberalization of abortion and divorce laws does not seem to be widespread or vocal. The use of contraceptives is widespread, and the state has instituted quite progressive policies toward violence against women, women's employment, and childcare policies, very much in line with those of the European Union. The Catholic Church, however, continues to be heavily involved in the primary and secondary educational system. Catholic rituals and holidays continue to be celebrated and honored by the state; but the state is otherwise separated from the church, and Spanish society seems to be becoming increasingly secularized, especially in the urban areas. Valiente's chapter illustrates how state feminism (implementing women's rights from the top down) has operated successfully in Spain in four issue areas, violence against women, abortion, gender equality in employment, and childcare. She explains these policies in some detail to show that Spain in the 1990s has been moving to conform with the rest of the European Union with regard to its gender policies.

In her chapter on the politics of implementing women's rights in Latin America, Laura Guzmán Stein notes that the Portuguese and Spanish brought the Roman Catholic Church by force to Latin America where Catholic beliefs have permeated the laws, customs, norms, language, institutions, and daily interactions of almost all Latin American peoples. The Catholic conquerors brought with them a very different understanding of sexuality, different ideas about the body, and a different social construction of gender than that of the indigenous populations they conquered. The cultural conflict was played out on women's bodies. Indigenous women were forced to cover themselves and submit to the subordinate position of women under Portuguese or Spanish law. Indigenous interpretations and reactions provided their own twists. Guzmán Stein explains how the legend of Malinche, the cult of the Virgin Mary or "Marianismo," and the idea of "Machismo" have been used in Latin America to blame women for all the evils of the Conquest, to reinforce women's subordination to men, and to secure women's ideal image as that of chaste motherhood. These interpretations are many and diverse, however, and need to be understood in context. The countries of Latin America are also diverse. Some, such as Costa Rica, Chile, and Uruguay, have smaller indigenous populations and are undergoing rapid modernization. Others with larger indigenous rural populations are more hierarchical and holistic in their political traditions with very different ways of organizing gender relationships. The impact of globalization, including industrialization, rural migration to urban areas, exposure to mass media, and access to education and waged employment for young women is changing traditional indigenous value systems and challenging both Catholic beliefs and Catholic hierarchies. In this context, Guzmán Stein discusses the success that many Latin American feminists have had in promoting women's health issues as a way of approaching the abortion question.

The chapters on Turkey, Iran, Egypt, and Bangladesh are written by women from quite different perspectives within the Muslim world. Ayşe Güneş-Ayata, in her chapter on Turkey, focuses on the impact of westernization and modernity as imposed on an Islamic country from the top

down by a secular military elite as early as 1923 and the rise of an Islamic
fundamentalist political party in the 1980s and 1990s. The attempt to
"modernize" and secularize turned the upper classes in Turkey toward
Europe, both economically and socially. This included changing the role
of women in society through education and participation in the workforce. Changes in women and men's attire, especially the ban against
women wearing headscarves (turban) in government offices and universities, were some of the initial symbolic implementations of this policy
course. Güneş-Ayata shows how the secular women's movement in
Turkey is divided between the older Kemalist secularists and the younger
secularists who often are European- or American-educated and bring
with them Second Wave European feminist ideas. She also traces the rise
of Islamist women's groups as they grew in the 1980s to oppose secular
westernized policies. The intense struggle between the United Nations-
inspired and -supported "National Machinery" or women's ministry in
charge of promoting women's equality, the secular feminists, and the increasingly well-organized Islamist women in the Welfare Party has resulted in an extraordinary struggle over the wearing of headscarves. It
also has changed the composition and policies of the women's ministry,
and forced secular women's rights advocates to fight to retain policies allowing women to work in the paid labor force. Although the delegates to
the Beijing Conference were primarily secular and proud of Turkey's
progress in implementing aspects of the Platform for Action, on their return to Turkey they found that Islamist forces were challenging popular
support for their policies. Turkey's politics today are an example of the
consequences of "top-down" modernization by a secular elite class over
a period of almost seventy years.

In the chapter on Iran, Mehranguiz Kar identifies and discusses the
ideas and political positions of a spectrum of women in Iran today. She
groups these into three general categories: conservative religious women,
reformist religious women, and secular-reformist women. Using her own
personal history as a case example, she identifies and discusses some
hopeful areas of convergence that have developed between reformist religious women and reformist secular women on policies such as divorce
law, custody rights over children, and alimony. Her chapter illustrates the
dynamic relationship between religious conservatism, nationalism, and
anti-westernism in Iran, the lively interest in intellectual debate and publication regarding women's issues in Iran in spite of the regime's authoritarian rule, and the continuing struggle of reformist women to build
consensus on at least some issues that advance women's rights in Iran.

In describing the conditions of women in Bangladesh, Najma Chowdhury shows how an indigenous women's movement is working with sup-

port from many international NGOs, including the United Nations, to advance women's rights. These groups are supported by the 1971 Constitution that in principle, on most issues, recognizes all citizens to be equal. Bangladesh, however, is a very poor country with a low literacy rate (22 percent for women, 42 percent for men), where a large proportion of the population adheres to traditional patriarchal beliefs with regard to the status of women. Unlike Iran, where religious debate over the interpretation of Islamic texts is lively and flourishing, in Bangladesh the Arabic Quran is inaccessible to most and the low literacy rate does not encourage scholarly writing and debate about religious re-interpretations. Instead, Islamic ideas often are mixed with traditional patriarchal beliefs and practices and used to continue to subject women to non-Islamic practices, such as honor killing, as well as to those supported by Islamic law, such as unequal inheritance. In this situation, the state walks a very precarious line between its need to please international aid granting institutions and its need to maintain the support of those with "fundamentalist" patriarchal views in the society. The state's dominant strategy is to give lip service to women's rights while in practice doing little to implement women's rights policies. Chowdhury uses the example of the institution of the United Nations backed "national machinery" policy to illustrate the process. The "national machinery" to initiate and coordinate the advancement of women was approved and created by the Bangladesh government. The political situation in the country, however, has marginalized the agency and made it practically unable to implement women's equality policy in any significant way. Chowdhury also shows how the Bangladeshi women's movement has focused on violence and inheritance as two issues of the Beijing Platform for Action that have particular relevance for Bangladeshi women.

The chapter on Egypt by Heba Ezzat presents a different perspective from the other authors in the book writing about Islamic contexts. Ezzat articulates the position of an educated Muslim woman who deeply resents the attempts by the state and ruling elites to impose a western, secular view of the world on Egyptian society and Egyptian women. Her position, however, is not that women should stay at home and perform only family duties. Instead, she notes that over the centuries since the founding of Islam, social custom, poverty, and illiteracy have often changed the intent of the Quran to circumscribe the lives of Muslim women in ways that are not in keeping with Quranic origins. She argues that rules and restrictions governing polygamy, divorce, dress, and other matters varied by time period and by region. Ezzat looks back into Egyptian history to identify Islamic women leaders, many of whom supported women's education. She also cites Islamic modernist scholars who have argued for more education for women and have spoken out against common abuses in the areas of polygamy and divorce. She notes that Egyptian women at the turn of the twentieth century were writers and intellectuals. Today, in spite of the Egyptian state's bias toward secular feminists, Islamic women continue to participate as an often unrecognized opposition, an opposition that would define and fashion an Islamic religious modernity as opposed to a secular western modernity. This Islamic modernity applauds women's education as well as women's participation in the workforce, in the society, and especially in the family. Its strategies differ from those of the secular feminists. It uses the veil as a means of obtaining political space to enable women to be in the public sphere without experiencing an enormous backlash. It is geared more to the action of organizing women than to articulating theory about women. Women in the Islamist women's movement have been mobilized with the aid of reforms that have taken place in the 1990s, reforms that have given women the right to be in public, the right to elect and be elected to parliament and other representative bodies, and the right to travel without a male member of their families, if safety precautions have been secured.

Throughout different chapters of this book certain paradigms emerge as connecting themes: the ongoing tension not only and simply between modernity and tradition, secularity or religiosity, but also between competing notions of modernity, modernization and traditionalism. The real line of demarcation seems to be between those forces who are committed to democracy, freedom of choice, and equal human/women's rights, and those who support authoritarianism, discrimination, and gender hierarchy under a religious or secular guise. Each chapter indicates that while feminism and the women's movement has become more global than ever before, sisterhood is not global, nor is it local. Women's solidarity has to be negotiated within each specific context.[2]

NOTES

1. For a complete report on the Fourth World Conference on Women that includes a listing of countries with reservations along with the written reservations themselves, see the United Nations Department for Policy Coordination and Sustainable Development (DSCSD). The "Report of the Fourth World Conference on Women (Beijing 4–15 September 1995)" is posted on the website gopher://gopher.undp.org:70/00/un-confs/women/of/a—20en./

2. This emphasis on contextualization of feminist struggle and the significance of coalition building for women's movements rather than ideologies, grand theories, and abstract notions like "global sisterhood" is stressed more recently by scholars such as Misciagno (1997); Rupp and Taylor (1999); and Sharoni (2001).

REFERENCES

Afkhami, Mahnaz, and Erika Friedl, eds. 1997. *Muslim Women and the Politics of Participation: Implementing the Beijing Platform.* New York: Syracuse University Press.

Amnesty International Index. 2000. ACT 77/008/2000.News Service: 105.

Gorji, Monir, and M'asoumeh Ebtekar. 1995. "The Life and Status of the Virgin Mary." In the "Special Edition for the Beijing Conference." *Farzaneh* (Journal of Women's Studies and Research). 33, 46.

Huntington, Samuel P. 1993. "The Clash of Civilizations?" *Foreign Affairs*, Vol. 72, no. 3 (Summer): 22–49.

Misciagno, Patricia S. 1997. *Rethinking Feminist Identification: The Case for De Facto Feminism.* Westport, CT: Praeger.

Moghadam, Valentine. 1995. "On the Muslim-Catholic Coalition and Other Conference Highlights." *AMEWS (Association for Middle East Women's Studies)* Newsletter. 10: (November 3).

Rumsey, Sunni. 2000. "UN Beijing Plus 5: An Expected Outcome for Women." *Dialogue.* (July): 6.

Rupp, Leila J. and Verta Taylor. 1999. "Forging Feminist Identity in an International Movement: A Collective Identity Approach to Twentieth Century Feminism." *Signs: Journal of Women in Culture and Society*, vol. 24, no. 21: 363–386.

Sharoni, Simona. 2001. "Gender, Conflict, and Peacebuilding: A Critical Overview of Theory and Practice." Paper presented at Conference on Gender in International Relations: From Seeing Women and Recognizing Gender to Transforming Policy Research at the University of Southern California. February 2–3.

Tohidi, Nayereh. 1996. "'Fundamentalist' Backlash and Muslim Women in the Beijing Conference: New Challenges for International Women's Movements." *Canadian Woman Studies.* 16: 3 (Summer): 30–34.

Woodman, Sophia. 1995. "Preparing for a New Era? Slouching Toward Beijing." *China Rights Forum.* (Summer): 24–25.

CHAPTER 2

WOMEN REDEFINING MODERNITY AND RELIGION IN THE GLOBALIZED CONTEXT

Nayereh Tohidi and Jane H. Bayes

To answer or attempt to explain some of the questions posed in chapter 1, such as why some Catholics have united with some Muslims to oppose equal rights for women, why some groups of men and especially women keep emphasizing male-female differences rather than gender egalitarianism, and why women's status, especially their sexuality, has become such a focus of attention especially in nationalist and ethnonationalist religious contexts, we concentrate in this chapter on three topics or issues to provide background and insight. The first topic is how the Catholic and Muslim religions recognize women. The second concerns the historical similarities and differences between Catholic and Muslim responses to modernity in different contexts. The third concerns the centrality of religion and spirituality to social change for women and women's agency in redefining and transforming parameters of modernity and religion.

HOW THE CATHOLIC AND MUSLIM RELIGIONS RECOGNIZE WOMEN

WOMEN AS MOTHERS: SIMILARITIES BETWEEN CATHOLICISM AND ISLAM

Islam and Christianity have many similarities. Originally Islam was part of a single religious tradition that included Judaism and Christianity.

Muslims fully recognize Abraham, Moses, Jesus, the Virgin Mary, and other pre-Islamic figures, and the Quran incorporated, in some form or other, many stories to be found in the Bible including those of the creation and fall, among others. Islam is now the world's second-largest religion, after Christianity.

Both Catholic and Muslim religious canons recognize women as something more than symbols of community or family honor and more than the chattel or the property of men.[1] Both Catholicism and Islam profess belief in a universal God who recognizes both men and women as equally capable of choosing good over evil before God. Women are recognized as having moral or spiritual qualities as well as having prescribed functions, especially those of motherhood, domesticity, and nurturing, yet women remain inferior to men because these functions make them weak, unable to reason, inadequate to engage in public or political activities. Women are seen as complementary to men, not as equal. Both the Christian and the Muslim religions have a prescribed "place" for women in the community as a whole, and do not recognize women and men as autonomous individuals. Both religions emerged in societies organized along patriarchal lines in which the family and not the individual was the building block of social order. Patriarchy entails "cultural constructs and structural relations that privilege the initiative of males and elders in directing the lives of others" (Joseph 1999, 12). In such a context, individuation, autonomy, and separate selfhood for men and especially women are not valued or supported. Family or community is valued more highly than the person (Joseph 1999, 13). This is yet another aspect of the conflict between premodern religions and individual-centered modernity and the principle of citizenship.

The official authorities in both religions limit acceptable sexuality to heterosexual relationships within marriage. With regard to birth control, Muslim ulama (religious scholars), while often opposing it, have taken different positions and in some cases (as recently in Iran) opposite positions at different times. Most of the leading medieval ulama found birth control permissible with the wife's consent (Musallam 1983). Many Muslim ulama permit abortion, although they differ on the stage of fetal development beyond which abortion becomes prohibited (al-Hibri 1993, 4–6). In the Catholic tradition, while dissenting views and practices surround the issues of contraception and abortion, the official position of the church (the Vatican) and the church hierarchy holds artificial contraception as unethical and abortion as not permissible (Maguire 1993).

One significant difference between the Catholic and Muslim religions with regard to women's bodies and sexuality is that Islam, unlike Catholicism, does not limit the purpose of sexual intercourse to procreation and sees "legitimate" sexual acts for both men and women as an important and God-given source of pleasure. Women's sexuality is considered very potent, hence the control of their seductive power (*fitna*) is necessary (Sabbah 1984).

Both the Roman Catholic and the Muslim religions are often associated with autocratic governments having laws, special male officers, and bureaucratic organizations. Neither Roman Catholic nor Islamic authorities will allow women to hold higher positions of religious authority. Both exercise executive, legislative, and judicial functions. Both cross the boundaries of nation-states, yet the histories, the customs, and the cultures of specific localities shape the practice of each religion. Neither religion is monolithic or unified, although the Roman Catholic religion has a centralized organization, whereas the Islamic religion does not. Each contains within it many schisms, disagreements, and conflicts. Both Catholicism and Islam are global religions whose influence is present on all continents and whose current strength and distribution has been shaped by political history and population demographics (see Appendix for a brief survey of each religion's historical expansion).

Catholics in 1999 were concentrated primarily in Latin America (454.1 million), and in Europe (285.7 million), with significant numbers also in Africa (118 million), Asia (117.3 million), and North America (70.7 million). Muslims, in contrast, were most highly concentrated in Asia (807 million) and Africa (310.5 million), with significant numbers also in Europe (31.2 million), and fewer in North America (4.3 million) and Latin America (1.6 million) (*World Almanac and Book of Facts 2001* 2001, 692).

Historically, both Islam and Catholicism are similar in that they are monotheistic. Both have an element of egalitarianism in that they recognize all humans, whether male or female, as equal before God. Both appeared during a millennium when new conceptions of the transcendental and the worldly were institutionalized in the Middle East and Mediterranean regions through existing religions such as Judaism and Zoroastrianism (Eisenstadt 1993, 1999). Both call for a renewal of the earthly world as a form of stewardship for the divine. The political order is the primary locus of the mundane and as such is lower and subservient to the transcendental. The god/king (king seen as shadow of God on earth, *zelollah*) is challenged by the idea of a secular ruler accountable to a higher order. A system of laws and rights emerges along with intellectual male elites (popes, bishops, clergy, priests, ulama, *muftis*, *ayatollahs*, and *mullahs*) who are the propagators and rulers of the new religious and moral order. The order is hierarchical, communal, and authoritarian. As we will see in chapter 3, some of these general assumptions are being challenged by modern feminist theorists. Religious elites who mediate the transcendental cooperate or compete with political elites to support or undermine various conceptions of the mundane. Both religions have written scriptures (the Bible and the Quran) that contain contradictory statements and injunctions concerning women.

The origins story of Adam and Eve, whereby Eve is created from Adam's rib and, in turn, becomes the source of evil that tempts Adam to partake of the forbidden apple, is the biblical account in Genesis 2:18–24. This story asserts that God created man first and that man is primary, that a woman is responsible for man's fall from grace, and that woman is created as companion or in some interpretations simply for men (Stowasser 1994; Hassan 1995, 4–5). Later in Genesis, the Bible presents a different, more egalitarian, origins story by stating that "[T]his is the book of the generations for Adam. In the day that God created man, in the likeness of God made he him; Male and female created he them; and blessed them, and called their name Adam, in the day when they were created" (Genesis 5:1–2). In contemporary Roman Catholic theology, a heated debate rages over the promotion by the church of the hierarchical creation story as opposed to the egalitarian creation story. Both scriptural passages are legitimate stories in the Catholic Bible of the creation of man and woman; however, the traditional teaching has emphasized the hierarchical story (interview with Susan Maloney by the authors, December 2000). Currently feminist theologians are challenging the traditional interpretations of these stories.

The Quranic stories of creation and fall are slightly but significantly different from the biblical stories. The order in which the first couple was created is not indicated in the Quran. The Quran gives no indication that Eve was created from Adam's rib, yet, in Islamic traditionist literature, Eve is referred to as created from a rib. This, as Leila Ahmed, Riffat Hassan, Jane Smith, Barbara Stowasser, and others have argued, is an example of the assimilation of the scriptural and social traditions of Christian and Jewish populations into the corpus of Islamic tradition once Islam conquered the adjacent territories (Ahmed 1992, 4). The Quranic origins story then does not privilege men over women; however, the Quran does contain passages that are used to justify what is perceived to be the self-evident truth that women are not equal to men. One of these is that men are the rulers or managers in relation to women. Another is the Quran's statement that women should inherit only half of what a man inherits, and the third is that, according to the Quran, a woman's worth as a witness is worth only one half of that of a man, and due to counting less than men as witnesses, women are less than men in intellect (Stowasser 1994, 33; Hassan 1995, 4).

Along with Eve, the Virgin Mary is another important icon symbolizing some traditional views of women within Catholicism. Her qualities of caring and nurturing are sacred, while her sexuality has been combined with the promotion of virginity. Her ideological power is accessed through motherhood. Both Muslim and Catholic beliefs and practices proscribe a specific place or space for women in the hierarchy of the social order. The first priority for both Catholic and Muslim women is to bear children within the institution of marriage.

Catholicism, like Islam, is practiced differently in almost every culture and even within cultures. Islam and Catholicism as practiced in the daily lives of religious women and men does not necessarily follow or reflect Quranic or biblical scriptures. This makes the enterprise of defining a religion extremely thorny because it involves defining a set of praxi, praxi that are infinitely varied in their exact forms, but are recognized by their practitioners to be "Catholic" or "Muslim." Any attempt to simplify descriptions of the two religions must of necessity fall short and be subject to criticism. Nevertheless, a modest attempt (however imperfect) is in order. The main purpose here is to demonstrate how processes of reform and democratization within religion take place in an interaction with socio-economic changes and democratization in broader society, including family structure and gender roles. As Nikki Keddie (2002) argues, a nuanced perspective sees that women's roles and status at any stage of history reflect historical, social, and cultural circumstances, among which religion, however important, is only one of the variables.

CATHOLIC GENDER RELATIONS IN THE TWENTIETH CENTURY

A model of proper gender relations propagated by the Catholic Church today can be identified officially because, unlike Islam, the Catholic Church has a central organization, and also because Pope John Paul II, as the head of the church, has clearly articulated his position on women in the 1990s. The Pope's position is not that of all Catholics. The Catholic Church has undergone significant schisms in the twentieth century. As explained by Susan Maloney in chapter 3 of this book, feminists have disagreed with much of the traditional church doctrine on women. Some have spoken out and have officially broken with the church, although many still consider themselves Catholic. Liberation theologians in Latin America are famous for their rebellion against the human rights violations of the military dictators that the official Catholic Church supported in the 1970s and 1980s. In Spain, during the 1960s and 1970s, many clerics and members of the Catholic Church began to break away from the conservative Catholic Franco regime to help make possible the transition that occurred after Franco's death.

This book is about the different ways that Catholic and Muslim women are attempting to interpret or rewrite Catholic and Muslim models of gender relationships to include women's rights in various contexts. Because of the institution of the Catholic Church, the Pope's position has to be a major part of the discussion. At the beginning of the twentieth century, the decrees of the First Vatican Council of 1869–70 governed the Catholic Church. These doctrines emphasized the church as a hierarchical institution, identical with the Kingdom of God, an institution autocratically centralized under the authority of the Pope. In spite of the social and intellectual ferment of the next ninety-three years, another ecumenical gathering of the church did not occur until 1962, when Pope John XXIII presided over Vatican II, the largest and most internationally diverse of all ecumenical councils.

Vatican II built on the critiques and theological writings of many Catholic theologians during the twentieth century to establish a somewhat more modern and liberal church (McBrien 1994, 683–86). Among the many changes were ones that moved the church away from understanding itself as a mystery or sacrament toward the concept of "the People of God." This was also a move away from a hierarchical institution toward a greater participation of the laity in the mission of Christ. Vatican I considered service to human needs a practice that might be a necessary preparation to preaching of the Word or the celebration of the sacraments but did not consider it an essential part of the church's mission. In contrast, Vatican II specifically declared that the mission of the People of God includes service to human needs. Another significant change provided for "collegial" governance rather than authoritarian domination by the Pope. Still another stressed that the church is a communion of churches expressed at the local and the universal levels through the collegiality of the bishops rather than always to be understood as the universal church centralized under the Vatican and the Pope. Vatican II stated that the church recognized that religious truth could exist outside of the Roman Catholic Church and should be respected. Perhaps the most encompassing reform of Vatican II over Vatican I was its recognition that the church is not identical with the Kingdom of God. Rather, the church and its mission are in subordination to the Kingdom of God, holy, yet always in need of renewal and purification (McBrien 1994, 683–86).

In general, Vatican II reforms internationalized, democratized, and deinstitutionalized the church, at least somewhat. Pope John Paul II, then Polish Bishop Karol Wojtila, participated fully in the Vatican II deliberations. Yet, once Karol Wojtila became Pope John Paul II in 1978, he ignored many of the Vatican II reforms and reasserted an authoritarian papacy. Not only did Pope John Paul II rule with limited institutionalized consultation, he went so far as to ban discussion on theological issues that were in dispute, such as the ordination of women. Pope John Paul II's conservative beliefs and doctrines have dominated the official church, although not necessarily the beliefs held by all Catholics. The political activism of Pope John Paul II, his authoritarian control of the church, and his personal religious and political ideas help explain the behavior of the Vatican delegation in Beijing at the United Nations Fourth World Conference on Women.[2]

THE POSITION OF THE POPE'S CATHOLIC CHURCH AND ITS BELIEFS IN THE TWENTIETH CENTURY

But why were the reform-oriented attempts of the 1960s (Vatican II) in which Pope John Paul II himself had taken part reversed in the 1980s and 1990s? How much of this regress can be attributed to the Pope's personal views and his position as a leader? What role have the sociopolitical changes of recent decades (specifically, globalization and changes in women's roles) played in changing the orientation of the Vatican and causing conservative reaction especially in regard to gender issues?

The disruption, social turmoil, and wider economic disparity generated by the forces of globalization, the feminization of the global labor force, and the demise of the Soviet Union has stimulated an anti-western, anti-modern, religious fundamentalist reaction in many parts of the world. Many are in search of explanations and more workable alternatives. Pope John Paul II, a moralist and philosopher, sees a breakdown of families, of societies, and of nations, which he attributes to an ideology of "radical capitalism," a capitalism that does not take account of moral or ethical values, a capitalism that increases the inequality between peoples, that promotes technology without values, and that promotes a "culture of death." The set of ideas that accompanies this position includes an explicit and firm conviction about the role of women as mothers in the family, primarily. During the 1990s, Pope John Paul II clarified his position on the status of women in a number of writings (see chapter 3 in this volume). His position is that men and women are basically different from one another and occupy complementary places in the world. Women should be treated equitably. They should not be beaten or abused. Both women and men should have adequate food, housing, and shelter. While women may be called on to work in the paid labor force, the primary focus is on the family. Women do not have the right to control their own bodies or sexuality. Furthermore, women cannot be priests in the church.

ISLAMIC GENDER RELATIONS: IN THEORY AND IN PRACTICE

Unlike Catholicism, Islam has no centralized organization or leader who can serve as the official voice or view of the religion. The two largest branches within Islam, Sunni and Shiite, differ little in their gender ideology. The main schism that divided the two branches initially was a dispute over who should lead the young Islamic empire after the Prophet's death in CE 632. Those who argued that leadership should be selected from among the Prophet's followers made up the majority (Sunni), and those who advocated leadership within the family circle most trusted by Muhammad and most familiar with his ideas and lifestyle, namely the Prophet's cousin and son-in-law Ali, made up the Shiite minority. This difference is still reflected in today's role of leadership among Sunnis and Shiis. Sunnis believe that the individual's relationship with God is direct and clerics are only guides or advisors, somewhat comparable to Protestant branches in Christianity. Shii clerics, however, have assumed the power to interpret God's will and word and direct the Muslim community, somewhat comparable to the Catholic Church in which clergy are more powerful. The more senior a Shiite cleric is, the more authority his *fatwa* (Islamic opinion or decree) carries in directing public opinion and behavior.

Iran is the only country in which Shiites constitute the majority of the Muslim population. Since the 1979 Revolution in Iran, the Shii clergy have seized state power and established a theocracy based on the rule of supreme jurisprudence, which gives a senior cleric ultimate power. This Supreme Leader, chosen by an eighty-member body of his peers, serves as the commander in chief, has veto power over the elected president and parliament, and makes top judicial appointments.

While it does not have a central organization, Islam does have sacred written texts: the Quran (believed to be God's Word transmitted through the Angel Gabriel to the Prophet and the early Muslim community), *Sunna* (the practice of the Prophet and the early Muslim community), *hadiths*, reports of the sayings or deeds of the Prophet transmitted by his companions), and *fiqh* (jurisprudence, religious law). Based on the mainstream scholastic doctrines, the Quran is divine speech (kalam Allah) delivered to Muhammad through the Angel Gabriel. As a consequence, the exact text is holy and cannot maintain its authority in translation. In the past, the orthodox doctrine concerning the nature of Quranic scripture as "eternal in God" was challenged by the Mùtazila (a rationalist school of Islamic theology) and, in recent years, it has been modified by modern epistemology that emphasizes the Quran's day-to-day cultural and temporal specificity versus its eternal nature (Rahman 1982; Stowasser 1994; Martin and Woodward 1997; and Shabestari 2000). The *ulama*, the scholars of Islam, debate to determine what is orthodox in Islam. Their job is to find a consensus for the *umma*, the entire Muslim community, on any issues raised. Debate among the clerical elite or ulama is an important element of Islamic tradition. In more recent modern times, gender issues and women's rights have become a subject of heated debates among ulama (Mir-Hosseini 1999).

The Quran states that men and women are equal before God. According to the Quran, God does not discriminate against women. In the eyes of God, men and women are equal. According to some feminist readings, not only does the Quran emphasize that righteousness is identical in the case of man or woman, but it affirms, clearly and consistently, women's equality with men and their fundamental right to actualize the human potential that they share equally with men (Hassan 1995, 12; Wadud 1999).

The Adam's rib story concerning the origins of women is prevalent in the Muslim world and mentioned in several *hadith*; however, the Quran, which is always the most authoritative text, tells an origins story that does not differentiate men from women (Hassan 1995, 5; Bodman 1998, 5). God creates *humanity*, not men and women per se. The Garden story is in the Quran, as is a serpent ("ash-Shaitan" or "iblis") whom God has ordered to tempt Adam and Eve. God tells the couple not to go near the tree. They disobey God together. They are told to leave the Garden, not because they have sinned but because they belong in the world. By disobeying God, the couple have transgressed the limits set by God and taken on the responsibility of choosing between good and evil. Both men and women are equally capable of making this choice (Stowasser 1994, Hassan 1995, 5). Both men and women can be righteous. Both can enjoy paradise, and both female and male believers are expected to engage in the five ritual duties of Islam: declaring the faith, prayer, fasting, almsgiving, and pilgrimage (Bodman 1998, 5).

When dealing with relationships between human beings, however, the Quran has a passage that is generally cited to support the belief that women are inferior to men and that women should obey men. According to the conventional interpretation of that passage:

> Men are the managers of the affairs of women because Allah has made the one superior to the other and because men spend of their wealth on women. Virtuous women are, therefore, obedient; they guard their rights carefully in their absence under the care and watch of Allah. As for those women whose defiance you have cause to fear, admonish them and keep them apart from your beds and beat them. Then if they submit to you, do not look for excuses to punish them; note it well that there is Allah above you, who is Supreme and Great. (Surah 4 An-Nisa': 34 A. A. Maududi's translation.)

In her comparison of various interpretations and exegeses ranging from classical traditionalist to modern, contemporary, and recent feminist ones, Barbara Stowasser shows how this pivotal Quranic verse on gender relations has been read differently in different times and contexts. She states that, "every 'reading' reflects in part the intention of the text as well as the 'prior text' of the one who makes the 'reading'; that is, the reader's own perspectives, circumstances and background. While a large variety of readings can thus coexist, mere relativism is prevented by the permanence and continuity of the Quranic text itself on which all readings converge" (Stowasser 1998,40). Some modernist Muslims, including Muslim feminists, have argued that since in modern times many women are engaged in paid employment and men are no longer the sole breadwinners, such a sex-based division of labor is no longer relevant. Paid maternity leave or parental support provided by the state and the employers mean that women need not be dependent on men for the management of their affairs (Hassan 1995, 130).

Meanwhile, gender inequality has continued both in practice and in traditional interpretations of the religious texts. According to the mainstream interpretation of the Quran, a man can have as many as four wives but only if he can treat them equally. A husband may obtain a divorce but must support his former wife if she is pregnant until the child has finished breastfeeding. The children of a marriage belong to the husband. A wife may obtain a divorce if her husband agrees; however, she often must forfeit the mahr (usually an agreed-upon sum of money or property) promised to her by the husband. Women can inherit half of what men can inherit, and a woman's worth as a witness is worth half that of a man. If a woman is accused of adultery, she may clear herself by taking the same number of oaths as a man, unless four eyewitnesses come forth to testify against her (Bodman 1998, 6).

Women in Islam do have certain rights under the Quran, the extent of which has depended not only on different interpretations but also on actual enforcement in various historical, sociopolitical, and cultural context. Some of these relate to a general philosophy about all human life. The Quran states that no human life should be taken except in the pursuit of justice, and all life is considered sacred. All human beings can rationally exercise free will, and know right from wrong, good from evil. This quality is what gives human dignity to all persons, both men and women. The Quran states that God gave human beings, both men and women, the gift of speech, including the faculty of reason and of self expression (Surah 55: Ar-Rahman: 3–4) (Hassan 1995, 118). Importantly, the Quran gives women the right to keep what they earn: "to men is allotted what they earn, and to women what they earn" (Surah 4: An-Nisa': 32).

Marriage in the Quran is a contract, not a sacrament, and is based on the consent of both parties (Surah 4: An Nisa': 3). According to some

Muslim feminist readings men and women are counseled by the Quran to have a loving mutual relationship in which men and women are protectors of one another. (Surah 9: At-Tawbah: 71). Men should provide maintenance for divorced women (Surah 2: Al-Bagarah: 241) and should treat abandoned wives kindly (Sura 4: An-Nisa': 129) (Hassan 1995, 137). The Quran prohibits a woman from being inherited against her will by male members of her dead husband's family (Surah 4: An-Nisa': 19). If a man is to marry, he should be able to provide for his wife. Those men who cannot afford to get married should "keep themselves chaste" until "God gives them means." Servant women and poor women should not be forced into prostitution (Surah 24: An Nur: 33).

In practice, however, *sharià* (Islamic way, including hadith, fiqh, and sunna) favors men overwhelmingly. Women are to be treated differently because they are mothers. In discussing the rights of women compared to the rights of men, the Quran does not state that men and women are equal, but, rather, that women shall have rights according to what is equitable (Surah 2; Al Bagarah: 228).

This brief review indicates that although the Catholic and Muslim religions are ruled by males, the official teachings of both religions counsel and attempt to provide some rules for fair and "equitable" (not equal) treatment for women as mothers and as human beings. The official teachings of the Quran, like those of the Bible, perceive women as human beings equal to men in the eyes of God. As to the relations between human beings, however, the Quran and the Bible vary between generalized declarations and specific decrees (Bodman 1998, 50).The cross-time, cross-class, and cross-cultural variability or diversity in the status of Catholic and Muslim women indicates that religion is not the only or even the primary variable in determining women's rights or in shaping gender relations. In the case of Islam specifically, the extent and forms of the implementation of *sharià* are indicative of the important role of many other factors that precede, interplay with, and/or supersede the role of Islamic scripture. For example, in her comprehensive review of the status of women in the Middle East since the rise of Islam, Nikki Keddie (2002) shows the significance of historical developments over the centuries that put women into their modern position. Some features seen as Islamic (such as veiling, polygamy, harems, clitoridectomy, honor-killing, and stoning) existed in many ancient civilizations of the Middle East, Africa, and the Byzantine Empire. Several scholars have documented the spread of veiling and seclusion, especially of elite women, and of strong male privilege in ownership, marriage and divorce (coded in Assyrian law) in pre-Islamic Middle East, Persia, and Greece (Lerner 1986; Ahmed, 1992). As Keddie argues, the creation of agricultural and pastoral modes of production and the emergence of agriculture in the pre-Islamic Mediterranean and Middle Eastern societies had already produced enough economic surplus to support the specialized occupations found in cities, states, and empires and to intensify a sex-based division of labor and separate male-female spheres. All three basic types of socioeconomic formations that existed in pre-Islamic Middle East (settled agriculture, nomadic pastoralism, and urban settlement) were patriarchal, but in different ways. While urban elite harems, slavery, concubines, veiling, and seclusion existed in pre-Islamic Middle Eastern empires, there was far less economic surplus, less gender segregation, no seclusion, and no large harems in agriculturalist and nomadic societies as all members (male and female) had to do physical tasks and take part in warfare and public life. However, Arab nomads, Keddie states, were very concerned about genealogical purity, and family and kin groups controlled women's sexuality and related actions. A Mediterranean emphasis on female virginity and chastity as central to male honor has been attributed to the difficult terrain and mixed settlement of the region and the prevalence of tribal groups, the effects of which continued through the centuries (Jane Schneider 1971, cited in Keddie 2002). In contrast, due to different histories and ecologies, the northern tribal people (Turks and Mongols) who increasingly ruled the Middle East from the eleventh century on (see the Appendix) had more egalitarian gender practices. Turkish and Mongol women usually did not wear the veil, exerted direct influence over major decisions, and could ascend the thrones as regents (Nashat and Tucker 1998, cited in Keddie 2002). As noted in the Appendix, in areas that were not conquered by Islam but where people converted to Islam gradually, like South East Asia, China, and Africa, women seem to have had more public roles. Local customs persist in some places. Minangkabau, a Muslim society of three million people in Indonesia, is matrilineal in inheritance and matrifocal in marriage (Whalley 1998).

As Muslims conquered new territories and as the Islamic community evolved and expanded from a tribal nomadic society in Arabia to one with a multi-ethnic urban and imperial state with written law, Islamic *sharià* was further influenced by the male supremacist ideas and patriarchal practices prevalent in conquered areas. From the eighth century, the caliphs (successor of the Prophet and head of the Muslim community), especially the Umayyads, emulating Sasanian (pre-Islamic Persian) kings, began to build large harems of wives and slaves and secluded their women. According to Keddie (2002), in the ninth century slightly varying schools of law developed, reflecting both the importance of patrilineal (agnatic) kin groups among the Arabs and the biased view of the time against women. Quranic verses were interpreted to mean strict veiling and women's subordinated position in marriage and in other areas and became sanctioned in Islamic law. In time, medieval Islamic society was more patriarchal than early Islamic Mecca and Medina, where women enjoyed more public roles. Many modern Muslim reformers, including Muslim feminists, believe that *sharià*—influenced by older religions, pre-Islamic tribal customs, and patriarchal Islamic imperial realities—is more gender-inequalitarian than the Quran. Therefore, they want to put aside these patriarchal features of Islam and concentrate their reinterpretation and reform efforts on the Quran (Mernissi 1991; Stowasser 1994; Hassan 1995; and al-Hibri 1997).

GLOBALIZATION, MODERNIZATION, AND RELIGION

GLOBALIZATION AS A CONCEPT

Globalization is a term that generally has become popular in academic literature in the last fifteen years to describe the remarkable and rapid movement of finance capital, goods, production, and people from a localized geographical area to a global context that extends beyond the borders of nation-states and to refer to the consequences of this rapid movement (Ohmae 1985,1990,1995; Sakamoto 1994; Sassen 1996, 1998; Burbach, Nunez and Kagarlitsky 1997; Mittleman 1997; Rodrik 1997; Schaeffer 1997; Bauman, 1998; Coleman and Underhill 1998; Falk 1999; Held et al. 1999; Gilpin 2000; Roberts and Hite 2000, Scholte 2000). The concept is somewhat murky as consensus does not exist concerning its exact meaning or definition. Some associate the term only with the changes in the global economy and society since 1970 (Ohmae 1995; Bauman 1998; Young 2001). Cairncross, for example, argues that the "death of distance" due to decreasing communication and travel costs and other technological developments (Internet, satellites, computers, mobile telephones, television) are responsible for many of these changes (Cairncross 1997). Others associate the term not only with the changes of the last part of the twentieth century, but also with the age of European imperialism and colonialism in the nineteenth and early twentieth centuries, or with the precapitalist empire building of the premodern world (Callinicos et al. 1994; Simms 2001). While most use the term to refer primarily to the global expansion of capitalism as a form of economic production, another group associates globalization with "cultural consciousness" or the permeability of societies and nations as they have become increasingly subject to "interference and constraints" from outside with regard to economic organization, consciousness of other societies, trade, migration, and communications (Robertson 1996, 5). Still others suggest that modern globalization in the twentieth century is a tranformative process, one that is akin to the Industrial Revolution in its impact on societies, economies, institutions of governance, and world order (Giddens 1990; Scholte 1993; Castells 1996; Held et al. 1999). Globalization from this point of view is replete with contradictions and is essentially a historical process whose outcome is not exactly predictable. Almost all societies have become interdependent and the new international division of labor that is forming new hierarchies and organizations that penetrate the boundaries of nation-states no longer conforms to the old North/South, First World/Third World divisions. Systems of production crosscut national geographic borders and tie institutions, governments, and households from different nations and continents in ever tighter interdependence. The role of the nation-state changes, as do the identities of peoples (Castells 1996; Ruggie 1996).

In each of these approaches, globalization refers to the movement and impact of something (capital, goods, commodities, ideas, institutions, religions, cultural practices) from one geographically contained area to a more global context. What differs is the content of what is moved and the impact that that content has on its new environment. This differs depending on the ideological approach of the analyst and the historical period under consideration. What is the relationship between certain ways of organizing economic production and the ideas (religious, ontological, philosophical, governmental) of the people who perform that work? What is the relationship between the belief systems supported by religious institutions, families, governments and the way that economic production is organized? What happens when the forces of globalization begin to industrialize a traditionally agricultural society not from within but from outside? What if the outside or foreign influence brought by globalization is not so much a different mode of production but, rather, is different ideas about the proper identity for women or about the proper role and organization of government? What difference does it make whether that preindustrial society has indigenous religious ideas and institutions that are Catholic, Muslim, Hindu, animist, or combinations thereof? What happens if elites in an agricultural or precapitalist society decide to pursue the perceived benefits of industrialization and economic globalization either with or without the adoption of the ideological and institutional relations of production that support industrialization in other already industrialized countries?

While this project began with a concern over the uniting of Catholic and Muslim women in Beijing at the United Nations Fourth World Conference on Women (FWCW) in 1995, the questions it raises address the relationship between the organization of any particular mode of economic production and the consequent necessity of certain relations of production. Is globalization today simply the transfer of industrialization and its accompanying ideological and social relations to preindustrialized countries another form of imperialism, or is it a transformative process that may lead to a new economic and political order as well as a new gender order? Our argument is that it is both.

THE EMERGENCE OF MODERNITY IN A CHRISTIAN CONTEXT

The term "modernity" is often used in contemporary intellectual discussion in reference to the new civilization developed first in Europe and North America over the last several centuries and fully evident by the early twentieth century (Cahoone 1996, 11). The essential features or traits of modernity that in combination (as a package) make it unique in human history include industry, technology, free markets and capitalism, science, a largely secular culture, liberal democracy, individualism, rationalism, and humanism. In the premodern, precapitalist period, both the Muslim and Catholic worldly kingdoms were religio-political systems. Religious ideas were central to the ideological legitimacy of government. While the Renaissance (fourteenth-seventeenth centuries) and the Reformation (sixteenth century) paved the way toward new thinking through the arts, literature, and religion, the Enlightenment (seventeenth and eighteenth centuries) provided the principal themes, conceptual frameworks, and philosophical foundations of modernity: rationalism, secularism, liberalism, humanism, and individualism. The American and French revolutions (1776 and 1789, respectively) provided the political and institutional framework of modernity: constitutional democracy, the rule of law, and the principle of sovereignty of nation-states. The Industrial Revolution that began in Britain (1750–80), provided the economic foundation: industrial production by a free labor force in urban settings, industrialism and urbanism as new modes of life, and industrial capitalism as a new form of appropriation and distribution (Giddens 1990, 1; Sztompka, 1994,70).

The exaltation of reason, science, and technology; of efficient productivity and creativity; of the rule of law instead of divine decree; of humanitarian regard for the rights of the individual "man," especially the right to be free from the oppression and corruption of governments, "a right claimed in blood in the French Revolution," have been among the positive achievements of modernity. Modernity did not come to Europe and America, however, without serious opposition and struggle, struggle that reached a climax in the great French and American revolutions but continued to smolder in Europe throughout the nineteenth century and even into the twentieth century. In France, the French Revolution led to an ongoing conflict between the liberal republicans and the Catholic monarchists throughout the nineteenth century.

Spain is a particularly interesting and graphic illustration of the resistance that modernity engendered in traditional agricultural Catholic communities. When liberal republican ideas infused France during the French Revolution, these same ideas made their way into Spain, beginning in 1808 with Napoleon's invasion. The Catholic Church played a major role in mobilizing nationalist and Catholic sentiments to oppose the French invasion, giving birth to "the two Spains," a Catholic Hispanic Spain as opposed to a liberal Europeanizing Spain (Casanova 1994, 76–77). Although liberal political institutions were intermittently installed during the period between 1810 and 1874, and again in 1930–36 with the Second Spanish Republic, the economy remained primarily agricultural, and the social structure primarily elitist and oligarchic. During the nineteenth and twentieth centuries, the conflict between conservative Catholic forces and compromise governments that melded some republican ideas with concessions to the Catholic Church erupted into civil war on three different occasions, once in the 1830s, once in the 1860s, and the last the Spanish Civil War of the 1930s, when Franco's forces won the day. Franco's 1936 military coup succeeded in overthrowing the Second Spanish Republic, founded in 1930. One of the first acts of the new regime was to order that school textbooks include Catholic doctrine and that educational activities be segregated by sex (Payne 1984,172). The liberal laws of the Second Republic were repealed, restrictions on women were reinstituted, including a repeal of women's right to vote, and legislation reverted to ideas based on the Commercial Code of 1829 and the Civil Code of 1889 (Kaplan 1992, 194).

In 1956, Franco relied on Opus Dei, an elitist, secret lay organization of professionals for expertise and economic advice, advice that moved Spain from an economic policy of protectionist import substitution to a more globalized export development strategy (Casanova 1994, 82). Ironically, this policy, initiated by staunch conservative Catholics, facilitated the rise of the liberal modernizing Spain over the traditional Catholic Hispanic Spain in the last quarter of the twentieth century. Opus Dei was important to the economic modernization of Spain, but they also were in the forefront of the conservative forces opposing the liberal social policies of the United Nations Platform for Action in Beijing.

Like many current conservative Muslim leaders, those in Opus Dei seem to be interested in being very selective in the aspects of modernity that they wish to import. They want the economic development and economic prosperity that modernization brings, but would like to constrain the social and political reforms (such as women's rights) that accompany modernization today.[3] When modernity and its accoutrements are brought through globalization to preindustrial or less developed or underdeveloped non-European societies, the struggle continues in new environments and in more complex contexts of which the United Nations Fourth World Conference on Women in 1995 was one.

MODERNITY IN MUSLIM CONTEXTS: COLONIALISM AND MODERNIZATION

In the East, specifically in Muslim societies, modernity has had a different history. By the eighteenth century, the Muslim world constituted a number of empires and a worldwide system of Muslim societies. Though interconnected by religious contacts and some common cultural values, these Muslim societies were very diverse (see Appendix). During this period of powerful Islamic empires, Muslims felt no need to emulate the West. Beginning by the late seventeenth century, however, a "certain stagnation among Muslims can be observed as a result of political weakness and the loss of many important areas after the opening of the sea passage to India and the rapid growth of European power" (Lapidus 1988: 551). The Islamic empire began to decline in power as it experienced some major losses to the Russian, the British, and other European forces. In the eighteenth and nineteenth centuries, the evolution of Muslim societies was diverted by European intervention. Driven by the need of industrial economies for raw materials and markets, and by economic and political competition with each other, European states established worldwide territorial empires. The British completed their colonization of India and Malaya, and established their influence in parts of the Middle East, East Africa, and West Africa. The Dutch had conquered Indonesia and the Russians (and Chinese) dominated Inner Asia. France, Germany, and Italy colonized the rest of Africa. By the beginning of the twentieth century, then, the European powers (and China) had completed their conquest of almost the entire Muslim world (Lapidus 1988, 551).

This European encroachment and colonialism created an acute intellectual and spiritual problem for pious Muslims. How could Islam, the perfected religion chosen by Allah, be in decay and retreat? What was the secret of European power and supremacy? If "modernity" with its industrial capitalism and its rational scientific ontology was responsible for this supremacy, how could it be combined with the truth of Islam? Although the response of people in Muslim societies to the challenge of modernity and to the colonial domination associated with modernism was different from place to place, two principal responses were generated by the Muslim elites in almost all Muslim regions (Lapidus 1988, 557). One was a progressive response coming from the newly formed intelligentsia and political elites (a new stratum of professional military, bureaucratic, or landowning intelligentsia, modern-educated middle-class professionals, and technicians) who were trained in western techniques and inspired by modern European values and accomplishments. They tended to redefine Islam to make it consistent with modern changes and European forms of the state and economy, hence favoring Islamic modernism or secular nationalism.

The second response was retrogressive in nature. It came from the older strata, that is, tribal leaders, merchants, traditional artisans, and commercial farmers led by ulama (Muslim scholars and clerics) and Sufis, whose lifestyles, beliefs, and material interests were challenged and jeopardized by modern ideas, secular education, and powerful European commercial and capital competitors. This group adhered to the revival of religious principles, reorganization of Muslim communities, and the reform of individual behavior in accord with fundamentals of Islam (Lapidus 1988, 557).

Not all members of the Muslim scholars (ulama) chose a retrogressive reaction to modernity. Scholars such as Egyptian Muhammad Abduh (1849–1905) and the subsequent *Salafiya* movement in Egypt, the Arab Middle East, and North Africa combined reformist Islamic principles with a modernist responsiveness to the political and cultural pressures of Europe and modernity. These scholars have tried to demonstrate the compatibility of science and religion, democracy and faith, modernity and tradition. This response emphasized a return to the Quran and the sayings of the Prophet, the right of independent interpretation and judgment in religious matters (*ijtihad*), abandonment of a stifling conformity to outmoded tradition (*Sunna*), and opposition to cultic Sufi practices (Lapidus 1988, 568).

The reformist political and moral response of ulama, tribal and urban communities to the internal transformation of the traditional structure of Muslim societies, particularly in regard to family and gender roles, all involved new interpretations of the Quran and of Islam. At the same time, such responses were attempts to create a self-identity different from that of the West in various parts of the Islamic world. For some elites (often military) especially in Turkey, Egypt, and Iran, the solution was to impose certain selective aspects of modernity such as capital penetration, uneven industrialization, selective technology, uneven urbanization, agricultural experimentation, and consumerism. Along with these often came certain negative as well as positive secondary cultural and social side-effects of modernity, branded later as "westernization," such as drug and alcohol abuse, sex tourism and sexual trafficking, high rates of divorce, the dissolution of the family, the demise of family values, sexual promiscuity, a sense of anomie, incoherence, insecurity, and alienation. Many positive components of modernity were absent or not allowed to be implemented, including democracy, genuine secularism, and equal civil rights, especially women's rights.

To become "modern without becoming westernized," some nationalist resistance movements against western colonial domination and neocolonial influence (in the Middle East as in Latin America and Southeast Asia) began to move toward a Soviet version of modernity. In response to this tendency and to preempt a communist insurgence in the mid-twentieth century, some western strategists such as W. W. Rostow (1960) formulated a more "comprehensive" development strategy under the rubric of "modernization" theory. Yet, many Muslim societies continued to suffer from structural duality and persistent incoherence. They lacked a domestically led self-sustained dynamism, social participation, and political representation. The gap between the marginalized "traditional majority" and the "westernized/modernized" privileged minority widened. Political repression and corruption created by a state-centered project of top-down modernization could not be mended by the "too little too late" interventions from outside. Although the influence and penetration of western advanced capitalism accelerated certain positive dimensions of technological and industrial capitalistic development in Muslim societies, an all-encompassing modernism was never implemented. The native regressive traditionalists were not alone in blocking the road to modern democratic changes in Muslim societies. Imperialism, too, as scholars such as Halpern have cogently described, "kept all transformers out of power and deliberately inhibited their work for at least the first of the twentieth century. The first generation of local ruling elites—and usually not only the first— often confused vivified Westernization with the genuine and world-wide movement of modernization" (Halpern 1977, 97).

GLOBALIZATION AND THE DYNAMICS OF MODERNIZING INFLUENCES OF DIASPORA CATHOLICS AND MUSLIMS

As Susan Maloney notes in chapter 3, the Catholic Church has a worldwide organization and bureaucracy that includes resources, personnel, and communication systems, which are used to spread the official word of the organized church. But these systems also can be used by modernizing elements, such as the Latin American liberation theologians, feminist theologians, or by groups such as the Sisters of Concern based in the United States (but administering reproductive health advice and aid to Catholics in Latin America, the Philippines, and elsewhere). Islam has no such unifying bureaucracy. However, the growing Muslim Diaspora in the West has been playing an increasingly important role in modernizing Islam. The globalizing media (satellite TV and the Internet), greater communications (air travel, telephones, and faxes), and increased economic penetration and interaction have served to "internationalize" and "de-territorialize" both Catholic and Muslim societies. Migrants moving to work in countries with gender equality laws gain new exposure and new ideas which they often communicate (but not necessarily implement) when they return. Both Muslim and Catholic populations have a greater consciousness of other societies and have ties to groups within other societies occasioned by migration, diasporation, and foreign aid (Robertson 1996, 5; Khosravi 2000).

Although Muslim diaspora communities are relatively small in number, have a young history and fledgling organizations, a confluence of factors has made their qualitative impact greater than their numbers. For example, American Muslims, numbering somewhere between three and ten million, make up only a tiny fraction of the roughly one billion Muslims worldwide, yet they are "among the freest, most educated, affluent and diverse Muslims in the world" (Watanabe 2000, 18). The Muslim immigrants (from more than fifty nations) in the United States, Canada, and Europe are provided with many civil rights and political freedoms that are usually unavailable to them in their countries of origin. By waging new debates about the fundamentals of Islamic faith and practice, tackling and criticizing oppressive traditions such as honor killing, domestic violence, spousal abuse, and male-biased family law through satellite TV and the spreading world of the Internet, American and European Muslim diaspora are slowly but steadily carving their modernizing and democratizing mark on the Islamic world, particularly with regard to changes in gender roles, gender attitudes, women's rights, and human rights (Eickelman, 1999; Watanabe 2000; Tohidi 2001). One example of the rise of the electronic *fatwa* is a Los Angeles-based site that receives 140,000 daily hits, more than half the visitors being outside the United States. As "one of the world's most popular Web sites on Islam," this site has tried to bypass the divides of cultures and religious sects (Watanabe 2000). During the Balkans conflict, when numerous Bosnian Muslim women were raped by Serbian soldiers, this site was flooded with queries about Islamic views on abortion. It responded with a neutral presentation of different views concerning the Islamic position on abortion.

Despite their lack of unity and questionable Islamic authority, the influence of the Muslim diaspora is further expanding by the growth of nonprofit organizations dedicated to bringing modern educational, healthcare, and business development to their homelands (Watanabe 2000, 18). The potent combination of modernity, democracy, equal rights, and piety demonstrated by many among the Muslim diaspora presents the Islamic world with a compelling alternative to extremism.[4]

GLOBALIZATION AND RELIGIOUS FUNDAMENTALISM

WHY IS GENDER SO FUNDAMENTAL TO RELIGIOUS CONSERVATIVES AND FUNDAMENTALISTS?

A strong tie has emerged between a conservative ideology of gender and the new religiopolitical movements known as fundamentalism, communalism, and Islamism in various western and eastern countries or the Global North and Global South. The conservative Muslim-Catholic alliance that emerged in Beijing to oppose the Platform for Action was not particularly fundamentalist. Fundamentalist and right wing conservative groups, however, have important ideological, economic, psychological, and sociological commonalities and concerns. Understanding the centrality of gender in fundamentalist thinking helps explain the attempt to exercise power over gender relationships and set limits on women's public life among those who oppose equal rights for women in an era of globalization. For lack of a better term and despite its definitional problems, we use the term fundamentalism here in reference to the new religiopolitical movements that pose themselves, in one way or another, as a political as well as ideological and sociocultural alternative to secular modern states and discourses (Keddie 1999).

An important distinction exists between fundamentalism in Christian and Islamic contexts. "Christian fundamentalism" usually indicates a literal interpretation of the text (scripture), whereas "Islamic fundamentalism" has been used in reference to different trends or movements, including "a return to the pure sources of Islam," and "a vying for power in the name of Islam (Haddad 1985, 234–59; Esposito 1997, 3)." The latter refers to the recent "global Islamic resurgence," described also as "political Islam" or "Islamism." Islamist groups use Islam as an alternative political ideology in opposition to liberalism, secular nationalism, and secular socialism to take over state power and to establish Islamic *sharià*. Islamism is, in part, a response to the failure of modern secular nationalist or socialist states in delivering a balanced economic, political, and cultural development. Islamism is, in part, a response to globalization, too, especially to the cultural aspects of globalization. As stated by an official in the Ministry of Religious Affairs in Indonesia (the world's largest Muslim population), "We are on the ship of globalism. But as globalism uproots, it invites a sense of localism and even tribalism to counter feelings of uncertainty. Islam could play an important role in easing Indonesia through the transition" (Wright 2000, 15).

In the Muslim context, we use the term "Islamism" or "Islamists" (rather than "fundamentalism" or "fundamentalists") to indicate a political difference between those who use Islam as an authoritarian and political ideology and those who consider Islam a religion only. "Islamic" for example, refers to those who are not necessarily Islamists, but who adhere to or are influenced by Islam as a culture or a religion. The dictates of adherents to Islamist movements, especially with regard to women and gender issues, have strong ideological, political, and authoritarian or totalitarian characteristics quite consistent with other "isms."

A quick reflection on the recently rising communalism, fundamentalism, and Islamism of 1970s, 1980s, and 1990s indicates that much more is involved than a genuine desire to defend religion, culture, communal, or national identity. The nostalgia of "fundamentalists" about the past is selective and the choice of which "fundamental" elements of the scripture or tradition to revive or retain are mostly male-centered. No fundamentalist groups are advocating the premodern medieval forms of political life, slavery, economic exchange, and so forth. Yet, they resort to extreme and violent measures, as in Afghanistan, Saudi Arabia, Pakistan, and, to a lesser extent, in Iran, to retain or revive patriarchal family codes and traditions like honor killing, stoning, veiling, and sex segregation. The gender-related issues that constitute the most hotly contested concern of almost all of the current fundamentalist or religiopolitical movements are hardly related to "defense of the fundamentals of religion" or "inerrancy of scripture." The few quranic verses that by the ninth century were interpreted to command veiling, in fact do not. For example, the verse (Surah 24: An-Nur: 31) that mentions the covering of women's ornaments and breasts in public, does not demand the veil (chador) so obsessively imposed on women in some Islamic contexts. Why should the Quran tell women to cover their breasts if the whole body had to be covered?

The current fundamentalism and Islamism, then, cannot be reduced simply to a religious revival or religious reaction. Neither is it simply a single reaction against modernity and the West taken as a whole. Islamists and various other fundamentalists both adopt and reject aspects of western modernization. For example, fundamentalist groups have effectively adopted some of the most modern technologies, sciences, and sophisticated organizational skills, including the Internet and the computerized Bible and the Quran. As scholars such as Hawley and Proudfoot (1994), Esposito (1997), and Hatem (1998) have argued, fundamentalism is a post-Enlightenment and modern phenomenon—both a reaction to modernity (and, we would add, to globalization) and a creature of it.

No one summary can possibly include the many nuances of fundamentalism, communalism, and Islamism in various contexts. Yet, the effects of these movements on women, at least in the short run, possess some remarkably common patterns. Comparative studies of fundamentalisms show that almost all fundamentalisms have conservative and retrogressive gender ideologies (Lazarus-Yafeh 1988; Riesebrodt 1990; Hardacre, 1993; Marty and Appleby 1994; Hawley and Proudfoot 1994; Brink and Mencher 1997; Bodman and Tohidi 1998; Keddie 1999). Control of women, sex segregation (if not physically, then conceptually), and the use of physical and spatial means to obscure feminine sexuality completely often figures critically in the discourse and politics of fundamentalists. For example, based on a comparison between American Protestant fundamentalism in the 1910s and 1920s and the Shiite Iranian "fundamentalism" in the 1960s and 1970s, Martin Riesebrodt (1990) cast fundamentalism as a "patriarchal protest movement" (Hawley and Proudfoot 1994, 26). In an interesting sociopsychological analysis of fundamentalist ideologies of gender, and in explaining why gender is such an important part of the meaning of fundamentalism, Hawley identifies three themes or elements: otherness, nostalgia, and religious machismo (Hawley and Proudfoot 1994, 25–34).

These psychological and ideological attributes are interconnected to broader societal and structural conditions, including the sense of humiliation, anxiety, and frustration because of rapid modernization and globalization. One consequence of the accelerated globalization is a relativization of societal, cultural, and religious boundaries or ideological standpoints that have heretofore been absolute. This has made the issues of otherness, in-group/out-group relations, and particularly the need to recover a distinctive identity a central concern for many in developing societies. Such concerns or anxieties are reflected in an extreme degree among the social strata that make up the constituencies of fundamentalist movements. They perceive the de-localizing and relativizing changes (brought by outsiders) as threatening, marginalizing, and chaotic. As Fatima Mernissi (1993) and Karen Brown observe, fundamentalists in general are often preoccupied with matters of boundary definition. "In groups led by men whose identity is constructed in important ways by their confrontation with an external 'other,' great weight falls on the need to control the other 'others' [women] in their midst" (Brown, cited in Hawley and Proudfoot 1994, 27).

Therefore, the moral decline decried by fundamentalists "shifts with relative ease between laments about fallen women and denunciation of outsiders" (Hawley and Proudfoot 1994, 26). In both Catholic and Muslim postcolonial contexts, women are blamed for failing to preserve the native culture and old traditional orders. Men are seen as becoming modern, while women are seen as becoming westernized or westoxicated. Guzman (see chapter 6 in this book) shows that in Latin American Catholic context, most of the folk myths blame women for all evils in the region. The male mestizo carries the sign of victory for having fought against the conqueror, while the female is blamed for the downfall of the native culture because she established an alliance with the conqueror and betrayed her people. This is the legend of Malinche, a legend that helps mestizo men justify their own superiority over women "who cannot be trusted." In many Muslim contexts, too, according to an "Islamic domino theory," outsiders select women as the best way to penetrate Muslim boundaries. The theory holds that imperialist outsiders often use the women of a Muslim nation to disrupt the traditional family, unravel the moral fabric of the healthy society, undermine its cultural identity, and, finally, dominate its economy. Modern or modernized women, then, are believed to be operating as the "fifth column of western imperialism" (Haddad 1985; Moghadam 1993; Najmabadi 1994; Tohidi 1994).

This dynamism explains, in part, why to secure the home front and focus on the family and women as a means of protecting the nation, its values, and its youth from the intruding global forces, have been common responses among religionationalists (Brand 1998; Keddie 1999; Ezzat, chapter 10 in this book). In many Muslim societies, while social institutions such as the military, economy, political, educational, and legal have been secularized and westernized (to various degrees), family law pertinent to marriage, divorce, child custody, and inheritance has remained either untouched or mildly reformed. "What could this indicate other than the resistance of patriarchy?" asks Shirin Ebadi, an Iranian feminist lawyer (Telephone interview by Nayereh Tohidi, Tehran, Iran, May 31, 1999). Why, with the stroke of a pen by an ayatollah, can usury be called a "processing fee" in Islamic banks, hence no longer forbidden, but even to modify slightly men's unilateral right to divorce, women have had to struggle for years (Ebadi 1999)? Conscious or unconscious patriarchal motivations behind many of the morality campaigns and programs of Islamists and conservative Catholics directed at reinforcing the traditional family, women's "authentic identity," and "motherhood duties," and blocking the implementation of reproductive rights are not hard to understand.

Another paradox or contradiction in the new Islamist opposition movements is that the Islamist male elite cannot gain women's support without letting women mobilize and be actively present in the public and political domain. While the men mean to use the mobilized women as auxiliary forces in their campaigns to seize state power, they do not know what to do with them after taking power and consolidating an Islamist state. Islamists in opposition should be distinguished from Islamists in positions of power. As the case of the "Islamic Revolution" in Iran has shown, the mobilized and politicized Islamic women are not going to allow the male leadership to return them to the "house of obedience" to play solely wifehood and motherhood roles. Already awakened to their own political agency, these women begin to demand a larger social space, civil rights, and equal status.

Another dimension to this fascinating gender dynamism is that after taking state power, some members of the Islamist male elite, especially the ones involved with modern economic activities and equipped with modern education, do not feel as insecure and powerless (mostaẓàf)[5] as they used to feel during their marginal and subordinate status under the westernized state. Depending on how strong the pressure for reform and equal rights is and how significant a role their female constituencies play in helping them to retain the state power, these Islamist elite tend to become flexible and pragmatist with regard to women's social roles. Gradually they concede a limited number of reforms and civil rights to women, as seen again in the case of postrevolutionary Iran in recent years.

To understand why so many women join the Islamist movements in the first place, one has to account for these women's ambivalence toward westernized modernization. The impact of western-oriented modernism on Muslim women has been uneven, complicated, and contradictory. While the effect of the European encroachment has been decidedly negative in certain respects, the overall impact of modernity on Muslim women has been broadly positive. As Leila Ahmed has demonstrated, modernist changes gradually dismantled the social institutions and mechanisms for the control and seclusion of women and for women's exclusion from the major social domains of activity. The premodern social system in the Middle East "had combined the worst features of a Mediterranean and Middle Eastern misogyny with an Islam interpreted in the most negative way possible for women, and the Middle Eastern women have no cause to regret its passing" (Ahmed 1992, 128).

Yet, because of the aforementioned colonial and postcolonial, sociopolitical, cultural, and psychological contradictions, many Muslim women feel ambivalent if not resentful toward some aspects of western modernism to the extent that many have joined neopatriarchal Islamist movements. As discussed earlier, the process of change, development, and modernization from premodern to modern in many Muslim societies has been associated with western colonial domination or neocolonial influence, hence seen as westernization. This process of development has been characterized as "distorted" (Sharabi 1988), "deformed," "underdeveloped," "dependent," and "neocolonial" (Alavi and Shanin 1982; Amin 1998). However labeled, the resulting pattern for the Muslim societies experiencing this kind of modernization or globalization has been "structural dualism" (Cardoso 1982, 112–27), an uneven economy, and cultural lag. The bizarre and extreme duality, incoherence, and inequality in every dimension of the many Muslim societies of the 1970s and 1980s can be exemplified in the juxtaposition of the miniskirts and the veil, "discotheques and mosques, modern luxury hotels and squalid mud huts, nuclear energy programs and the fuel of animal droppings, F-16s and old rifles and daggers, palaces and tents, computerized libraries and omnipresent illiteracy" (Bill and Leiden, 1984, 2–3). For example, the widening urban-rural gap and growing mal-distribution of wealth and acute class polarization contributed to political repression and bureaucratic corruption, leaving no place for democratic and more even-handed development.

Such structural dualities and failures of secular and western-oriented modernization and globalization have contributed to the growing appeal of Islamism as an alternative not only among many Muslim men, but also among a large number of Muslim women. As Bauer (1997, 223) notes, an increasing number of studies on women and fundamentalism have been emphasizing the active and positively constructive, rather than the passive and reactionary involvement of better educated women in religious movements (El Guindi 1983; Mir-Hosseini 1996; Hale 1997; Hegland 1997; Afshar 1998; Fernea 1998; Karam 1998; Najmabadi 1998; Afsaruddin 1999; Ameri 1999). They point to the "existential side of women's experience"(Friedl 1997, 155); the "mixed blessing of women's fundamentalism" (Hegland 1997, 179); or the "democratic impulses within these patriarchal movements" (Bauer 1997, 226). As Ezzat argues (see chapter 10 in this book), many Muslim women join Islamists not to return to a traditional subservient and secluded role but, on the contrary, to find a legitimate and sanctioned milieu for social presence and political activism. Despite the desire of their male leaders, some Islamist movements then may become, paradoxically, a detour toward modernization of traditional layers of women in transitional Muslim societies.

WOMEN NEGOTIATING MODERNITY

While women in the Christian West have a long history of negotiating for equality and thereby engendering modernity, women in the Muslim context face different problems in negotiating modernization. In the western-Christian contexts, many anti-modern patriarchal traditionalists as well as some modernist conservatives have resisted egalitarian changes in gender arrangements. It has taken western women two centuries of fierce struggle (which continues today) to avail themselves of the egalitarian themes of modernity. Initially, the egalitarian goals of modernity and its call for "liberty, equality, and fraternity" were meant for men only. Many basic concepts and doctrines of modernity and modern democracy such as individual autonomy, citizenship, civil rights, civil society, and social contract theory were construed from an androcentric or male normative perspective. Long before or along with postmodernists, feminists have criticized (both capitalist and socialist versions of) modernity and have tried to deconstruct the masculinist and androcentric conceptualization of modernity and modernization (Wollstonecraft 1792; Smith 1977; Jaggar 1983; Hartsock 1983; Harding 1986; Shiva 1988; Marshall 1994; Pateman 1988,1989).

In the modern West, the women's rights movement and feminist criticism drew attention to the incomplete and biased nature of such modernist projects as liberal democracy and its rival, social democracy (DuBois 1978; Rowbotham 1992). Only after the emergence of the women's movement and the institutionalization of the right of universal suffrage in modern western countries have democracy and citizenship begun to assume a more gender inclusive frame of reference in the project of modernity. But this very frame of reference, masculine or otherwise, is yet to be institutionalized in the modern Muslim world. Moreover, what has further complicated the feminist struggle in the Muslim context is the very association of certain feminist issues such as unveiling with the colonial and Orientalist discourse. For example in Egypt, as Ezzat (chapter 10 in this book) states, feminism has been blamed as "western missionary conspiracy."

In the Muslim world, the factors of colonization and the anti-colonial secular or religious nationalism have complicated the modern versus anti modern alignments. In order to fight western/European encroachment, many Muslim modernist liberals, including women's rights advocates and feminists, have felt compelled to unite forces with retrogressive anti-modern religionationalists (as in Algeria, Iran, Palestine, and Lebanon). For instance, some scholars have argued that because of more extensive and severe French domination in Algeria, the patriarchy has been more persistent in this society than in the neighboring Tunisia and Morocco (Knauss 1987). Women in this situation are caught in a web of contradictions and are, unfortunately, often compelled to postpone women's rights and feminism and give priority to the battle over nationalist goals and ethnoreligious identity politics. If some of them choose to insist on the priority of their feminist agenda, they may reluctantly find themselves in alliance with repressive yet secular and modernist military states (like in Turkey and Algeria) in order to prevent a more sexist and religiously conservative opposition from taking state power. Women's movement and feminist strategizing around such dilemmas has to be most delicately contextual.

WOMEN AND RELIGION

While respecting the many people who hold their religious beliefs to be true and immutable, our approach to religion in this book is more sociological than confessional. While some of us as contributors to this volume are believers and some atheist, we all have tried to understand and study the given religions without the rancor, dogmatism, competitiveness, and contempt that typically characterize sectarian religious or anti-religious writings. We all recognize religion as a major mover and motivator in

human culture and history (Gross 1996, 7). Our cross-cultural, comparative approach is based on the belief that "to know one religion is to know
none." [6] Religion, as defined by W. C. Smith (1963), is something that one
does, or that one feels deeply about, or that impinges on one's will, ex-
acting obedience or threatening disaster or offering reward or binding one
to one's community. Religion is a system of symbols, rituals, beliefs, and
practices based on recognizing the sacred. Our focus here is not on the
content of religious belief systems that vary cross-culturally and over time,
but on similarities and differences in the shared *functions* and *consequences*
of religion and religious beliefs in affecting gender relations and women's
status, roles, and rights in contemporary Catholic and Muslim societies.

Both the Catholic and the Muslim religions originated in preindustrial,
premodern social orders. Both have waged battles and wars in coming to
terms with modernity. Both the Muslim and Catholic religions, like all religions, exert power and influence by virtue of the way they organize people's
lives. They each provide a framework, a language, a common set of concepts and values by which large numbers of people live, believe, worship,
and gain a sense of community. They are "Ideological Apparati" (Wingrove
1999). Religious systems, like ideological systems, structure and reflect a society's perception of the cosmos and the social world. Religion, however, is
more than ideology. It is a multidimensional institution with more than simply a corpus of directly scriptural beliefs and rites. These dimensions include: intellectual or philosophical (ideological and doctrinal dogma); ritual
(symbols, myths, rites); experiential (emotional, spiritual); ethical and legal;
organizational (church, mosque, etc.); and material (architecture, build-
ings, arts) (Smart 1977; Glock and Stark 1965; Malekian 2001).

Women make up the majority of followers of world religions. For effective feminist strategizing, a realistic assessment and understanding of the
role of religion in women's lives, especially in shaping women's status is
necessary. Modern scientific advances and secularism have not eroded religion or spiritual needs in many women and men's lives. Secularism does
not mean atheism or anti-religiosity. Modernity and secularism have been
associated with religious diversification, plurality, and tolerance. While
the significance or influence of certain dimensions of religion (*i.e.*, doctrinal and dogmatic) might have been minimized in modernized and secularized contexts, the experiential, spiritual, and ritualistic dimensions
have kept their vitality and sociopsychological functions.

Sociological theories of religion, such as the "symbolic interaction"
theory of Peter Berger, consider all society, including religion, to be a
human construct. Religion is a human or social product that continuously
interacts with its producer (Berger 1969, 3). But when religion is constructed, it works as the definer of the sacred, the profane, the good, and

the bad through everyday rituals. Why should society construct the sacred (the very concept that has many implications for women and the regulation of sexuality)? Echoing Durkheim's insights on social cohesion and social control as important functions of religion, Berger explains that the sacred legitimizes and stabilizes social life. As a human creation, society is inherently precarious and subject to disruption. Placing everyday events within a "cosmic frame of reference" confers on the fallible, transitory creations of human beings "the semblance of ultimate security and permanence" (Berger 1969, 35–36).

The history of each religion (Islam, Christianity, and any other religion) is the history of dialogue or interaction between two realms: the realm of religious scripture and symbols, as these interact with the realm of the material and cultural world of everyday reality. While a very important factor, religion is only one determinant of women's status and role in society. Political and socioeconomic conditions are equally if not more important (Kandiyoti 1991; Keddie 1991, 2002; Moghadam 1993; Brand 1998; Haddad and Esposito 1998). The position of women in religious systems is often a reflection, however oblique, of women's status in society. Religion, in its turn, shapes and mediates women's status. Through a process of "symbolic interaction," then, any given religion can be reconstructed toward a more gender egalitarian orientation. To avoid essentialism, we have tried not to view Catholicism, Islam, or any religion as a reified, ahistoric, static, and monolithic entity. From our perspective, despite religion's often valuable function of providing a certainty, permanence, and strength especially in times of disruption and chaos, no religion has been able to escape change and transformation. Certain forms of religious praxis, such as Liberation Theology, have been at the heart of resistance and social change movements.

We also see an important distinction between any formal, official, organized, or clergy centered religion as opposed to the informal, non-organized, daily religious practices and experiences that are officially viewed as "incorrect." An ongoing tension exists between religious authority and spiritual experience or religious practice. Many women perceive or experience religion or faith in a way that is not clergy-centered but, rather, personal, existential, or spiritual (Buchanan, 1996). Women have a tradition of being religious innovators. For example, women have been active as mystics and in heretical movements, including goddess worshiping and paganism that have provided a forum for the alienated and oppressed (McLaughlin, 1979). The first Muslim representative of "genuine love mysticism" was a woman, Rabi'a al-Adawiyah or Rabi'a of Basra (d. 801), who was one of the great early formative influences in the development of Sufi doctrine in Islamic tradition (Esposito 1998, xiii).

She was seen one day in the streets of Basra, carrying a bucket in one hand and a torch in the other. Asked the meaning of her action, she replied: "I want to pour water into Hell and set fire to Paradise so that these two veils disappear and nobody worships God out of fear of Hell or hope for Paradise, but only for the sake of His eternal beauty." (Schimmel, 1992, 105)

WOMEN'S BODIES/SPIRITS AS A SITE OF CONTROL AND A SITE OF RESISTANCE

As demonstrated during the United Nations Fourth World Conference on Women in Beijing, in both Catholicism and Islam, the power of religious hierarchies over women is manifested more clearly in various kinds of spiritual authority to regulate women's bodies, especially their reproductive practices, abortion rights, and sexual expressions, veiling, and honor killing. Women's bodies and spirits have been both a site of battle for political power among men and a site of resistance against patriarchal oppression among women. The exaltation of men through images of the highest spiritual being as male (images of a male God or savior, for example), or the abrogation to them of highest spiritual authority (the Pope, the Ayatollah, for example) have implied that women are inferior both in body and in spirit. Women's bodies tend to be valued or devalued in relation to their function as signs of men's status. Religious authorities, as in Iran, Algeria, Afghanistan, Nicaragua, and Vatican, "have often made women's bodies a sort of battleground, a turf on which they and the state authorities allied with or opposed to them play out their own power struggle" (DeLamotte 1997, 17). In response to this reality, contemporary liberation theologians such as Maria Clara Bingemer and a growing number of Muslim and Christian feminists see spirituality as conceptually and politically inseparable from liberatory action (DeLamotte 1997, 15). In contrast to those who set spirituality apart from women's material reality, some feminists, resisting inside or outside of religious authority systems, have located a source of oppression in women's lives at the disjunction between spirit and body. In their postcolonial discourses, many feminists of the Global South, women of color, including spiritual feminists, have noted the linkage between religion or spirituality and women's body or sexuality. The Mexican-American feminist writer, Cherrie Moraga, for instance, has cogently shown this interconnection:

> Women of color have always known although we have not always wanted to look at it, that our sexuality is not merely a physical response or drive, but holds a crucial relationship to our entire spiritual capacity. Patriarchal religions—whether brought to us by the colonizer's cross and gun or emerg-

ing from our own people—have always known this. Why else would the female body be so associated with sin and disobedience? Simply put, if the
spirit and sex have been linked in our oppression, then they must also be
linked in the strategy toward our liberation. . . . To date, no liberation
movement has been willing to take on the task. To walk a freedom road
that is both material and metaphysical, sexual and spiritual. Third World
feminism is about feeding people in all their hungers. (Moraga 1983, 132)[7]

As argued by DeLamotte (1997, 14), this passage by Moraga is valuable
because it models a way to move beyond sorting women's experience into
binary oppositions of soul and body, spiritual and sexual desire, religious
life and erotic life, material needs and spiritual needs. If the double territory of body and spirit has been a site of control and oppression of women,
how, in resistance, have women been able to transform that colonized territory into a site of freedom and empowerment?

FEMINIST TRANSFORMATION OF
RELIGION AND SPIRITUALITY

In modern times, the rise of feminism, feminist theology, and feminist spirituality has led women to challenge the exclusion of women from religious
authority and the patriarchal bias of religion in many traditions. As discussed by Susan Maloney in this volume (chapter 3), Catholic women in
the United States have responded to the patriarchal dimension of the
Catholic religion in various ways. Feminists elsewhere also have used different strategies in dealing with sexist religions and religious institutions.
Briefly stated, feminists have adopted three different approaches; rejection, revision, and reconstruction.

Some feminists who view religion as a key factor in the subordination and
oppression of women have rejected religious traditions in their entirety. They
have either dismissed religion altogether or fought against it from within.
The second approach has been that of feminists who have religious convic-
tions, but who are critical of the patriarchal orientation and sexism of their
religious traditions. Believing that misogyny is not the whole story of any religion, they try to change and reform their traditions from within. They seek
to revise by retrieving, reclaiming, and discovering a "usable past," or the
"ideals or moments of realization of human wholeness" (McLaughlin 1979,
94–96) that would legitimate an equal place for women today. The third approach, of a more radical or revolutionary nature, seeks to "deconstruct, sub-
vert, and reconstruct" the past and present of a given tradition. Both
believers and non-believers operating from within and from outside of various religious traditions have pursued this approach. The underlying argument for them is that unless the traditional notions of gender are removed

from people's understanding of God, women will never share equally with men in the church (or mosque) *or* outside of it. For example, feminist theologian Mary Daly puts it bluntly: "If God is male, then male is God" (Daly 1973). Another example is Rosemary Radford Ruether who represents the Women-Church movement within a Catholic context. She reflects "the perspective of religious feminists who seek to reclaim aspects of the biblical tradition, Jewish and Christian, but who also recognize the need both to go back behind biblical religion and to transcend it" (Ruether, 1986, 3–4).

Within all three Semitic or Abrahamic religions (Judaism, Christianity, and Islam) and others such as Hinduism and Buddhism, we find a process of feminist reform and reinterpretation occurring. Feminist theology and the feminist spirituality movement have a longer and stronger background in Christian tradition than they do in Islam.[8] This goes back to the longer experience of European white Christian women with modernity, secularism, and feminism. Yet, a growing feminist revision, reinterpretation, and reconstruction of religion in various traditions among women of color, lesbian women, and third world feminists, including Muslim feminists has contributed to the inclusiveness, enrichment, and diversification of the global feminist movement, especially spiritual feminism.[9]

CATHOLIC AND MUSLIM FEMINISM: PERILS AND PROMISES

Both Catholic and Muslim feminists are trying to adjust their religious traditions to a more egalitarian modern reality. While Catholic or other spiritual feminists have a longer history and a more mature and established place within western feminism (Braude 1989; Pellauer 1991), Muslim feminism is a new, still undefined, and more contested arena. Compelled by the growing Islamist environment since the 1970s and/or out of personal and spiritual conviction, many Muslim women have attempted to change and improve women's roles and rights within an Islamic framework. They seek to redefine, reinterpret, and reform Islam to be a more women-friendly and gender egalitarian religion. This seems to be their way both of negotiating modernity and challenging the pre-modern traditional patriarchy. A growing body of literature and scholarship concerned with the study of the nature, variations, strengths, and weaknesses of Muslim feminism in recent decades reflects this trend of resistance, revision, and reform within the Islamic tradition.[10] A basic claim among various religious feminist reformers, including Muslim and Christian feminists, is that their respective religions, if understood and interpreted correctly, do not support the subordination of women.[11] These reformers maintain that the norms of society and the norms of God are at odds. An egalitarian revision, therefore, is not only possible but necessary. In reclaiming the "egalitarian past," reformist feminist scholars note that before these religions became closely associated with state power (in the first through fourth centuries of Christianity and in the early years of Islamic tradition in the eighth century), women did hold positions of leadership.

While modernist rational attempts to reinterpret or reform Islam emerged almost a century ago by theologians and jurists such as the Egyptian Muhammad Abduh (d. 1905), feminist reinterpretation of Islam is quite recent. The Quran, seen as the "eternal and inimitable" text, provides for Muslims both the foundational basis and the point of convergence of many different, human interpretations in the light of specific socioeconomic and political situations (Stowasser 1998, 30). Feminist Muslims such as Azizah al-Hibri see flexibility and evolution as "an essential part of Quranic philosophy, because Islam was revealed for all people and for all times. Consequently, its jurisprudence must be capable of responding to widely diverse needs and problems. . . . Muslims rely on *ijtihad* which is the ability to analyze a Quranic text or a problematic situation within the relevant cultural and historic context and then devise an appropriate interpretation or solution based on a through understanding of Quranic principles and the *Sunnah*" (al-Hibri 1993, 2).

An important challange for Muslim feminists as writers such as Roald (1998, 41) have argued, is that the Quran is seen as the "word of God" and consequently is immutable. In response, Muslim modernists and feminists have noted that the symbolic wording of the Quran is not critical. Rather the *interpretation* of the Quran by men forms the basis of Islamic law, application, and practice. This male (*ulama*) monopoly of authority to interpret the Quran or engage in *ijtihad* is what Muslim feminists are challenging now. As Erika Friedl explains:

> Theoretically these texts are beyond negotiation because they are claimed to emanate from divine or divinely inspired authority. Practically, however, the Holy Writ has to be translated, taught, and made understandable to the faithful, especially to illiterate and semiliterate people who cannot read original Arabic texts. . . . This means it has to be interpreted. Interpretation is a political process: the selection of texts from among a great many that potentially give widely divergent messages, and their exegesis are unavoidably influenced, if not outrightly motivated, by the political programs and interests of those who control the formulation and dissemination of ideologies (Friedl 1997, 146).

During the past two decades, such a reform-oriented religious feminism—known in the West as "Islamic feminism" or "Muslim feminism"[12]—has grown among Muslim women in different Muslim societies. This trend emerges in primarily modern cities among the highly educated, urbanized upper- and middle-class Muslim women who adhere to their religious traditions and hold Islam as a significant component of their ethnic, cultural, or even national identity. Their views, behaviors, and politics contain both practical and ideological inconsistencies and contradictions. These women, especially the elite among them, are pushed forward by the expanding processes of modernization, increased levels of education, globalization, and the discourses of democracy, women's rights, and feminism. Not only are they influenced by modernity; as highly educated professional women, they themselves have become agents of change and modernization (Moghadam 1993). Regardless of the Islamist or Islamic causes for which they are campaigning, women are increasingly engaged in religious, cultural, and social life outside the private realm, and in arenas that were earlier rendered inaccessible to women—whether they be physical spaces, such as the mosques, or intellectual arenas, such as learned theology debates (Ask and Tjomsland 1998, 7).

At the same time, however, these women are pulled back by the traditionalist conservative forces, the rise of identity politics, ethno-religio-nationalism, and Islamism. Under the contradictory pressures of modernism and traditionalism, Muslim feminism seems to be, among other things, a theological challenge to a theological imposition, a way of resistance to the patriarchal reading of Islam, an attempt to legitimize or "nativize" feminist demands in their community, demands that would otherwise be cast as western imports. As Leila Ahmed argues, "reforms pursued in a native idiom and not in terms of the appropriation of the ways of other cultures" would possibly be more intelligible and persuasive to more traditional classes (and not merely to modern upper and middle classes) and possibly, therefore, they may prove more durable (Ahmed 1992, 168).

What can be troubling in regard to religious feminism, be it Islamic or Christian, is the tendency toward sectarianism or totalitarianism. The real danger is when a single brand of ideological feminism, be it secular Marxist or religious Islamic (in this case Islamist) presents itself as the only legitimate or authentic voice for all women or the "true path for liberation," negating, excluding, and silencing other voices and ideas among women in any given society. Appreciation for ideological, cultural, racial, sexual, and class diversity is critical for local and global feminist movements.

For effective feminist strategizing, the importance of dialogue, conversation, and coalition building among women activists of various ideological inclinations cannot be overemphasized. The feminist movement is not one movement but many. What unites feminists is a belief in the human dignity, the human rights, freedom of choice, and the further empowerment of women rather than any ideological, spiritual, or religious stance. Secularity works better for all when secularism means impartiality toward religion, not anti-religionism. Some secularist and Marxist feminists have treated Muslim or Christian feminists as rivals or foes of secular feminism and have been preoccupied with academic concerns over their philosophical and ideological inconsistency and postmodern limits (as if various brands of secular feminism are free from such limits).[13] We may see religious and spiritual feminism, including Muslim feminism, as a welcome addition to the wide spectrum of feminist discourse, as long as these religious feminists contribute to the empowerment of women. In some contexts, they may be very effective agents of women's empowerment. When their discourse and actions impose their religious strictures on all, however, or when they coopt the meaning of feminism to fight against equal rights for women or women's empowerment, or when they cooperate with and serve as arms of repressive and anti-democratic Islamist states, Muslim feminism is not helpful. Muslim feminism has served women's cause when it complements, diversifies, and strengthens the material as well as spiritual force of the women's movements in any given Muslim society.

The chapters that follow are written by feminists who have different perspectives with regard to how women should be empowered in their respective contexts. In no way should the inclusion of a Catholic feminist or a Muslim feminist in this mix be understood as the sanctioning of a religious state, even though some religious feminists may find a religious state desirable. Our observations indicate that religious theocratic states are not able to empower women nor are they able to provide an inclusive democracy for their citizens.[14] Religion is important but should be separated from state power. Muslim feminists seem to be an inevitable component of the ongoing change and development of Muslim societies as they face modernity. In the short run, Muslim feminists may serve as a sort of Islamization of feminism for some. In the long run, in a society that allows for and protects open debate and discussion, Muslim feminism can facilitate the modernization and secularization of Islamic societies and states. Negotiating modernity takes many forms.

NOTES

1. See Leila Ahmed (1992) for a discussion of women as honor or women as chattel. See also Bayes (1998) for a discussion of types of gender regimes.
2. For more information concerning Pope John Paul II's life and thinking, see George Weigel (1999), Karol Wojtyla (1981), and Tad Szulc (1995).
3. A distinction should be made between *modernity*, *modernism*, and *modernization*. Whereas the terms *modernity*, *modernized*, and *modern* refer to an historical era and a whole way of life associated with the Enlightenment, rational thinking, science, democracy, free markets, and liberal thought, *modernism* has been used in ambiguous ways in reference to

cultural aspects (arts, literature, architecture, music, dress code, etc.) that reflect a modern or modernized society that can be—and often are—adopted in non-modern societies (Cahoone 1996, 13). As discussed in this chapter, we use "modernization" not only in reference to the process of implementation or expansion of modernity. We also refer to a deliberate strategy of foreign policy theorized by western policy makers to export selective aspects of modernity into the non-western world. Modernization, in this sense, involved a neoimperialist expansion of markets, economic penetration, and cultural diffusion from the modern West or North toward the premodern East or South that, while facilitating some progressive changes, brought about a mostly top-down, incoherent, and uneven process of abrupt change through authoritarian state power.

4. Sulayman Nyang, cited in Watanabe 2000, 18.

5. For further analysis on this, see Tohidi 1994, 132–135.

6. As cited in Gross (1996, 8), this famous statement was made by Max Muller (1823–1900), one of the founders of comparative studies in religion.

7. Cited in DeLamotte (1997), 13–14.

8. See, for example, Mary Daly (1973); Judith Plaskow and Carol Christ (1989); Elizabeth Schussler Fiorenza (1992); Rosemary Ruether and Catherine Keller (1995); and Rita Gross (1993 and 1996).

9. See for instance, Katie Cannon (1988); Christine Downing (1989); Paula Cooey, William Eakin, and Jay McDaniel (1991); Leonard Grob, Riffat Hassan, and Haim Gordon (1991); Lina Gupta (1991); Virginia R. Mollenkott (1992); Rita Gross (1993); Ursula King (1994); Arvind Sharma (1994); Ada Maria Isasi-Diaz and Yolanda Tarango (1995).

10. See for instance, Smith (1985); Mernissi (1991); al-Hibri (1992); Ahmed (1992); Hassan (1995); Hoodfar (1996); Tohidi (1996 and 1998); Bauer (1997); Najmabadi (1998); Haddad and Esposito (1998); Fernea (1998); Roald (1998); Abu-Lughod (1998); Badran (1999); Mir-Hosseini (1999); Wadud (1999); Keddie (1999); Moghadam (2000).

11. See, for instance, Mernissi 1991, part 2; Ahmed 1992, p. 67, or Hassan 1995.

12. Rather than "Islamic feminism," perhaps it is more accurate to call this trend "Muslim feminism" and its advocates "Muslim feminists." Muslim feminists and Muslim modernists, like the various schools within secular feminism and modernism, might be better evaluated for their contribution to practical sociocultural change toward tolerance, democratization, human/women's rights, and civil rights, rather than their ideological validity or coherence.

13. For extensive discussions on the debate over "Islamic feminism" in the context of Iran and views of writers such as Moghissi, Mojab, Shahidian, Najmabadi, Mir-Hossein, and Tohidi, see Moghadam 2000 and see also Tohidi 1996, part 1.

14. For a concrete example of the violation of human rights and civil rights of religious and ethnic minorities under religious states, see Sanasarian (2000) on the case of the Islamic Republic of Iran.

REFERENCES

Abu-Lughod, Lila. Ed. 1998. *Remaking Women: Feminism and Modernity in the Middle East*. Princeton, N.J.: Princeton University Press.

Afshar, Haleh. 1998. *Islam and Feminism: An Iranian Case Study*. London: Macmillan.

Afsaruddin, Asma. 1999. "Introduction: The Hermeneutics of Gendered Space and Discourse." In *Hermeneutics and Honor: Negotiating Female "Public" Space in Islamic/ate Societies*, ed. Asma Afsaruddin. Cambridge, Mass.: Harvard University Press.

Ahmed, Leila. 1992. *Women and Gender in Islam*. New Haven, Conn.: Yale University Press.

Alavi, Hamza, and Teodor Shanin, eds. 1982. *Introduction to the Sociology of Developing Societies*. New York: Monthly Review Press.

Ameri, Anan. 1999. "Conflict in Peace: Challenges Confronting the Palestinian Women's Movement." In *Hermeneutics and Honor: Negotiating Female "Public" Space in Islamic/ate Societies*, ed. Asma Afsaruddin. Cambridge, Mass.: Harvard University Press.

Amin, Samir. 1998. *Capitalism in the Age of Globalization*. London: Zed Books.

Ask, Karin, and Marit Tjomsland, eds. 1998. *Women and Islamization: Contemporary Dimensions of Discourse on Gender Relations*. Oxford: Berg.

Badran, Margot. 1999. "Toward Islamic Feminisms: A Look at the Middle East." In *Hermeneutics and Honor: Negotiating Female "Public" Space in Islamic/ate Societies*, ed. Asma Afsaruddin. Cambridge, Mass.: Harvard University Press.

Bauer, Janet. 1997. "Conclusion: The Mixed Blessings of Women's Fundamentalism: Democratic Impulses in a Patriarchal World." In *Mixed Blessings: Gender and Religious Fundamentalism Cross-Culturally*, eds. Judy Brink and Joan Mencher. New York: Routledge.

Bauman, Zygmunt. 1998. *Globalization: The Human Consequences*. New York: Columbia University Press.

Bayes, Jane. 1998. "Globalization and Gender Regime Change." Paper delivered at American Political Science Association Annual Conference in Atlanta, Georgia, September 3–6.

Berger, Peter. 1969. *The Sacred Canopy: Elements of Sociological Theory of Religion*. New York: Doubleday.

Bill, James, and C. Leiden. 1984. *Politics in the Middle East*. New York: Little Brown.

Bodman, Herbert L. 1998. "Introduction." In *Women in Muslim Societies: Diversity Within Unity*, eds. Herbert L. Bodman and Nayereh Tohidi. Boulder, Col.: Lynne Reiner.

Bodman, Herbert L., and Nayereh Tohidi, eds. 1998. *Women in Muslim Societies: Diversity Within Unity*. Boulder, Col.: Lynne Reiner.

Brand, Laurie. 1998. *Women, the State, and Political Liberalization: Middle Eastern and North African Experiences*. New York: Columbia University Press.

Braude, Ann. 1989. *Radical Spirits: Spiritualism and Women's Rights in the Nineteenth Century American*. Boston: Beacom Press.

Brink, Judy, and Joan Mencher, eds. 1997. *Mixed Blessings: Gender and Religious Fundamentalism Cross-Culturally*. New York: Routledge.

Buchanan, Constance. 1996. *Choosing to Lead: Women and the Crisis of American Values*. Boston: Beacon Press.

Burbach, Roger, Orlando Nunez, and Boris Kagarlitsky. 1997. *Globalization and Its Discontents: The Postmodern Socialisms*. London: Pluto Press.

Cahoone, Lawrence, ed. 1996. *From Modernism to Postmodernism*. Cambridge, U.K.: Blackwell Publishers.

Cairncross, Frances. 1997. *The Death of Distance*. Cambridge, Mass.: Harvard Business School Press.

Callinicos, Alex et al. 1994. *Marxism and the New Imperialism*. London: Bookmarks.

Cannon, Katie G. 1988. *Black Womanist Ethics*. Atlanta, Ga.: Scholar's Press.

Cardoso, F. H. 1982. "Dependency and Development in Latin America." In *Introduction to Sociology of Developing Societies*, eds. Hamza Alavi and Theodo Shanin. New York: Monthly Review Press.

Casanova, José. 1994. *Public Religions in the Modern World*. Chicago: University of Chicago Press.

Castells, Manuel. 1996. *The Rise of the Network Society*. Oxford: Blackwell Publishers.

Coleman, William D., and Geoffrey R. D. Underhill, eds. 1998. *Regionalism and Global Economic Integration: Europe, Asia and the Americas*. London: Routledge.

Cooey, Paula, William Eakin, and Jay McDaniel, eds. 1991. *After Patriarchy: Feminist Transformation of the World Religions*. New York: Orbis Books.

Daly, Mary. 1973. *Beyond God the Father*. Boston: Beacon Press.

DeLamotte, Eugenia. 1997. "Sexuality, Spirituality and Power." In *Women Imagine Change: A Global Anthology of Women's Resistance*, eds. Eugenia DeLamotte, Natania Meeker; and Jean O'Barr. New York: Routledge.

Donohue-White, Patricia. 1998. "The Feminist Pope: The Political Thought of Pope John Paul II." Paper delivered at the American Political Science Association Annual Convention in Atlanta, Georgia, September 1–6.

Downing, Christine. 1989. *The Goddess: Mythological Images of the Feminine*. New York: Crossroad.

DuBois, Ellen Carol. 1978. *Feminism and Suffrage: The Emergence of an Independent Women's Movement in America, 1848–1860*. Ithaca, N.Y.: Cornell University Press.

Ebadi, Shirin. 1999. "Negaresh-e sonnat ve moderniteh be barabari-ye zan ve mard." In *Jens-e Dovom*. 2 (Khordad 1378) (Tehran): 31–38.

Eickelman, Dale, and Jon Anderson, eds. 1999. *New Media in the Muslim World: The Emerging Public Sphere*. Bloomington: Indiana University Press.

Eisenstadt, S. N. 1993. "Religion and the Civilizational Dimensions of Politics." In *The Political Dimensions of Religion*, ed. Said Amir Arjomand. Albany: State University of New York Press.

Eisenstadt. S. N. 1999. *Fundamentalism, Sectarianism, and Revolution: The Jacobin Dimension of Modernity*. Cambridge, U.K.: Cambridge University Press.

El Guindi, Fedwa. 1983. "Veiled Activism: Egyptian Women in the Contemporary Islamic Movement." *Femmes de la Mediterraneed Peuple/Mediterraneens*. 22–23 (Jan-June).

Esposito, John L. 1997. "Introduction." In *Political Islam: Revolution, Radicalism, or Reform?* ed. John L. Esposito. Boulder: Lynne Rienner.

———. 1998. "Introduction." In *Islam, Gender and Social Change*, eds. Y. Y. Haddad and John Esposito. New York: Oxford University Press.

Falk, Richard. 1999. *Predatory Globalization: A Critique.* Cambridge: Polity Press.

Fernea, Elizabeth Warnock. 1998. In *Search of Islamic Feminism.* New York: Doubleday.

Friedl, Erika. 1997. "Ideal Womanhood in Postrevolutionary Iran." *In Mixed Blessings: Gender and Religious Fundamentalism Cross-Culturally,* eds. Judy Brink and Joan Mencher. New York: Routledge.

Giddens, Anthony. 1990. *The Consequences of Modernity.* Cambridge, U.K.: Polity Press.

Gilpin, Robert. 2000. *The Challenge of Global Capitalism: The World Economy in the 21st Century.* Princeton, N.J.: Princeton University Press.

Glock, Charles, and Rodney Stark. 1965. *Religion and Society in Tension.* Chicago: Rand McNally.

Grob, Leonard, Riffat Hassan, and Haim Gordon. 1991. *Women's and Men's Liberation: Testimonies of Spirit.* New York: Greenwood Press.

Gross, Rita. 1993. *Buddhism after Patriarchy: A Feminist History, Analysis, and Reconstruction of Buddhism.* Albany: State University of New York Press.

———. 1996. *Feminism and Religion: An Introduction.* Boston: Beacon Press.

Gupta, Lina. 1991. "Kali the Savior." In *After Patriarchy: Feminist Transformation of the World Religions,* eds. Cooey, Paula, William Eakin, and Jay McDaniel. New York: Orbis Books.

Haddad, Y. Yazbeck. 1998. "Islam and Gender: Dilemmas in the Changing Arab World" in *Islam, Gender and Social Change.* eds. Yvonne Yazbeck Haddad and John L. Esposito. New York: Oxford University Press.

———. 1985. "Islam, Women and Revolution in Twentieth Century Arab Thought." In *Women, Religion and Social Change,* eds. Y.Y. Haddad and Elison Banks Findly. Albany: State University of New York Press.

Haddad, Y. Yvonne, and John Esposito, eds. 1998. Islam, *Gender and Social Change.* New York: Oxford University Press.

Hale, Sondra. 1997. "Ideology and Identity: Islamism, Gender, and the State in Sudan." in *Mixed Blessings: Gender and Religious Fundamentalism Cross-Culturally.* eds. Judy Brink and Joan Mencher. New York: Routledge.

Halpern, M. 1977. "Four Contrasting Repertoires of Human Relations in Islam." In *Psychological Dimensions of Near Eastern Studies,* eds. C. Brown and N. Itzkowitz. Princeton, N.J.: The Darwin Press.

Hardacre, Helen. 1993. "The Impact of Fundamentalisms on Women, the Family, and Interpersonal Relations." In *Fundamentalisms and Society: Reclaiming the Sciences, the Family, and Education,* eds. Martin E. Marty and R. Scott Appleby. Chicago: University of Chicago Press.

Harding, Sandra. 1986. *The Science Question in Feminism.* Ithaca, N.Y.: Cornell University Press.

Hartsock, Nancy. 1983. *Money, Sex and Power: Toward a Feminist Historical Materialism.* New York: Longman.

Hassan, Riffat. 1995. "Women's Rights and Islam: From the I.C.P.D. to Beijing." Papers written for a Ford Foundation project in Cairo in 1994, for an International Planned Parenthood Federation Conference held in Tunis in July 1995, and for the Family Planning Association of Pakistan in April, 1995. Unpublished manuscript.

Hatem, Mervat. 1998. "Secularist and Islamist Discourses on Modernity in Egypt and the Evolution of the Postcolonial Nation-State." In *Islam, Gender and Social Change*, eds. Yvonne Yazbeck Haddad and John L. Esposito. New York: Oxford University Press.

Hawley, John Stratton, and Wayne Proudfoot. 1994. "Introduction." In *Fundamentalism and Gender*, ed. John S. Hawley. New York: Oxford University Press.

Hegland, Mary Elaine. 1997. "A Mixed Blessing: The Majales—Shià Women's Rituals of Mourning in Northwest Pakistan." In *Mixed Blessings: Gender and Religious Fundamentalism Cross-Culturally*, eds. Judy Brink and Joan Mencher. New York: Routledge.

Held, David, Anthony McGrew, David Goldblatt, and Jonathan Perraton. 1999. *Global Transformations: Politics, Economics and Culture*. Stanford: Stanford University Press.

al-Hibri, Azizah. 1993. "Family Planning and Islamic Jurisprudence." In *Religious and Ethical Perspectives on Population Issues*. Washington, D.C.: The Religious Consultation on Population, Reproductive Health, and Ethics.

———. 1997. "Islam, Law and Custom: Redifining Muslim Women's Rights." *American University Journal of International Law and Policy*. 12: 1–44.

Hoodfar, Homa. 1996. "Bargaining with Fundamentalism: Women and the Politics of Population Control in Iran." *Reproductive Health Matters*. 8 (November): 30–40.

Huntington, Samuel. 1998. *The Clash of Civilizations and the Remaking of World Order*. New York: Touchstone Books.

Isasi-Diaz, Ada Maria and Yolanda Tarango. 1995. *Hispanic Women: Prophetic Voice in the Church*. San Francisco, Calif: Harper and Row.

Jagger, Alison M. 1983. *Feminist Politics and Human Nature*. New Jersey: Rowman & Allanheld.

Joseph, Suad. 1999. "Introduction: Theories and Dynamics of Gender, Self, and Identity in Arab Families." In *Intimate Selving in Arab Families: Gender, Self, and Identity*, ed. Suad Joseph. New York: Syracuse University Press.

Kandiyoti, Deniz. 1991. "Introduction." In *Women, Islam and the State*, ed. Deniz Kandiyoti. Philadelphia: Temple University Press.

Kaplan, Gisela. 1992. *Contemporary Western European Feminism*. New York: New York University Press.

Karam, Azza. 1998. *Women, Islamism, and State: Contemporary Feminism in Egypt*. London: Macmillan Press.

Keddie, Nikki R. 1991. "Introduction." In *Women in Middle Eastern History: Shifting Boundaries in Sex and Gender*, eds. Nikki Keddie and Beth Baron. New Haven, Conn.: Yale University Press.

———. 1999. "The New Religious Politics and Women Worldwide: A Comparative Study." In *Journal of Women's History*. Vol. 10, No. 4 (Winter): 11–34.

———. 2002. "Women in the Middle East: Since the Rise of Islam." Forthcoming pamphlet by the American Historical Association, Washington, D.C.

Khosravi, Shahram. 2000. "An Ethnographic Approach to an Online Diaspora." In *ISIM* Newsletter. 6:13.

King, Ursula. 1994. *Feminist Theology from the Third World: A Reader.* New York: Orbis.

Knauss, Peter R. 1987. *The Persistence of Patriarchy: Class, Gender and Ideology in 20th Century Algeria.* New York: Praeger.

Lapidus, Ira M. 1988. *A History of Islamic Societies.* Cambridge: Cambridge University Press.

Lazarus-Yafeh, Hava. 1988. "Contemporary Fundamentalism-Judaism, Christianity, Islam." *The Jerusalem Quarterly.* 47: 27–39.

Mahdi, Akbar. 2000. "Zanan-e Iran, novgarayi ve mohajerat" (Iranian Women, Modernism and Immigration, in Persian) *Iranian Political Bulletin* (www.iranemrooz.de/maqal/mahdi825.html), accessed December 18, 2000.

Malekian, Mostafa. 2001. "Religion and Globalization." An interview with Fatema Sadeqi. In *Hambastegi* (a Tehran daily) (22 Dey 1379/January 11): 6.

Maquire, Daniel. 1993. "Poverty, Population, and Catholic Tradition." In *Religious and Ethical Perspectives on Population Issues.* Washington, D.C.: The Religious Consultation on Population, Reproductive Health and Ethics.

Marshall, Barbara L. 1994. *Engendering Modernity: Feminism, Social Theory and Social Change.* Boston: Northeastern University Press.

Martin, Richard C., and Mark R. Woodward. 1997. *Defenders of Reason in Islam: Mùtazilism From Medieval School to Modern Symbol.* Oxford, U.K.: Oneworld.

Marty, Martin E., and Scott Appleby, eds. 1994. *Accounting for Fundamentalisms: The Dynamic Character of Movements.* Chicago: University of Chicago Press.

McBrien, Richard P. 1994. *Catholicism.* San Francisco: Harper.

McLaughlin, Eleanor. 1979. "The Christian Past: Does It Hold a Future for Women?" In *Woman Spirit Rising: A Feminist Reader in Religion,* eds. Carol Christ and Judith Plaskow. San Francisco: Harper and Row.

Mernissi, Fatima. 1987. *Beyond the Veil.* Cambridge, Mass.: Schenkman Publishing Company.

———. 1991. *The Veil and the Male Elite: A Feminist Interpretation of Women's Rights in Islam.* Reading, MA: Addison-Wesley.

———. 1993. *Islam and Democracy: Fear of the Modern World.* Reading, Mass: Addison-Wesley.

Mir-Hosseini, Ziba. 1996. "Stretching the Limits: A Feminist Reading of the Sharià in Iran Today." In *Feminism and Islam: Legal and Literary Perspectives,* ed. Mai Yamani. London: Ithaca.

———. 1999. *Islam and Gender: The Religious Debate in Contemporary Iran.* Princeton, N.J.: Princeton University Press.

Mittleman, James H., ed. 1997. *Globalization: Critical Reflections.* Boulder, Col.: Lynne Reiner.

Moghadem, Valentine M. 1993. *Modernizing Women: Gender and Social Change in the Middle East.* Boulder, Col.: Lynne Rienner.

———. 2000. "Islamic Feminism and Its Discontents: Notes on a Debate." *Iran Bulletin* (www.iran-bulletin.org/islamic_feminism.htm).

Mollenkott, Virginia R. 1992. *Sensuous Spirituality: Out from Fundamentalism.* New York: Crossroad.

Moraga, Cherrie. 1983. *Loving in the War Years*. Boston: South End Press.

Musallam, Basim. 1983. *Sex and Society in Islam*. Cambridge: Cambridge University Press.

Najmabadi, Afsaneh. 1994. "Power, Morality and the New Muslim Womanhood." In *The Politics of Social Transformation in Afghanistan, Iran and Pakistan*, eds. Myron Weiner and Ali Banuazizi. Syracuse, N.Y.: Syracuse University Press.

———. 1998. "Feminism in an Islamic Republic: Years of Hardship, Years of Growth." In *Islam, Gender and Social Change*, eds. Yvonne Yazbeck Haddad and John L. Esposito. New York: Oxford University Press.

Ohmae, Kenichi, ed. 1985. *The Evolving Global Economy*. Cambridge, Mass.: Harvard Business Review.

———. 1990. *The Borderless World: Power and Strategy in the Interlinked Economy*. New York: Harper Business.

———.1995. *The End of the Nation State: The Rise of Regional Economies*. New York: The Free Press.

Pateman, Carole. 1988. *The Sexual Contract*. Stanford: Stanford University Press.

———. 1989. *The Disorder of Women: Democracy, Feminism and Political Theory*. Stanford: Stanford University Press.

Payne, Stanley G. 1984. *Spanish Catholicism: An Historical Overview*. Madison: University of Wisconsin Press.

Pellauer, Mary. 1991. *Toward a Tradition of Feminist Theology: The Religious Thought of Elizabeth Cady Stanton, Susan B. Anthony, and Anna Howard Shaw*. Brooklyn, N.Y.: Carlson Publishing.

Plaskow, Judith, and Carol Christ. 1989. *Weaving the Visions: New Patterns in Feminist Spirituality*. San Francisco: Harper and Row.

Rahman, Fazlur. 1982. *Islam and Modernity: Transformation of an Intellectual Tradition*. Chicago: University of Chicago Press.

Riesebrodt, Martin. 1990. *Fundamentalismus als patriarchalische Protestbewegung: Amerikanische Protestanten (1910–28) und iranische Schiiten (1967–79) im Vergleich*. Tubingen: J. C. B. Mohr (Paul Siebeck).

Roald, Anne Sofie. 1998. "Feminist Reinterpretation of Islamic Sources: Muslim Feminist Theology in the Light of the Christian Tradition of Feminist Thought." In *Women and Islamization: Contemporary Dimensions of Discourse on Gender Relations*, ed. Karin Ask and Marit Tjomsland. Oxford: Berg.

Roberts, J. Timmons, and Amy Hite, eds. 2000. *From Modernization to Globalization: Perspectives on Development and Social Change*. Oxford: Blackwell Publishers.

Robertson, Roland. 1996. *Globalization: Social Theory and Global Culture*. London: SAGE.

Rodrik, Dani.1997. *Has Globalization Gone Too Far?* Washington D.C.: Institute for International Economics.

Rostow, Walt W. 1960. *The Stages of Economic Growth: A Non-Communist Manifesto*. London: Cambridge University Press.

Rowbotham, Sheila. 1992. *Women in Movement: Feminism and Social Action*. London: Routledge.

Ruether, Rosemary Radford. 1993. "Christianity and Women in the Modern World." In *Today's Woman in World Religions*, ed. Arvind Sharma. Albany: State University of New York Press.

Reuther, Rosemary Radford, and Catherine Keller, eds. 1995. In *Our Own Voices: Four Centuries of American Women's Religious Writing*. San Francisco: Harper and Row.

Ruggie, John G. 1996. *Winning the Peace: America and World Order in the New Era*. New York: Columbia University Press.

Sabbah, Fitna. 1984. *Women in the Muslim Unconscious*. New York: Pergamon Press.

Sakamoto, Yoshikazu, ed. 1994. *Global Transformation: Challenges to the State System*. Tokyo: United Nations University Press.

Sanasarian, Eliz. 2000. *Religious Minorities in Iran*. Cambridge, UK: Cambridge University Press.

Sassen, Saskia. 1996. *Losing Control? Sovereignty in an Age of Globalization*. New York: Columbia University Press.

———. 1998. *Globalization and its Discontents*. New York: The New Press.

Schaeffer, Robert K. 1997. *Understanding Globalization: The Social Consequences of Political, Economic, and Environmental Change*. Lanham, Md.: Rowman & Littlefield Publishers.

Schimmel, Annemarie. 1992. *Islam: An Introduction*. Albany, N.Y.: State University of New York Press.

Scholte, Jan Aart. 2000. *Globalization: A Critical Introduction*. New York: St. Martin's Press.

Schussler-Fiorenza, Elizabeth. 1992. *But She Said: Feminist Practices of Biblical Interpretation*. Boston: Beacon Press.

Shabestari, Muhammad Mojtahed. 2000. *Naqdi bar qaraat-e rasmi az din* (A Critique of the Official Reading of Religion). Tehran: Tarh-e No.

Sharabi, Hisham. 1988. *Neopatriarchy: A Theory of Disordered Change in Arab Society*. New York: Oxford.

Sharma, Arvind, ed. 1994. *Today's Women in World Religions*. Albany, N.Y.: State University of New York Press.

Shiva, Vandana. 1988. *Staying Alive: Women, Ecology and Development*. London: Zed Books.

Simms, Marian. 2001. "Globalization, Democratization, and Gender: Some Lessons from Oceania." In *Gender, Globalization, and Democratization*, eds. Rita Mae Kelly, Jane H. Bayes, Mary Hawkesworth, and Brigitte Young. Boulder, Col.: Rowman & Littlefield Publishers.

Smart, Ninian. 1977. *The Long Search*. Boston: Little Brown.

Smith, Dorothy E. 1977. *Feminism and Marxism—A Place to Begin, A Way to Go*. Vancouver: New Star Books.

Smith, Jane. 1985. "Women, Religion and Social Change in Early Islam." In *Women, Religion and Social Change*, eds. Y. Y. Haddad and Elison Banks Findly. Albany: State University of New York Press.

Smith, Wilfred Cantwell. 1963. *The Meaning and End of Religion*. New York: Macmillan.

Stowasser, Barbara F. 1994. *Women in The Quran, Traditions, and Interpretation.* New York: Oxford University Press.

———. 1998. "Gender Issues and Contemporary Quran Interpretation." In *Islam, Gender and Social Change,* eds. Yvonne Yazbeck Haddad and John L. Esposito. New York: Oxford University Press.

Sztompka, Piotr. 1994. *The Sociology of Social Change.* Oxford: Blackwell.

Szulc, Tad. 1995. *Pope John Paul II: The Biography.* New York: Simon and Schuster.

Tohidi, Nayereh. 1994. "Modernity, Islamization and Women in Iran." In *Gender and National Identity: Women and Politic in Muslim Societies,* ed. Valentine Moghadam. London: Zed Books.

———. 1996. *Feminizm, Demokrasi va Eslam-gera'i* (Feminism, Democracy and Islamism). Los Angeles: Ketabsara.

———. 1998. "Conclusion: Issues at Hand." In *Women in Muslim Societies: Diversity Within Unity,* eds. Herbert L. Bodman and Nayereh Tohidi. Boulder, Col.: Lynne Reiner.

———. 2001. "The International Connections of the Women's Movement in Iran." In *Iran and the Surrounding World, 1501–2001: Interaction in Culture and Cultural Politics,* eds. Nikki Keddie and Rudi Matthi. Seattle: Washington University Press.

Tronto, Joan. 1996. "Care as a Political Concept." In *Revisioning the Political,* eds. Nancy J. Hirschmann and Christine Di Stefano. Boulder, Col.: Westview.

Wadud, Amina. 1999. *Quran and Woman: Rereading Sacred Text from a Woman's Perspective.* Oxford: Oxford University Press.

Watanabe, Teresa. 2000. "US Freedoms Give American Muslims Influence Beyond Their Numbers." *Los Angeles Times.* (December 29):18–19.

Weigel, George. 1999. *Witness to Hope: The Biography of Pope John Paul II.* Cliff Street Books/Harper Collins.

Whalley, Lucy A. 1998. "Urban Minangkabau Muslim Women: Modern Choices, Traditional Concerns in Indonesia." In *Women in Muslim Societies: Diversity within Unity,* eds. Herbert Bodman and Nayereh Tohidi. Boulder, Col.: Lynne Rienner Publishers.

Wingrove, Elizabeth. 1999. "Interpolating Sex." *Signs.* 24, 4. (Summer): 869–893.

Wojtyla, Karol. 1981. *Love and Responsibility,* trans. H. T. Willetts. New York: Farrar, Straus, Giroux.

Wollstonecraft, Mary. 1975. *A Vindication of the Rights of Woman* (1792). Baltimore, Md.: Penguin.

World Almanac and Book of Facts 2001. 2001. Mahway, N.J.: World Almanac Education Group.

Wright, Robin. 2000. "The Changing Face of Islam." *Los Angeles Times.* (December 27–29).

Young, Brigitte. 2001. "Globalization and Gender: An European Perspective." In *Gender, Globalization, and Democratization,* eds. Rita Mae Kelly, Jane H. Bayes, Mary Hawkesworth, and Brigitte Young. Boulder, Col.: Rowman & Littlefield Publishers.

CHAPTER 3

UNITED STATES CATHOLIC WOMEN: FEMINIST THEOLOGIES IN ACTION

Susan Marie Maloney

This chapter will explore how U.S. Catholic women are implementing the Platform for Action (PFA)[1] adopted at the United Nations Fourth World Conference on Women (1995) in Beijing, China. The first section, entitled Roman Catholicism: Church and State, describes the institutional organization of the Catholic Church and its status as a political state. As a branch of Christianity, Roman Catholicism is a church; as a political entity, the Catholic Church is the Vatican state. Various official agencies of the Catholic Church and Catholic groups are legally and politically autonomous from the institutional church but are embedded in the structure of the church for historical reasons. The distinction between official Catholic agencies and non-official autonomous Catholic organizations is critical to understanding the daily struggles Catholic women face finding practical opportunities to implement the PFA.

Feminist religious thought provides the religious theory that grounds much of the work of U.S. Catholic women implementing the PFA. As a perspective, it challenges the traditional interpretations within Catholic theology. As a motivation for action, it provides Catholic women with a religious authority based on their own experience. The second section, entitled Three Perspectives, identifies the diversity of these women's commitments to the PFA. I have named these perspectives holistic feminism, moderate feminism, and reconstructive feminism. The perspectives are based on the research and the interviews I conducted for this study. Each perspective is descriptive of some U.S. Catholic women working strategically to change the oppressive policies and conditions under which many women must live. The description of each is meant to serve and assist the reader in managing and synthesizing the dialectic between action and theory.

My research indicates that U.S. Catholic women hold a myriad of views on feminism (theory) and similarly scores of ideas for implementing the PFA (action). The arbitrary creation of the three perspectives of feminism is to provide the reader with (1) a clear understanding of some of the theological differences among U.S. Catholic women working for the PFA; (2) a manageable framework for explaining the work of U.S. Catholic women implementing the PFA; and (3) an insight into how some Catholic women influence international policy and discussion, shape Catholic Church opinion, and mobilize local Catholic women to support particular PFA commitments. In order to give a concrete example of the enthusiasm and commitment of U.S. Catholic women to the PFA, at the end of this section I provide a brief sketch of one woman's commitment to the PFA.

The third section, entitled Catholic Feminist Scholarship, offers a brief summary of the work of scholars who reconstruct Catholic theology from a feminist perspective. Their scholarship advances not simply areas of compatibility between Catholic thought and feminist theory but also suggests new understandings of Catholicism based in the experience of women. Although their writings are not directly related to the implementation of the PFA, their work and those of other feminist scholars have a profound religious significance for U.S. Catholic women implementing the PFA. Their theological writings provide (1) the theological grounding on which Catholic women may stand to critique sexist, unjust policies and practices both in the church and in society, and (2) the religious language so necessary to validate and motivate Catholic women to act for the implementation of the PFA.

ROMAN CATHOLICISM: CHURCH AND STATE

Roman Catholicism is a church organized and governed by a rigid hierarchical system of authority. The Pope is the spiritual leader of all Roman Catholics. He is elected by an international council of cardinals. The Vatican is the central office of the Roman Catholic Church, comprised of many agencies devoted to the administration of the temporal as well as the spiritual needs of Roman Catholics. Vatican City is the territorial state as well as a commonly interchangeable name for the Holy See (Derr 1983,

27).[2] The Pope, as bishop of Rome, heads the Holy See.[3] The diocese of Rome functions as the preeminent seat of spiritual as well as temporal power among Roman Catholic dioceses. Each bishop directs a diocese that is in union with the Pope. With the local bishop as the sole legal authority, each diocese is incorporated as a legal, separate entity within a country. The Pope, in consultation with the curia and the bishops of the church, is the prime interpreter of Catholic teaching. Each diocese, however, issues its own pastoral directives and guidelines based on the teachings of the universal church.

International church efforts dealing with doctrine, theology, humanitarian aid, religious education, health systems, evangelization, and other church endeavors are dependent on the cooperation of each national body of bishops with the Vatican curia. The curia is the administrative arm of the Holy See with its international offices located at Vatican City in the center of Rome, Italy. On the national level the United States Catholic Conference (USCC) is the association of U.S. bishops. Whereas any single bishop has pastoral and legal authority in his own diocese, the USCC is dependent on each local bishop to collaborate with USCC agencies that function to carry out the mission of the Roman Catholic Church in the United States.

The Pope is both a spiritual and secular leader. He functions as the head of the universal Roman Catholic Church and the Vatican state. Through spiritual proclamations, religious treatises, political statements, educational exhortations, books, media interviews, appointment of delegates to international meetings, visitations with heads of state, and personal visits to dioceses and nations, the Pope is a major figure on the political and religious scene. Whenever he speaks, he proclaims the doctrine and teachings of the Roman Catholic Church, whether addressing the United Nations or a small impoverished parish. His influence on the world of religion, politics, and society, as well as on millions of Roman Catholics is profound and unparalleled by any other contemporary Catholic figure.[4]

WOMEN AND THE ORGANIZATIONAL STRUCTURE OF THE CATHOLIC CHURCH

Contrary to common misconceptions, women hold many positions within the institutional church. These women are employed by the church or serve as volunteers within church agencies. A woman who heads a diocesan office of Catholic Charities or Pastoral Ministries would be an example of this first category. In these positions women working in church agencies are dependent on male ecclesiastics for appointments to church committees, approval of policy statements, and the use of resources at their disposal (*i.e.*, budgets).

Many Catholic women not employed by the institutional church direct women-led organizations, or work in centers that promote social justice based on a progressive understanding of church teaching. Such agencies are related to, but not dependent on, hierarchical church authorities for institutional and material resources. A woman who is the non-governmental organization (NGO) representative of her religious community of sisters, or a woman employed by an independent Catholic agency (women's shelter) would be an example of this second category.

These two classifications offer a structural explanation of the relationship between U.S. Catholic women working for the PFA and the U.S. Catholic Church. The next section will examine three distinct perspectives of feminism: holistic, moderate, and reconstructive. I will consider each of these perspectives in relation to the implementation of the PFA.

THREE PERSPECTIVES

Pope John Paul II selected Mary Ann Glendon (Bole, 1995), as chair of the Vatican delegation to the UN Fourth World Conference on Women. A law professor at Harvard, mother, grandmother, and scholar, Glendon's appointment was symbolic and strategic (Butterfield 1995). For some, Glendon's appointment symbolized the Pope's commitment to the leadership of women. For others, her selection was a strategic move that highlighted U.S. Catholic women's support for Catholic teaching on reproductive issues.

In addition to being the first U.S. woman to head a Vatican delegation to a UN conference, Glendon has become known as the chief promoter of holistic feminism.[5] The feminism of the 1970s, she writes,

> is distinguished by its sour attitude toward family life, its rigid party line on gay rights and abortion, and its puzzling combination of sexual anger with sexual aggressiveness. . . . [N]ew feminism is a house with many rooms, inclusive rather than polarizing; open minded rather than dogmatic. (Glendon 1995d, 47)

Glendon's definition of holistic feminism does not critique any forms of hierarchy or patriarchy, or any structures of church authority. Rather, holistic feminism uses the traditional theological sources to promote the concept of woman primarily as wife and mother. This is based on an immutable, static, and unchanging view of the nature of human beings. It draws not only on medieval notions of woman from the theologian Thomas Aquinas but on more recent papal teachings by John Paul II.[6]

In the document *Mulieris Dignitatem,* John Paul II (1988) proposes a theology of woman rooted in the book of Genesis. Adam and Eve as human beings are made in the image and likeness of God and both reflect the love of the Creator God. Their creation establishes equality between the sexes and their relationship before God guarantees the sanctity of marriage. This biblical interpretation of equality means that men and women are created to complement one another. This concept of complementarity is not only biological and sociological but, for proponents of holistic feminism, it reinforces heterosexual marriage and the family as central religious symbols for the Catholic Church.

For centuries, the church's ecclesiology (self-understanding) has been based on this nuptial analogy. Women as loving wives and mothers are to image the church as the Bride of Christ, while Christ is the Bridegroom. The church is the temporal and institutional manifestation of the union Christ has with its earthly members. For many, this analogy may seem strange. Yet, for centuries, Christian (not only Catholic) tradition has taught that woman and her role should be seen primarily in relation to marriage and family. Marriage and the family has been the quintessential analogy to express the love of God (male) for his church (female).[7] Thus, to challenge this notion of the supernatural and "natural" order of hierarchy is to challenge a sacred system of religious symbols. Symbolic representation of the sacred is at the heart of all religions. When moderate or reconstructive feminists challenge the image of woman as other than bride, wife, and mother, they question a key religious analogy revered by the Roman Catholic Church.

Pope John Paul II and adherents of holistic feminism have made some accommodation to widen the image of women (Navarro-Valls 1995). For instance, Vatican documents acknowledge women's oppression and condemn the objectification and exploitation of women. They also advance a concept of "equality with dignity" that "promotes women's exercise of all their talents and rights without undermining their roles within the family" (Glendon 1995a, 204).

Holistic feminism also claims theoretical ground from Catholic social teaching. The cornerstone of Catholic social teaching rests on the dignity of the individual as the unique image and reflection of the loving God. It promotes the full expansion of human rights of individuals, family, regions, cultures and all nations.[8] The policy implications of this social teaching coupled with the centuries old symbol system of the church as the bride of Christ is reflected in the following statement by John Paul II. "No program of 'equal rights' between women and men is valid unless it takes this fact [women's special role as mother] fully into account" (John Paul II 1988).

The appropriation of the term "feminism" by conservative U.S. Catholic women demonstrates the dynamism and power of feminist thought.[9] Women and men who have not historically been aligned with the movement are seeking to acknowledge some of the issues it claims, and to capitalize on its strength and influence (Tong 1993). Appropriation of the term "feminism" is an attempt to redefine the term within a traditional Catholic context. Finally, holistic feminism challenges the more liberal and radical Catholic feminists to be more attentive to and inclusive of women who primarily define themselves as wives and mothers.[10]

HOLISTIC FEMINISM AND THE IMPLEMENTATION OF THE PFA

The fourteen women and nine men in the Vatican delegation to Beijing in 1995 represented nine countries and five continents. The delegation included Archbishop Renato Martino, permanent observer of the Holy See to the United Nations, and Dr. Joaquin-Valls, the official press person for the Vatican. Under Glendon's leadership, the delegation's mandate was

> to make the documents issued by the conference more responsive to the actual lives of women, and, second in keeping with the Catholic Church's traditional mission to the poor—to be a voice for the marginalized and voiceless women who can seldom make themselves heard in the corridors of power. (Glendon 1996, 32)

Considering that the aim of the Vatican delegation was to focus on the social and economic issues of women, as well as to avoid an outright confrontation with abortion rights advocates, the emphasis on diplomacy and discussion may be seen as a positive action to support the PFA. Arguments with feminists were not to be the Vatican's legacy to Beijing. The delegation did not want to repeat the negative impact associated with the Vatican following the 1994 UN Conference on Population and Development held in Cairo.[11]

Widely published in Catholic journals and newspapers, Glendon's final statement to the UN Fourth World Conference on Women consisted of a pronouncement that the Vatican's endorsement of the PFA was contingent on how compatible the resolutions were with Catholic social teaching. "Certainly the living heart of these documents lies in their sections on the needs of women in poverty, on strategies for development, on literacy and education, on ending violence against women, on a culture of peace, and on access to employment, land, capital, and technology" (Glendon 1995b, 233).

Despite this broad endorsement, the final Vatican delegation statement written by Glendon resoundingly critiques portions of the final PFA document.[12] These criticisms of the PFA include the denunciation of the emphasis on individualism, an attack on the exaggerated attention on sexual and reproductive health needs of women rather than nutrition and disease related issues, and the absence of stronger language affirming the family as the basic unit of society. The statement also reiterates Vatican opposition to abortion, artificial contraception, and the use of condoms as a family planning measure or in HIV/AIDS prevention programs (Glendon 1995c, 235–36).

The relationship between those who hold the perspective of holistic feminism and the implementation of the PFA needs close analysis. Three significant areas emerge. First, holistic feminism, following traditional Vatican teaching, gives considerable attention to the statistics of the historical oppression of women with a special emphasis on poverty and the lack of economic resources for women. As an implementation, this starting point is an important commitment on the part of the Vatican and adherents to holistic feminism to raise public consciousness about the real (and not stereotypical) women living in poverty. Most women in poverty have children and need to merge the cares of family life with a participation in the broader social and economic order. Holistic feminism, following the Vatican's acknowledgment of the material reality of women living in poverty and their lack of access to resources, adds considerable moral weight to the term "feminization of poverty." The linking of work, women, and poverty by the Vatican delegation is an important admission that poverty has a gender.

Second, prior to the UN Fourth World Conference on Women, Pope John Paul II had responded to a request by UN Secretary General Boutros Boutros-Ghali that heads of state make specific commitments to improve the lives of women in connection with the Beijing Conference. In a remarkable address, the Pope committed

> all of the over 300,000 social, caring and educational institutions of the Catholic Church to a concerted and priority strategy directed to girls and young women, and especially to the poorest; appealed to all men in the church to undergo, where necessary, a change of heart, and to implement, as a demand of their faith, a positive vision of women; and requested that the women of the church assume new forms of leadership in service while asking all institutions of the church to welcome this contribution of women. (quoted by Glendon 1995a, 204–05

Some U.S. Catholic women employed by the Catholic Church appeal to this papal address in order to advance the well-being and recognition of women within church structures (Sheila Garcia, telephone interview by the author, Washington, D.C., July 15, 1997).[13] For some observers, this Papal statement may be too little and too late. Its significance, however, lies in the fact that women's talents, leadership skills, and experience are here acknowledged by the male authorities of the church. For women dependent on the church for employment, this highlighting of the institutional church's own inadequate treatment of women results in notable benefits to them. Catholic women know that the institutional policies of the church, along with its well-known prohibition forbidding women to serve as priests (Congregation for the Doctrine of the Faith 1995), prevent both its members and the wider public from hearing the message of any Catholic proclamation without prejudice. The Pope's statement and its promotion by those holding a traditional (holistic feminist) stance toward the PFA should not be underestimated as mere lip service, nor exaggerated as a full endorsement of women's rights. Instead, it should be seen as an acknowledgment of the concrete oppression of women within the church and society.

The third area of analysis of holistic feminism and the implementation of the PFA is the recognition of the relationship between sexuality and violence against women. Glendon's statement indicates a welcome emerging alignment in Catholic thought between the public and private spheres of women's lives. The Vatican delegation concurred with the PFA

in dealing with the question of sexuality and reproduction, where the former affirm that changes in the attitudes of both men and women are necessary conditions for achieving equality and that responsibility in sexual matters belongs to both men and women. Women, are moreover, most often the victims of irresponsible sexual behavior in terms of personal suffering, disease, poverty, and the deterioration of family life. (Glendon 1995a, 205)

In the above statement, Glendon expands the Vatican stance from violence against women as chiefly seen as exploitation of cheap labor, particularly of young girls, to include the issue of violence in the home. This shift of emphasis is important because it more readily reflects the reality of women's lives. Whether working or unemployed, women are vulnerable to violence in the private sphere of their lives. Although previous church documents have linked violence and the home, Glendon's comments suggest that the church may be willing to make the connections between religious teaching, violence, women, and the home. Noteworthy is the fact that Glendon's statement was published in several Catholic journals and newspapers.

In sum, holistic feminism is the ideology underpinning the traditional stance of the Vatican about women and issues affecting their lives. What it adds to the discussion of the PFA is an emphasis on the connection between the practical lives of women and Catholic teachings about women. While holistic feminist analysis has made a positive step in focusing on poverty, Catholic institutions, and violence against women, this analysis tends not to emphasize direct action.

MODERATE FEMINISM

Moderate feminism, unlike holistic feminism, challenges the hierarchical and patriarchal nature of the Catholic Church. Its theological principles are grounded in both the experience of women and the social teaching of the Catholic Church. Drawing on the stories of women, it gives priority to the daily reality of women's lives. The stories, shared experiences of women across cultures, give rise to the awareness of sexism as a constituent component of the economic, political, social, and cultural oppression of women. Using the life stories of women as the entry point to a consciousness-raising method called "the praxis cycle," moderate feminism aims to connect the local issues of women with the global realities of all womankind.

Theological reflection is a component of this praxis cycle, a step in a method to empower women. Women from the moderate feminist perspective reflect on passages from a variety of religious texts, whether biblical or inspirational tracts. Theological symbols in moderate feminism rest less on Catholic tradition and dogma and more on pragmatic approaches to religious rituals. Clearly Catholic in identity but not exclusively so, moderate feminists make alliances with women of other faiths. The defense or criticism of church doctrine is not central to moderate feminism. Moderate feminists tend not to defend church doctrine but, rather, to incorporate the experience of women with Catholic social teaching in order to advance the empowerment of women.

The primary religious image of the church used by moderate feminists is the metaphor of the church as the People of God (Abbott 1966).[14] This figure of speech, adopted from the Vatican II document *The Dogmatic Constitution on the Church*, represents a modern and dynamic self-understanding of the church in today's world.[15] For Catholics of the post-Vatican II era, this metaphor means that all members of the church are valued, responsible Catholics accountable for the work and mission of the church. The shift of the primary religious analogy of the church from the Bride of Christ to the People of God has profound implications for Catholic women. This is not a minor metaphorical change. The shift represents a move away from women being envisioned as dependent individuals (brides) to being imaged as independent adults (responsible persons) within a religious community.

This religious image coupled with Catholic social teaching arms moderate feminists to enter the battleground of politics and the international economic order. They have both the organizing metaphor of a moral community and the strong tradition of Catholic social teaching that emphasizes human dignity and the duties of the responsible person.

Moderate feminism uses the social sciences to inform its analysis for further action. It incorporates the most recent findings in science, politics, economics, anthropology, and technology to analyze women's issues. It is committed to coalition building for action. Moderate feminism finds its Catholic identity in the Catholic social teaching and its feminist identity from liberal U.S. feminism.[16] Some moderate feminists ignore Catholic teaching on sexuality and its policy implications, stating that other Catholic organizations have sexual issues as a priority. This position does not promote nor does it repudiate traditional church teaching on sexuality. Using Catholic social teaching as its theoretical base, moderate feminism promotes human rights, advocates the participation of women in the political process, advocates economic justice for women, and emphasizes the principles of freedom and equality. Moderate feminism seeks to bring about change on behalf of women both within church structures and in the political sphere.[17]

The blend of the practical life experienced by most U.S. Catholic women, for example, the notion of the supreme right of the individual, mixed with the communitarian theory from Catholic social teaching places moderate feminists in a unique position within U.S. culture and the church. They can dialogue easily with conservative Catholics (the organizing metaphor of *The People of God* is well within church teaching), while negotiating with reconstructive feminists on economic and educational issues.

MODERATE FEMINISM AND
IMPLEMENTATION OF THE PFA

An impressive amount of follow-up action to the UN Fourth World Conference on Women has been, and continues to be initiated, organized, and executed by moderate U.S. Catholic feminists. Many of these women are presently working in church offices, charitable agencies or organizations which have as a focus the promotion of women's issues. After having experienced the energy, enthusiasm, and dynamism of the NGO conference and the PFA adopted by the official delegates, these women "brought home" the tenacity and power to make the vision a reality.

The moderate approach to action for U.S. Catholic women is defined as those strategies that promote the PFA agenda *within* the institutional church and *outside* or in alliance with non-church groups (Curran 1985). This distinction from other approaches is important because many of the women working from this perspective carry a "double burden" to promote the PFA. The "double burden" for these women is the challenge to respond to both their commitment to women's issues and their commitment to the Catholic Church. For most of these women, their task is to balance their public obligations to the church (many hold official staffing positions within the church) and to devote time to the strategic planning so necessary to implement the PFA. To do this, many of the women have successfully linked the long tradition of Catholic action in social service and educational arenas with the PFA. One strategy is to connect the Catholic Church's commitment to the poor in a global feminist perspective. Another strategy is the incorporation of the PFA as a component of prayer services and of adult education study group guides.

Moderate Catholic feminist women are laying the groundwork for long-range systemic change by using their positions of influence to implement the PFA in three major ways. These are: coalition building, publications, and relations with the U.S. government and NGOs.

Coalition Building. Five months after the PFA was adopted, the Catholic Coalition in the United States on the UN Fourth World Conference on Women was formed. The members included staff of several diocesan offices, personnel from the national offices of the USCC, representatives from the International Catholic Child Bureau Board, directors of diocesan Catholic Charities, members of religious orders of women, heads of the Catholic Health Association, Global Catholic Relief Services, National Catholic Educational Association, the Center of Concern, Catholic Daughters of the Americas, and other agencies. The purposes of this coalition were: (1) to collaborate on the implementation of the PFA in the priority areas of poverty, violence, and the girl child; and (2) to explore ways to commit Catholic institutions to the care of girls and young women, especially the poorest (Donna Hanson, interview by the author, Spokane, Wash., August 11, 1997).[18]

This group has identified several projects. An example of one project is the joint response of the coalition to the preparatory documents for a special Synod for the Americas (A synod is an international meeting called by the Pope with a very focused international agenda dealing with specific church issues). By responding to the pre-synod materials that shape the synod agenda from a PFA perspective, these Catholic women have shown not only a commitment to the PFA but demonstrated a very sophisticated strategy to keep the church and the Pope accountable to their public commitment to women. This preparatory document links the person of Jesus Christ as evangelizer with the social and political priority of women's lives in the PFA. One could say that this document has two foci. Using religious terms, it addresses issues of importance to the ecclesiastical authorities, such as the centrality of Jesus Christ in the church, ritual, and faith formation. However, it also adroitly demonstrates that religious dogma and teaching must have practical moral content if the Catholic Church is to be credible in the social and political arenas (Working Group 1996, 2). In short, the coalition document argues that the Catholic Church cannot proclaim the love of Jesus Christ in contemporary times and avoid the issues of poverty, violence against women, and education for the girl child. An institutional manifestation by the church of Jesus' love for all humankind must address specifically the devastating statistics on the abuse of women.

Publications.   One of the most impressive actions that furthers the commitment to the PFA are the publications that have been issued by U.S. Catholic women. Many such publications exist, but of unusual educational value and practicality is the work of Maria Riley, O. P. For over twenty-five years, Riley has been active in the women's movement (Maria Riley O. P., Telephone interview with the author, May 20, 1997).[19] As coordinator of the women's project at the Center of Concern,[20] Riley has positioned herself as a leader and liaison between Catholic groups and the larger Washington, D.C. interest groups on behalf of women. Of particular note is her work *Women Connecting Beyond Beijing* (Riley 1996a, 1996b). In this publication, she has designed a study-reflection-action packet that, in three sessions, synthesizes the massive PFA documents into manageable increments for small groups. Using a creative pedagogical tool entitled PFA Women's Empowerment Agenda, Riley's book shortens the PFA and enables women to see the connection between the global crises of women and local issues that many women deal with on a daily basis.

Contrary to a common public perception about Catholic publications, these materials are not directed to a "Catholic only" audience. They make no mention of the Holy See's participation in the UN Conference or of a particular "Catholic agenda." The focus, rather, is on developing a process that empowers women to take seriously their own local issues and see how they reflect, and are related to, the global situation of women as a whole. These materials are carefully crafted to highlight the similarities—not the differences—among women. The materials are interfaith in perspective and do not mention any religious dogma and obligations that may create a barrier among women. The only reference to a religious practice is an invitation directed to the facilitator to open each session with a prayer/reflection time. The interfaith nature of the publications reflects a respect for religious diversity and emphasizes the desire for social justice as a religious virtue that transcends religious affiliation.

U.S. Government and Non-Governmental Relations. Another impressive action that furthers the commitment to the PFA by moderate feminists is the relationship being established between U.S. women's groups, government, and NGOs. With the exception of the President's Interagency Council on Women established in 1995, the U.S. government does not have a permanent national coordinating body to address U.S. women's agendas and issues. The United States is one of a few countries in the world that lacks such a national coordinating agency for NGOs.[21] This lack of government sponsored structure seriously restricts the political potential of U.S. women committed to the implementation of the PFA. It also hinders any national focus on the issues of women in the United States. Each of the four UN World Conferences on Women has recommended some form of national coordination.

In response to this institutional void, independent women's agencies organized and created the U.S. Women Connect organization, a network that developed after the 1995 UN Fourth World Conference on Women in Beijing out of a series of consultations between 1996–99 with representatives of over one hundred U.S. women's organizations and NGOs. Its mission is to connect together U.S. women and girls working for rights and empowerment, and to link them with other activists and advocates around the globe.

U.S. Women Connect is governed by a fifteen member board elected in June 1999, whose members encompass the diversity of women and girls throughout the United States.[22] Some Catholic women have taken leadership roles in the formation of this group. The establishment of this much-needed national coordination agency indicates a clear alliance by Catholic women with political and non-religious groups. This alliance demonstrates a political sophistication U.S. Catholic women have acquired. The networks forged are based not on political expediency but, rather, on a deep commitment to change political and social policy for the well-being of all women of the world.

Of emerging interest and a potential political influence is the voice of the religious communities of women who hold NGO status at the United Nations. Several independent orders of Catholic women have established NGO offices to promote issues pertinent not to internal church matters but, rather, to concerns of justice, peace, international development, and women (Catherine Ferguson, interview by author, Los Angeles, Calif., July 26, 1999).[23] Not given adequate coverage by the media, over seventy religious orders of Catholic women issued a joint statement to the official delegates of the UN Fourth Conference on Women, Beijing, 1995.[24] This statement reflects the emerging political involvement of women in Catholic orders.

Although not explicitly stated, the establishment of these NGOs indicates a growing discomfort with the Vatican's stance toward international efforts on behalf of women. The presence of feminist women in Catholic orders offers an alternative Catholic voice to the international women's movement and challenges the traditional practice of the Vatican speaking solely on behalf of all Catholics. Many religious orders of Catholic women operate international institutions with numerous schools, hospitals, and social service agencies under their control. These resources can easily provide sites throughout the world that can link local empowerment projects for women with their sisters in other regions around the globe. Many of these communities are becoming increasingly aware that their "sisters" in other national regions are not simply those who have religious status with the church but *all women* who either work on behalf of the poor and disenfranchised or who are vulnerable themselves.

Many of these Catholic orders of women have used their status as stockholders to raise justice issues on world trade and banking. As participants in the international economic order, they have increasingly become aware of the systemic injustice that women suffer. This awareness has intensified the urgency with which they support the implementation of the PFA.

RECONSTRUCTIVE FEMINISM

Reconstructive U.S. Catholic feminists seek to shape and advance the sexual and reproductive ethics of the Catholic Church. Their theological theory is grounded in the moral capacity of women to make sound and responsible decisions about their lives.[25] Unlike holistic feminism, reconstructive feminism gives greater emphasis to the Catholic social teaching tradition of the church. It emphasizes the church teaching of the dignity of the individual human being as the *imago dei*.[26] Reconstructive feminism also draws on the Catholic teaching of the primacy of conscience. Church teaching instructs that the individual's conscience can be judged by God alone. "For man [sic] has in his heart a law written by God. To obey it is the very dignity of man; according to it will he be judged. Conscience is the most secret core and sanctuary of a [man]. There [he] is alone with God whose voice echoes in his depths" (Abbott 1966, 213). Grounded in the tradition of Catholic human rights theory and the primacy of conscience, reconstructive feminism speaks to Catholic women familiar with U.S. culture and the tradition of individual liberty and equality. Grounded in Catholic human rights theory and the primacy of conscience, reconstructive feminism presents a strong challenge to the Vatican perspective on the PFA and to holistic feminism.

Reconstructive feminists support feminist activists and scholars working to align progressive Catholic thought on reproductive ethics with Catholic social teaching. Their theoretical ground is a critique of the Catholic Church's view on women and a woman's ability to make decisions for herself. Reconstructive feminists seek to empower women to take control of their lives and align themselves with political feminists from political movements. Unlike moderate feminists, reconstructive feminists do not ignore the sexual teachings of the church; rather, they make it a priority to challenge the church's paternalistic teaching (Kissling 1996).

Strategies used by reconstructive feminists are education, media exposure, publications, and advocacy for public policy issues that promote social justice and the welfare of women. Emphasis on health issues, violence against women, discrimination, and sexual rights are priorities for reconstructive feminists. In recent years, reconstructive feminists have been sensitive to the cultural understandings of feminism. Alliances to implement the PFA have been made that respect cultural differences, encourage financial support, but not dependence, and see each regional feminist endeavor as a movement of sisters in cooperation, not sisters in competition.

RECONSTRUCTIVE FEMINISM AND
THE IMPLEMENTATION OF THE PFA

Catholic feminists who oppose the church's teaching on abortion and sexual ethics have a reconstructive approach to action on behalf of the PFA. Well organized and supported by pro-choice funding, Catholic feminists from this approach seek "to advance the health and fight against violence against women" priorities of the PFA. They seek to influence Catholic social teaching with an emphasis on gender analysis of issues. Discourse, advocacy, and education are the strategies used by radical Catholic feminists. Catholics for a Free Choice (CFFC), under the leadership of Frances Kissling, is an example of the reconstructive approach to the implementation of the PFA. CFFC publishes a monthly news journal and pamphlets. It provides a speakers bureau. CFFC lobbies U.S. representatives with the intention of offering an alternative voice of Catholic opinion on social policy dealing with reproductive rights of women, healthcare issues, and international health policy (Kathy Toner, telephone interview by author, May 22, 1997).[27]

Of special importance is CFFC's effort to promote women's reproductive rights in Latin America. With technical assistance and support from CFFC, three organizations have become an important force for Catholic women. Catolicos por el Derecho a Decidir/Mexico (CDD/Mexico), Catolicos por el Derecho a Decidir/Latin America, and Catolicas pelo Direito de Decidir/Brazil (CDD/Brazil) are each independent, active networks set up to educate and empower women within their own countries about health issues, birth control, and abortion.

These organizations form a collaborative partnership and make a concerted effort to respect cultural differences, understandings, and religious sensibilities in the promotion of reproductive rights (Kissling and Hunt 1995). They are not duplicates of CFFC. Rather, CFFC aids in technical assistance, providing speakers, board development, information sharing, and program planning. CFFC's success at assisting in the organization of regional partnerships can be verified by the opposition to its existence. The Brazilian bishops' conference issued a public statement that denounced CFFC as a bogus Catholic organization. "It [CFFC] cannot be considered a Catholic organization because it defends points that are in total contradiction with church teachings" (*National Catholic Reporter* 1997, 7). In reply, Brazil's Catholics for a Free Choice representative said, " . . . We want to open the possibility of being a Catholic and keeping our faith, but at the same time living a liberating sexual experience, more autonomous, open to the right to choose" (*National Catholic Reporter* 1997, 7)

Another CFFC project is *Catholics for Contraception*. This is a broad based long-term project aimed to increase public awareness about Catholic support for family planning, especially in developing countries (*Conscience* 1997, 30). The importance of this initiative lies in the separation of the discussion of abortion from the issue of birth control. Statistics indicate that over 85 percent of U.S. Catholics support some form of artificial birth control. This move to organize around birth control rather than fuse the two issues enables CFFC to reach out to more progressive Catholics who oppose abortion according to traditional church teaching but support artificial birth control contrary to church teaching. According to CFFC reports, this strategy has been very successful in the approval of appropriations by the U.S. Congress for international family planning programs. A Catholic voice present at Congressional hearings on these programs supported the right to contraceptives but not the right to abortion. This strategy of compromise is important to the implementation of the PFA, considering the strength of the U.S. Catholic Bishops lobbying arm in Washington, D.C. (*Conscience* 1997, 30).

In late 2000, CFFC published a follow-up pamphlet entitled *Catholic Voices on Beijing: A Call for Social Justice for Women*. The purpose was to articulate the views of Catholic women and men who see the PFA to be compatible with "the broad teachings of the church, particularly Catholic social justice teaching" (Beijing Plus 5 Working Group 2000, 3). This is an example of educational materials created by reconstructive feminists to promote a living and vibrant tradition of teaching and moral continuity within the church.

Implementation of the PFA is not only the concern of U.S. women who hold a particular perspective on feminism. Many Catholic women promote the PFA through singular educational endeavors. To represent the work of the individual Catholic woman, I have included a brief example of the efforts of one woman.

THE INDIVIDUAL U.S. CATHOLIC WOMAN AND IMPLEMENTATION OF THE PFA

A large percentage of the forty thousand participants at the NGO Forum for the UN Fourth World Conference on Women were Roman Catholic women. These were individuals sponsored by religious institutes (members and non-members), local churches, women's organizations, social service agencies, the business community, the U.S. government,[28] and self-financed groups. Most of these women did not attend with any church status.[29] Almost all of these women have gone back to their respective countries to promote the PFA (Chittister 1996). The following example helps to illustrate the energy, dynamism, talent, and commitment of individual Catholic women to the implementation of the PFA.

Cecilia Calva has been a member of the Sisters of the Holy Names of the California Province for over thirty years. Most of her time has been in ministry to the Latino/a community. For ten years, she served in the state of Chiapas, Mexico organizing and educating members of the local Catholic parish, mostly women, for leadership roles in both the church and society. Cecilia attended the NGO Forum and pledged to discuss the PFA and its twelve "critical areas of concern" in whatever venue available. As a bilingual person, Cecilia is committed particularly to the empowerment of the U.S. Latinas. In the first year after the UN Conference, Cecilia spoke to over twenty groups about her experience. Her commitment took her into high school and college classrooms, senior citizens centers, convents, parish councils, and civic groups. The enthusiasm and commitment of individual women like Cecilia have increased the awareness of the plight of the world's women and continues to foster a commitment in others to implement the PFA.

CATHOLIC FEMINIST SCHOLARSHIP—
THE UNDERLYING DIFFERENCE

Allegiance to the PFA is but one fundamental concern for U.S. Catholic women. Whether one professes a holistic, moderate, or reconstructive feminist perspective, at the heart of women's issues rests the question: How do Catholic women reconcile Catholic teaching and feminist thought? Both Catholic feminist theology and feminist theory have many variations, subtleties, and substantive differences (Tong 1989, 23).

For the past thirty years, feminist theologians have challenged the Catholic Church to re-examine its teaching and treatment of women. Many eminent feminist scholars have contributed to the reconstruction of Catholic theology. They object to the underlying sexism and patriarchy that undergirds traditional Catholic theology. In an attempt to illustrate some general similarities and differences in this extremely complex body of thought about the nature of women, sexuality, the social teaching of the church, and political action, this section presents the work of five Catholic feminist theologians.

ELIZABETH SCHÜSSLER-FIORENZA

Elizabeth Schüssler-Fiorenza's ground-breaking work, *In Memory of Her* (1985), is a sophisticated theological study of the re-interpretation of the Christian Scriptures. In this work, Schüssler-Fiorenza deconstructs the methodology used in traditional biblical studies and offers new forms of critical analysis based on innovative and creative feminist scholarship. She offers a methodology that deconstructs the patriarchal sources of Christian scripture and promotes the idea that the first Christians were a community of disciples with shared authority among equals—not a hierarchy of males. Her work offers a vision to Catholic feminists of a new biblical authority of interpretation. This new feminist interpretation provides theoretical grounds for advocating the ordination of women to the priesthood, and for leadership roles for women in the Church and society (Schüssler-Fiorenza 1993).

ROSEMARY RADFORD RUETHER

Whereas Schüssler-Fiorenza's work is in biblical studies, Rosemary Radford Ruether's scholarship focuses on systematic theology. Her most significant work, *Sexism and God-Talk: Toward a Feminist Theology* (1983), challenges the sources and categories of traditional Catholic teaching. Her overriding criteria are "whatever diminishes or denies the full humanity of women must be presumed not to reflect the divine" [and] "what does promote the full humanity of women is of the Holy" (Ruether 1983, 19). Using these two criteria, Ruether deconstructs the teaching of the church around issues of the role and mission of the church in the world, moral norms, exclusive language, and the understanding of Christ as the Savior. Her work, more practical than Schüssler-Fiorenza's, gives Catholic women the theological foundation on which to question traditional practices of the local church (Bianchi and Ruether 1992). Ruether, a scholar-activist, holds that the commitment of the Catholic Church to social justice should include a concrete commitment to women. Ruether's work is complemented by the work of moral theologian Christine Gudorf.

CHRISTINE GUDORF

Catholic ethicist Christine Gudorf in her popular and scholarly work, *Body, Sex and Pleasure: Reconstructing Christian Sexual Ethics* (1994), draws on scripture, natural law, and historical and contemporary sources to craft a systematic reconstruction of Catholic sexual ethics. Her critique of the church's teaching of procreationism is unsurpassed by any recent scholar. Many argue that the Catholic Church will not be able to change and renew its teaching on birth control and abortion until women theologians challenge the deep-structured anthropological, dualistic, and anti-body ideals of traditional Catholic theology.

Gudorf's work offers women a way to understand and revere the experience of sexual pleasure and their bodies from a theological moral stance. She argues that violence against women is a private domestic issue as well as a public social problem, a problem that is sustained by traditional religious texts promoting the subservience of women to men. By exposing the historical and the cultural origins of misogynist church teaching about women and attitudes toward the human body, Gudorf's feminist insights provide Catholic women with an ethical language based on their own experience as women. Of particular significance is Gudorf's argument that the traditional Christian virtues of charity and justice must be linked with the contemporary struggle for woman's rights and control of their bodies.

MARIA PILAR AQUINO

Unlike Schüssler-Fiorenza, Ruether, and Gudorf, Maria Pilar Aquino, in her text, *Our Cry for Life: Feminist Theology from Latin America* (1994), sets forth a theology that gives recognition to the struggle and liberation of Latina women's experience. The lives of Latina women are the source of theological reflection and action for Aquino. Using feminist analysis to amend and correct the androcentric positions of liberation theology, Aquino challenges both traditional theological concepts and androcentric interpretations of liberation theology. Based in the experience of Latin America women, Aquino's work has great influence among women, especially U.S. Catholic Latinas. The process of dialogue, discussion, and exchange among differing sectors of women results in a particular theological perspective for Latina women. As a religious studies professor in a U.S. Catholic college, Aquino's goal is to give voice to and to contextualize the experience of Latina women struggling to create new ways of living in church and society, thus enabling both women and men to attain human dignity.

M. SHAWN COPELAND

M. Shawn Copeland writes from an African-American womanist experience. Womanist theology grounds its self-understanding in the struggle for survival of the African-American community. In womanist theology, the concept of God through the person of Jesus is not necessarily always a God of liberation but, rather, a God of resistance. To resist injustice, exploitation, and slavery is central to womanist theology. Womanist theologians challenge the racism and ethnocentric notions inherent in Catholic theology. Basing their theology primarily on the experience of women in the black community, womanist theologians argue that theology is learned in the context of family and home, not initially in the church. Catholic womanist theologians have raised the consciousness of the U.S. Catholic Church through the denunciation of racism within church and society and the reconstruction of theology based on the experience of African-American women.

These scholars have contributed to the retrieval of Christian sources of thought that expose the sexism embedded in Catholic theology. They have introduced the new sources, based on women's experience, for the construction of a new feminist Catholic theology. The desire to remain Catholic but denounce the sexist norms and practices of the Catholic Church and renew the spiritual lives of women and men is at the heart of their work. They are not only models of committed Catholic women who question authority but who serve as leaders both in church and society. Their scholarship acts as a motivation for women working to implement the PFA. Their work is both scholarly and practical—linking a religious vision of a just and peaceful world with women's liberating actions for change.

CONCLUSION

U.S. Catholic women, whether operating from a holistic, moderate, reconstructive, or individual perspective, are involved in the implementation of the PFA. At first glance, one sees that implementation is devoted to eliminating the suffering, discrimination, and sexist practices under which many women live. The priorities of the PFA have been taken to heart by U.S. Catholic women. On reflection and analysis, however, my research reveals that U.S. Catholic women see that the Catholic Church and some of its more blatant sexist practices hinder them from assisting other women in need. This is not a new reality for them but, rather, a deeper realization of the long-term implications and emotional costs to women of the sexist teachings and practices of the Catholic Church.

Finally, the strength of the implementation of the PFA for U.S. Catholic women will be the common ground on which Catholic women, from whatever perspective, may act and work together on behalf of all women. In my discussions with U.S. Catholic women committed to the PFA, it was of great concern to discover that women from the differing perspectives had little or no communication with one another. The strength of the U.S. Catholic women implementing the PFA lies in their access to institutional power, projects, programs, and their contacts with grassroots women. If U.S. Catholic women could collaborate on a massive scale to promote at least one of the PFA priorities within the U.S. Catholic Church, such an action would make a world of difference for many women and a different world for U.S. Catholic women.

NOTES

1. The Platform for Action consists of twelve priorities for the lives of women and girls. They are: violence against women, women and armed conflict, human rights, women and poverty, women and the economy, institutional mechanisms, education and training of women, women and health, women and the media, women in power and decision making, women and the environment, and the girl child. (Riley 1996a, 3).

2. Derr writes, "To be precise, one must say that the 1929 treaty that created the sovereign state of Vatican City was concluded between Italy and the Holy See, the latter functioning as a legal personality prior to the emergence of its own territorial state. . . . Nevertheless in common practice the Holy See and the Vatican state are indistinguishable, . . . it has some of the formal apparatus of a nation, notably, a diplomatic corps with accreditation to many other governments. It can enter into treaties and concordats with other nations" (Derr 1983, 27).

3. The Holy See refers to the authority of the Pope as the preeminent bishop of the Catholic Church and the political entity he heads is officially titled

the Vatican state. The Vatican state holds permanent observer status at
the United Nations. The Holy See is a derivative from the Latin term
sedes, meaning seat: the seat (or throne) of power and authority.

4. Estimates indicate there are 995 to 1,044 million Roman Catholics in the
world with about sixty-two to seventy-one million in the United States
(World Almanac and Book of Facts 2001, 692). Roman Catholics constitute about twenty-three percent of the United States population and
about seventeen percent of the world population (1999 Catholic Almanac 1998; www.nccbuscc.org).

5. Glendon uses the term "holistic feminism." *Origins* quotes Glendon as
saying "The church has a holistic feminism that takes into account all of
the complicated parts of women's lives and all of the roles women play in
a complex modern society" (*Origins* 1995, 189, col. 3).

6. Most notable is the Papal document *Mulieris Dignitatem* (John Paul II
1988). This includes the reflections of John Paul II on Catholic conceptions of womanhood, marriage, defense of Catholic teaching against feminism, and an emphasis on nurturing and caring as special feminine
qualities (Segers 1996, 586–615).

7. The term "Holy Mother the Church" is a title commonly used by the Pope
and Catholics in reference to the entire Roman Catholic Church.

8. See "Pacem in Terris," a historic papal encyclical by Pope John XXIII issued on April 11, 1963. It is *the* papal document that delineates the social
doctrine of the church and its advocacy of full human rights for all (John
XXIII 1977).

9. This same phenomenon occurs in the Reformation churches. Conservative Protestant women have claimed the term "biblical feminist" to de-
note a particular interpretation of the Bible that supports patriarchal texts
while, at the same time, the promotion of issues relative to women war-
rant the term "feminist."

10. One group that may be classified as operating from a holistic feminism
perspective is Women Affirming Life, headquartered in Gaithersburg,
Maryland.

11. The Vatican's emphasis on the social and economic aspects of women's
plight reflects the church's long-held social teaching. The media representation of the Vatican stance as anti-woman in Cairo was of serious concern
to Glendon and the delegation. She writes, "We hoped to avoid the situation that developed at the UN's 1994 Conference on Population and Development in Cairo, where an abortion rights initiative led by a hard-edged
U.S. delegation pushed all other population and development issues into
the background. The Holy See's efforts to correct that skewed emphasis
never got through to the public. . . . For the most part, the press accepted
the population lobby caricature of the Vatican at Cairo as anti-woman,
anti-sex, and in favor of unrestrained procreation" (Glendon 1996, 30).

12. The Holy See was one of forty-three nations that had partial consensus
on the documents of the Fourth World Conference on Women and ex-

pressed serious reservations on some of the concepts used in them (Glendon 1996, 223–236).

13. Sheila Garcia was a staff member of the United States Catholic Conference (USCC) Office of Family, Laity, Women and Youth, July 15, 1997.

14. Since the close of the Second Vatican Council in 1965, the Catholic Church has promulgated, taught, envisioned, and proclaimed itself as the People of God.

15. Most of the women I interviewed who were employed by the Catholic Church used the metaphor of the People of God for the church.

16. Liberal feminists maintain that women's subordination " . . . is rooted in a set of legal and customary constraints that block women's entrance into or success in public life. Because society has the false belief that women are, by nature, less intellectually and physically capable than men, it excludes women from the academy, the forum, and the marketplace" (Tong 1998, 2).

17. Two organizational examples of moderate feminism are the Women's Project at the Center of Concern, and Network, a social justice lobby founded by members of religious communities of women. Both of these groups are headquartered in Washington, D.C.

18. In 1997, Donna Hanson was the Diocesan Director of Catholic Charities, Spokane, Wash., and Chair of the Catholic Coalition on Women to Follow-up the UN Fourth Conference on Women, Beijing, 1995.

19. Maria Riley, O.P. is a member of the Order of Preachers (O.P.), which is a part of the Dominican Order. She was one of the major PFA organizers in the U.S. Catholic Church. As Coordinator of the Women's Project at the Center of Concern, she has used her position to link U.S. Catholic women and the larger political arena. She provided many contacts, documents, and suggestions for this research project.

20. "The Center of Concern is an independent, inter-disciplinary team engaged in social analysis, theological reflection, research, education, and policy advocacy. Guided by a global vision, and rooted in a faith commitment, current programs focus on women in development and the global women's movement. The Center holds consultative status with the United Nations" (Riley 1996a, title page).

21. All the information on the establishment of a National Action Agenda Agency for Women has been obtained from the coordinating committee minutes, personal notes of Maria Riley, and notes from my interview with Maria Riley in February 1997.

22. For more information on U.S. Women Connect see www.uswomencon.com, accessed by the author on September 9, 2000.

23. The Sisters of Loretto and the Sisters of Mercy of the Americas are two of the Catholic orders of women who hold independent NGO status at the United Nations. Other religious orders of women are exploring ways to influence the work of the United Nations. Catherine Ferguson SNJM is a member of the Sisters of the Holy Names of Jesus and Mary (SNJM).

24. "As Catholic women religious from the Asia-Pacific, Africa, Latin America, Europe and North America, participating in the NGO Forum '95 and the Fourth World Conference on Women, we stand in solidarity with all women participants. Our commitment to live out the Gospel impels us to raise our voices with theirs to insist that the delegates to this UN Conference ratify and implement a platform of action which effectively addresses the militarization, racism, structural adjustment programs, narrow fundamentalist interpretations and patriarchal structures which contribute to the feminization of poverty and do violence to women and girl children everywhere. Compelled by the Gospel imperative to 'act justly', we call upon the United Nations and our respective governments to commit themselves to work for peace, equality and sustainable development. Furthermore, we challenge the United Nations, all Governments, NGOs, Churches, and other institutions working for human rights, to develop effective mechanisms of accountability to convert these commitments into concrete, measurable actions" (A Statement to the Delegates to the UN Fourth World Conference on Women, Beijing, China 1995 signed by seventy-nine Roman Catholic women's congregations (orders) and issued in Sept. 1995, Beijing, China. Photocopied public statement).

25. Catholics for a Free Choice (CFFC) is one of the most notable organizations that fits my description of a reconstructive Catholic feminist perspective.

26. *Imago Dei* is the Latin term for the image of God. Catholic tradition teaches that each individual is a unique reflection of God. This is the theological basis for Catholic human rights theory. Each individual human being qua human being has guaranteed rights by her/his very existence (John XXIII 1977).

27. Kathy Toner, a staff member of Catholics for a Free Choice provided much of this information.

28. Approximately twenty percent of the official U.S. delegation to Beijing were members of the Roman Catholic Church. Interview and personal memo from Maria Riley, May 1997.

29. The Vatican delegation to the UN Fourth World Conference on Women did not attend the NGO Forum in Huairou. Its members were at the Vatican conferring with the Pope prior to the opening of the official UN conference. Interview with Donna Hanson, August 11, 1997.

REFERENCES

Abbott, Walter S. J., ed. 1966. *The Documents of Vatican II.* New York: America Press.

Aquino, Maria Pilar. 1992. "Perspectives on a Latina's Feminist Liberation Theology." In *Frontiers of Hispanic Theology in the United States,* ed. Allen Figueroa Deck. New York: Orbis Books.

————. 1994. *Our Cry for Life: Feminist Theology from Latin America*. New York: Orbis Books.

Bianchi, Eugene C., and Rosemary Radford Ruether 1992. *A Democratic Catholic Church*. New York: Crossroads.

Beijing Plus 5 Working Group. 2000. *Catholic Voices on Beijing: A Call for Social Justice for Women*. Washington, D.C.: Catholics for a Free Choice.

Bole, William. 1995. "Who will push the Catholic view of women in Beijing?" *Our Sunday Visitor*. (30 July): 3.

Butterfield, Fox. 1995. "U. N. Women's Forum Is a Test for Pope's Advocate. An Interview with Mary Ann Glendon." *New York Times* (August 29) A3.

Chittister, Joan. 1996. *Beyond Beijing: The Next Step for Women: A Personal Journey*. Kansas City: Sheed and Ward.

Congregation for the Doctrine of the Faith. 1995. "Inadmissibility of Women to Ministerial Priesthood." *Origins*. 25, no. 24 (November 30): 401–05.

Copeland, M. Shawn. 1996. "Wading Through Many Sorrows: Toward a Theology of Suffering in Womanist Perspective." In *Feminist Ethics and the Catholic Moral Tradition*, eds. Charles Curran, Margaret Farley, and Richard McCormick. New York: Paulist Press.

Curran, Charles. 1985. *Directions in Catholic Social Ethics*. Notre Dame, Indiana: University of Notre Dame Press.

Conscience: A Newsjournal of Pro Choice Catholic Opinion. 1997. "CFFC Notebook." 28: no. 1 (Spring): 30.

Derr, Thomas Sieger. 1983. *Barriers to Ecumenism: The Holy See and the World Council on Social Questions*. New York: Maryknoll.

Glendon, Mary Ann. 1995a. "Vatican Delegation in Beijing." *Origins*. 25, no. 13 (September 14): 203–06.

————. 1995b. "The Bitter Fruit of the Beijing Conference." *The Wall Street Journal* (September 18) : A22.

————. 1995c. "Vatican Stance: Women's Conference Final Document." *Origins*. 25, no. 15 (September 28): 233–36.

————. 1995d. "Obsolete Feminism in Beijing." *New Perspectives Quarterly*. 12, no 4 (Fall): 47–48.

————. 1996. "What Happened at Beijing." *First Things* (January): 30–36.

Gudorf, Christine. 1994. *Body, Sex and Pleasure—Reconstructing Christian Sexual Ethics*. Cleveland: Pilgrim Press.

John XXIII. 1977. "Pacem in Terris." In *Renewing the Earth: Catholic Documents of Peace, Justice and Liberation*, eds. David Obrien and Thomas A. Shannon. New York: Image/Doubleday.

John Paul II. 1988. *Mulieris Dignitatem: Apostolic Letter on the Dignity and Vocation of Women*. Vatican City: Rome, Italy. (Accessed at www.american.edu.catholic /church—December 5, 2000).

Kissling, Frances. 1996. *The Vatican and Politics of Reproductive Health*. Washington, D.C.: Catholics for a Free Choice.

Kissling, Frances, and Mary Hunt, eds. 1995. *Equal is as Equal Does: Challenging Vatican Views on Women*. Washington, D.C.: Women-Church Convergence.

National Catholic Reporter. 1997. "Bishops Repudiate Choice Group." (July 18): 7–8.

Navarro-Valls. J. 1995. "Position of the Vatican's Beijing Delegation." *Origins.* 25, no. 12 (September 7): 187–91.

1999 Catholic Almanac 1998 at www.nccbuscc.org, website of the National Council of Catholic Bishops U.S. Catholic Conference. Accessed January 15, 2001.

Origins Catholic News Service Documentary Service. 1995. 25, no.12 (September 7): 189.

Riley, Maria O. P. 1996a. *Women Connecting Beyond Beijing.* Washington, D.C.: Center of Concern. [Participant's Booklet.]

———.1996b. *Women Connecting Beyond Beijing.* Washington, D.C.: Center of Concern. [Facilitator's Booklet.]

Ruether, Rosemary Radford. 1983. *Sexism and God-Talk: Toward a Feminist Theology.* Boston: Beacon Press.

Schüssler-Fiorenza, Elisabeth. 1985. *In Memory of Her.* New York: Crossroads.

———. 1993. *Discipleship of Equals: A Critical Feminist Ekklesialogy of Liberation.* New York: Crossroads.

Segers, Mary. 1996. "Feminism, Liberalism and Catholicism." In *Feminist Ethics and the Catholic Moral Tradition,* eds. Charles Curran, Margaret Farley, and Richard McCormick. New York: Paulist Press.

Tong, Rosemarie. 1989. *Feminist Thought.* Boulder, Colo.: Westview Press.

———. 1993. *Feminine and Feminist Ethics.* Belmont, Calif.: Wadsworth.

Working Group of National Catholic Organizations Engaged In Follow-up on the UN Conference in Beijing 1996. "Special Synod for America: 'Lineamenta' Questionnaire Responses." (Fall). Unpublished minutes.

World Almanac and Book of Facts 2001. "Adherents of All Religions by Six Continental Areas, Mid-1999." Mahwah, NJ: World Almanac Education Group.

CHAPTER 4

IMPLEMENTING THE BEIJING COMMITMENTS IN IRELAND

YVONNE GALLIGAN AND NUALA RYAN

INTRODUCTION

As a postcolonial country with a legacy of nationalist engagement and a historically strong adherence to the Roman Catholic religion, one would expect only modest advances in women's rights. Yet, such is not the case. Ireland has undergone a remarkable change in the last thirty years with regard to the relationship between the Roman Catholic Church and the state and with regard to the implementation of women's rights. Whereas over 90 percent of the Irish population are born as Catholics, recent years have seen a growing secularization of Irish society accompanied by significant improvements in the role and status of women. All of this change has coincided with mammoth infusions of foreign direct investment in the island's economy. Today, foreign firms employ almost half of the country's labor force and account for two-thirds of its output (Economist 2000, 21).

Irish society is in a period of transition and the Roman Catholic Church has a waning influence on the shape of public policies, not least on policies related to women's rights. This chapter explores the relationship between church and state, and assesses changing norms and values in a traditionally religious society. It evaluates the role of the women's movement in highlighting the politics of women's rights and assesses the strength of Christian feminism. In Ireland, a consensus on beliefs and values between political nationalism and religious authoritarianism shaped public policy since the foundation of the state in 1922. This alliance fostered support for conservative social norms for over seventy years and led to the enactment of repressive legislation on women's rights, particularly in the 1920s and 1930s. Today, Irish society is changing, bringing with it a significant alteration in the formerly close relationship between the Roman Catholic Church and the state. This change is at its most stark in relation to popular attitudes toward religion. In terms of the rights of women, attitudes among political leaders and decision makers have evolved from denial in the 1950s to, at best, a benign patriarchy in the 1990s, with occasional demonstrations of a radical commitment to gender equality. Although the extent to which the principle of women's rights is realized through supportive public policies is an issue of constant debate, the status of women in Irish society today is better than it was a generation ago.

The transition from tradition to modernity often can be a painful social and political process. This has been the Irish experience since the early 1970s, when the process of change was initiated through economic reform. As old, safe, and accepted social and moral values were contested, Irish society became the site of extensive political conflict. The tone of this conflict was captured in the debates around differing conceptions of women's rights. If, as survey evidence indicates, Irish public opinion is becoming more liberal and secular, this move is not a simple, neat unilinear one. Instead, it involves a process whereby old and new values compete for dominance. This conflict takes place at many levels and over many issues, but is arguably most visible in the politicization of social and moral issues such as divorce and abortion. This mixture of traditional and modern value systems inevitably impacts on the status of women in Ireland and on their progress toward equal citizenship with men. Historically, the Roman Catholic Church and the state have enjoyed a close relationship buoyed by popular support for this arrangement. In this environment, the women's movement has articulated an agenda of change. The state has responded, but the women's movement has been highly critical of the government's slow pace in implementing the commitments Ireland entered into during the 1995 United Nations Conference on Women (Women's NGO Beijing Coalition 2000).

CHURCH AND STATE

The dominance of Roman Catholic dogma and the authoritarian interpretation of Catholic teachings characteristic of Irish religious leaders has been a hallmark of Irish politics and public policy both before and since the foundation of the state in 1922 (Whyte 1980). The close connections between popular movements for independence and church representatives during the nineteenth century helped to lay the basis for a symbiotic relationship with the leaders of the new state. As Coakley (1993, 31) notes, the Irish population embraced Catholicism wholeheartedly and quite uncritically. The role of the church as an institution of significance in people's lives was further augmented by its dominant presence in the education system.

The close connection between nationalism and Catholicism was exemplified in the actions of the leaders of the 1916 Easter Rising, according to Condren. The failed nationalist rebellion, the execution of its leaders and their subsequent elevation to political martyrdom, she argues, was an illustration of blood sacrifice used to justify war and political violence, but also used to underpin religious beliefs. By mystifying the "motherland" and glorifying the sacrifice of young men, this tradition elevated women to an idealized state similar to that of the Virgin Mary, while "simultaneously keeping real women in their place." This had "devastating consequences for women in the post-revolutionary Ireland because their 'purity' became the indicator of national identity over 'pagan' England: a situation which led to repressive reproductive legislation and social norms which contemporary Irish women are heirs"(Condren 1995, 180).

Scholars have repeatedly shown how Catholic Church teachings influenced the social policies that the leaders of the new state introduced (Rumpf and Hepburn 1977; Whyte 1980; Fanning 1983; Breen et al. 1990). The social conservatism of the first independent government in 1922 was clearly manifest in policies that removed many of the rights of citizenship from women, such as holding employment and serving on juries (Valiulis 1995, 117–36). This perspective on the role of women in the new state was reinforced by Catholic social teaching that sought to circumscribe the role of the state—a view formally expressed in the 1931 papal Encyclical, Quadragesima Anno, and echoed some years later by a prominent nationalist leader, Eamon de Valera. De Valera suggested that, under his leadership, Catholic corporatism would characterize the institutional arrangements of the nation and "the state would be confined to its proper functions as guardian of the rights of the individual and the family, coordinator of the activities of its citizens" (Breen et al. 1990, 28).

The Catholic Church exercised enormous influence over Irish governments in all matters of public morality from the 1920s to the 1970s. In addition to the enactment of legislation designed to protect Irish morality (such as the Censorship of Publications Act 1929, the Public Dance Halls Act 1935, and the Criminal Law [Amendment] Act 1935), two significant events underscore the confessional nature of the state in this period. One, the 1937 Constitution, was heavily influenced by the Catholic code on social principles. Article 41 recognized the traditional family as "the natural primary and fundamental unit group of Society, and as a moral institution possessing inalienable and imprescriptible rights, antecedent and superior to all positive law" and was guaranteed state protection. In order to secure the special position of the family, a ban on divorce was introduced and the primacy of parents in the education of their children was recognized in the constitution. Article 41 also defined women's citizenship, expressing a Roman Catholic view of womanhood combined with a strongly patriarchal view of gender relations:

> In particular, the State recognizes that by her life within the family home, a woman gives to the State a support without which the common good cannot be achieved. The State shall, therefore, endeavour to ensure that mothers shall not be obliged by economic necessity to engage in labour to the neglect of their duties in the home.

Thus, the Constitution reinforced a role for women as envisioned by nationalist leaders and church authorities—as passive caretakers, homemakers, and economic dependants, corresponding to the reality of the majority of women's lives at the time.[1] Catholic teaching on ownership of private property was expressed in Article 43, and, in Article 44, the special position of the Catholic Church in Irish society was given constitutional recognition. In the words of one historian, Ireland of the 1930s and 1940s was governed by a "system of mutually reinforcing political and episcopal visions" (Fanning 1983, 158).

The second event, the crisis over mother and child health services in 1951, illustrates the continuing influence of Catholic leadership on the political elites of the day.[2] The radical minister for health, Noel Browne, sought to introduce a free public health care policy for all mothers and children under sixteen years. Episcopal opposition to the plan reflected the unease within government circles on the policy, and, combined with the opposition of party political and medical interests, brought about a defeat of the policy and the resignation from office of Dr. Browne.

The basis of church disapproval of the plan rested in the interventionist role envisaged for the state in this policy, a role that infringed on the precepts of Catholic social teaching. The decision by the government to abandon the mother and child scheme in apparent deference to the view of the Irish bishops was greeted with charges that the Catholic Church rather than elected representatives governed the state (Whyte 1980, 231–2). Indeed, this charge had some substance, for, in a parliamentary debate following the resignation of Dr Browne, his party leader and deputy prime minister in the government, Sean McBride, declared, "Those of us in this House who are Catholics, and all of us in the Government who are Catholics are, as such of course, bound to give obedience to the rulings of our Church and of our hierarchy" (Whyte 1980,

232). This example of the close relationship between church and state, then, serves to highlight the constraints on the expansion of the welfare state in Ireland in direct contrast to many other European countries during the 1940s and 1950s.

Since the 1970s, as the discussion on the contraception issue below shows, the influence of the Catholic Church on public policy has become less directly interventionist at the government level. The church continues assiduously to defend its own interests, particularly in the area of education and on issues with a moral dimension. Yet, the wishes of the church are a declining, if still important, influence on both the government and the people.

CHURCH AND CITIZENS

The unquestioning deference of the population to Catholic Church teaching began to wane in the 1970s as the economic revitalization program introduced in the 1960s began to result in a growing prosperity. Overtly, very little appeared to change. In this period of economic modernization, popular support for the church in the form of attendance at weekly mass did not decline from the levels of earlier decades. Surveys of mass attendance in this decade record over 90 percent weekly mass-going by Irish Catholic adults (Whyte 1980, 382). Over 90 percent of the population described themselves as Catholics. Yet, behind the high levels of outward profession of faith were forces acting to change the relationship between the church and society, and between church and state.

Ironically, one of the factors of change in this area was the growth of the ecumenical movement in the Catholic Church worldwide represented by Vatican II, which became a feature of Irish Catholicism in the 1960s but was embraced more fully by the Irish hierarchy in the 1970s. Interdenominational services, meetings of representatives from all religions on the island of Ireland, and a general opening up of the Catholic hierarchy to other views characterized this ecumenism. With the opening of a space for dialogue between religions, various Protestant denominations began publicly to express liberal views on social issues such as contraception and, later, divorce. The control of education by the Catholic Church was being critically examined, with a growing demand from some sections of the urban middle class for nondenominational, or at least interdenominational, schooling (Whyte 1980, 353–5). Critical voices began to emanate from within the church, with a new generation of clerics concerned at the lack of response of the institutional church to extensive social problems of poverty, unemployment, emigration and discrimination. Symbolizing the new era, a constitutional referendum in 1972 removed the special position of the Roman Catholic Church from the Constitution with the consent of the church hierarchy and the support of all parties in parliament.

By 1988–89, weekly mass attendance levels had dropped to 82 percent (Pollack 1991), a decrease of 9 percent compared to a similar survey in 1974. Clericalism was still a strong feature of Irish life, a fact reinforced by studies comparing popular support for a religious view on a range of issues in Ireland and the European Union. Such investigations found that, as late as 1990, the Irish were significantly more supportive of Catholic Church statements on public affairs than other Europeans (Coakley 1993, 41). During the 1980s, when constitutional referenda on abortion (1983) and divorce (1986) resulted in significant majorities for outcomes favored by the church, the tentative liberalism of the 1970s appeared to have disappeared and popular attitudes seemed to have once more become synchronized with religious beliefs and values.

Such was not to be the case. The authority of the Catholic Church was greatly weakened in subsequent years, in part as a consequence of a growing secularization and urbanization of Irish lifestyles, in part because of the revelations of sexual scandals among leading figures in the Irish hierarchy and, more disturbing, continual charges of sexual abuse of children by priests and nuns.

From the early 1990s, public confidence in the supreme authority of the Catholic Church has eroded. In 1996, 92 percent of the population professed to be Catholic, yet weekly church attendance had dropped to 66 percent, as compared with 79 percent in a similar poll 1991 and 85 percent in 1986. More strikingly, in 1996, only 21 percent of Catholics followed church teaching when confronted with serious moral decisions, while 78 percent preferred to follow their own conscience (Pollack 1996). In July 1997, 71 percent of Irish people held little or no confidence in the capacity of Catholic bishops to provide leadership, ranking them with trade union leaders (72 percent) and government ministers (74 percent) as failed leaders (Kerrigan 1997). Whether or not the trend toward a greater degree of secularization in Irish society will continue, the current position indicates a church in crisis and a disillusioned congregation for whom the Catholic Church holds little relevance.

The recent rapid decline of the Catholic Church as a moral arbiter cannot be attributed solely to revelations of clerical sexual proclivities. Popular disaffection with church leadership on family affairs was evident from the 1970s onward as fertility, birth, and marriage patterns slowly began to converge toward European, or more modern norms. Even as the hierarchy pronounced on the evils of contraception in 1973, a majority of the population was in favor of some reform of the law on contraception, the fertility rate was on the brink of decline, and increasing numbers of couples were choosing to cohabit outside the traditional bonds of marriage (Galligan 1998a, 26–28).

Growing urbanization (and, for some, growing affluence), increased exposure to the media, the decline of agriculture as a way of life, the growth of employment in the services sector, and entry to the European Economic Community (now the European Union), all contributed to break the monolithic society of past generations. By 1996, family size had fallen to 1.8 children, as compared with 3.5 children in 1971, marking the fastest recorded decline in average family size in Europe and North America in this period. The birthrate, too, declined from 23 percent in 1971 to 13 percent in 1994. Yet, the number of children born out of wedlock, 20 percent of all births in 1996, came close to the European average.

The growing number of women in the workforce from the 1970s onward, a product of increased educational opportunities for women, of growing female employment in multinational industries located in Ireland, and of high male unemployment rates, heralded a modification of traditional family roles. Although in 1994 Ireland still had one of the lowest levels of participation in employment by women in Europe, with just over one-third (35 percent) of women in the labor force, the striking factor was the increase in married women's employment. In 1971, 14 percent of women who worked outside the home were married; in 1994, this had risen to 45 percent and continued to increase thereafter (Durkan 1995, 7).

This trend was indicative of a significant change in popular attitudes towards women's participation in paid employment in the space of a generation. By 1990, one-half of all women and 40 percent of all men were supportive of women having both a career and a family. Support for this lifestyle was most marked among young, employed middle-class women (Henley 1990, 12). Perspectives on the roles of women and men within the home reflected a shift toward supporting more equal roles, with 46 percent of the view that equal roles represented the ideal arrangement in a family as compared with 30 percent support for such a proposition in 1982 (Henley Centre Ireland 1990, 13–14). Although these attitudes represent a significant shift in support for women's equality in a short space of time, Irish men and women remained less egalitarian in their views on gender role within the family than citizens of other European Union countries (Wilcox 1991, 131). Within Ireland, though, attitudes toward women's role in society varied according to age, gender, and marital status. The most liberal positions on women's role were espoused by young women and men, married working women, and married men. The most conservative views were held by older women and men, single men, and married women engaged exclusively in home duties (Galligan 1998b).

This latter constituency has found a political voice in the rise of as yet tiny conservative Catholic parties in the 1990s, such as the National Party and the Christian Solidarity Party.

The rapid social and attitudinal change suggests that a considerable shift in cultural values took place in Ireland during the twenty-five years between 1971 and 1996. Although this would appear to contradict the high levels of weekly mass observance noted during the 1970s and 1980s, Inglis has argued that religious attitudes were changing, with a growing number of Catholics prepared to make decisions independently of clerical guidance (Inglis 1987, 221–22, quoted in Coakley 1993, 42–43). Whyte (1980, 12–13), too, noted this tendency, commenting that "Irish Catholics . . . are able to compartmentalize their loyalties, and to accept the church's authority unquestioningly in one sphere at the very time that they challenge it in another."

The opening of a gap between the church and the people has been evident in political issues in the 1990s. Although a referendum to include a ban on abortion in the Constitution was carried by a two-thirds majority in 1983 and a referendum on the removal of the ban on divorce in the Constitution was defeated by a similar margin in 1986, the 1990s has seen a strengthening of the liberal vote on moral issues. Some commentators pointed to the election of a liberal, feminist candidate to the office of President in 1990 as a tentative indicator of an upswing in support for progressive views in Ireland. While the successful election of Mary Robinson was due to a number of factors, the outcome of this particular electoral contest more closely resembled the politics of modern Ireland than the traditional dominance of the office by the largest political party, Fianna Fail.

A further illustration of the conservative-liberal cleavage in society came in the guise of the 1992 abortion referendums. The blanket nature of the ban on abortion introduced into the Constitution in 1983 was modified by the Supreme Court in 1992 in the case of a fourteen-year-old rape victim, identified as "X," who wished to travel to Britain to obtain an abortion. The Attorney General, the chief legal officer of the state, sought an injunction in the High Court to prevent the abortion, as Article 40.3.3 of the Constitution claimed to protect the right to life of the unborn child. This injunction was granted. On appeal, the Supreme Court found that the clause in Article 40.3.3. addressing the "due regard to the equal life of the mother" meant that a suicidal woman did have a right to an abortion.

In a subsequent three-fold referendum designed to place abortion and the related issues of travel and information within a regulatory framework, the proposal to limit abortion to circumstances where the life of the mother was in danger was rejected while the ancillary proposals to lift the restrictions on travel and information on abortion services in other European Union countries were passed.[3] The votes on travel and information, carried with, respectively, 62 percent and 60 percent support, clearly indicated a divide along liberal and conservative lines. When compared with the referendum results of 1983 and 1986, a clear correlation appeared between the geographical and political party distribution of liberal and conservative support in the travel and information results (Kennelly and Ward 1993, 125–26). The support for the liberalization of public policy on travel and information was highest in urban areas, particularly Dublin, and in constituencies immediately west and south of the capital. The "yes" vote closely matched Labor Party support in these areas. The "no" vote to both issues was highest in rural constituencies and in areas of the west.

The result of the abortion referendum is more difficult to interpret, as the proposal was rejected by liberals and conservatives alike. In a subsequent survey that sought information on why people voted against the abortion amendment, the liberal-conservative divide clarified. A majority of voters in Dublin and the south of Ireland (59 percent and 53 percent, respectively) believed that the proposal would not protect the rights of the mother. The majority of the electorate in the west, northwest, and midlands (64 percent and 51 percent respectively) were of the opinion that the amendment would not rule out abortion. The total national figure on this issue showed an even split, at 48 percent, between supporters of both liberal and conservative positions (Kennelly and Ward 1993, 129). The referendum results and the subsequent opinion poll indicated that the liberal vote gained ground between 1986 and 1992, while the position of conservatives eroded from a two-thirds majority to about 50 per cent in the same period.

The results of the second divorce referendum in 1995, then, should have come as no surprise. Given the even split between the forces of change and tradition evident in 1992, the outcome of the divorce poll was in the balance. The constitutional amendment to permit divorce in certain restricted circumstances carried by a wafer-thin majority, 50.3 percent. During the course of the campaign, the Catholic Church made its opposition to any relaxation in the constitutional ban on divorce very clear, claiming that this measure would undermine the traditional Irish family. In a marked change from former times, an all-party consensus in parliament emerged on the need for some form of legislation to regularize marriage breakdown and subsequent relationships.

The national pattern of liberal and conservative support evident in the 1992 referendums reappeared in the close outcome in favor of amending the traditional position and permitting divorce. This result reinforces the evidence indicating a trend toward support for secular attitudes and a waning of religious influence in Irish society. Nevertheless, one cannot say that Ireland is a secular society. Support for traditional religious and moral beliefs remains strong, particularly in rural areas among people over forty-five years of age and in farming communities. What these referendum results show is that this support has suffered a significant drop in a relatively short space of time. Whether the liberal-conservative divide will remain poised on an even balance as we head into the twenty-first century is another matter.

THE WOMEN'S MOVEMENT

The modernization of Irish society throughout the 1960s created a space for new political discourses—in particular, discourses based around new social movements. Ireland was not immune from the civil liberties protests and the emergence of feminism elsewhere in the world. The civil rights movement in Northern Ireland and the re-emergence of nationalist politics in that province in the late 1960s encouraged the development of an emerging critique of women's rights on the island. In Ireland, action campaigns and protests focused on poverty and social exclusion in inner city Dublin acted as a catalyst for feminist politicization. There existed, too, a significant network of women's rights groups, some organized on a national basis, that were open to advancing the cause of women in a more visible manner than before. Although tensions existed between the older, more institutionalized feminists and their radical sisters, Connolly (1996, 55) notes that their political agendas were similar.

The primary difference between the two derived from preferred strategy—persistently lobbying the state for moderate, gradual legislative change on the one hand, and engaging in controversial, direct action tactics (pickets, protests, expressive action) on the other. Even though these methods were more concentrated in each sector, each drew on the same repertoire of tactics (and symbols, ideologies, and resources) in a strategic fashion when the need arose. For example, the fight for change through the courts was utilized both by mainstream and autonomous feminists, as were petitioning, mass meetings, and demonstrations.

In the early days of the women's liberation movement, radical feminist action drew the ire of the Catholic Church, expressed most often from the pulpit at Sunday mass. Of equal concern to the hierarchy was the feminist demand for a reform of the contraception laws—a demand that united moderate women's groups and the women's movement for a decade (Galligan 1998a, 142–160). Legislators, too, were unwilling to contemplate this reform. Yet, the fiction of prescribing the pill as a cycle regulator, exempting it from the anti-contraceptive laws, was widespread. Mary Henry, an outspoken liberal doctor, observed at the time that "The Pill was a God-send for both Irish doctors and women because it is perfectly obvious that it had nothing to do with sex" (Solomons 1992, 23). This issue took almost a decade to resolve and was the focus of controversy for almost all of that time. The hold of the Irish hierarchy on policy was diminishing, however. Whyte pointed out that the Irish bishops, while condemning any attempt to introduce birth control measures, explicitly recognized that lawmakers had a duty to consider legislating for matters contrary to Catholic moral teaching.

They (the bishops) disclaimed any suggestion that the state was obliged to defend by legislation the moral teaching of the Catholic Church. "There are many things which the Catholic Church holds to be morally wrong and no one has ever suggested, least of all the Church herself, that they should be prohibited by the State." The issue, they claimed, which legislators had to decide was: "[W]hat effect would the increased availability of contraceptives have on the quality of life in the Republic of Ireland?" The implications for this for the future were important. It meant that in the bishops' eyes, legislators were free to make up their own minds about the balance of advantage in such moral issues, and—if they came to the conclusion that the law need no longer prohibit what was condemned by Catholic moral principles—then they were entitled to do so (Whyte 1980, 407- 08).

The willingness to reform the contraceptive laws rested in the hands of politicians. While the church consistently spoke against the introduction of any reforms in this area, the bishops were prepared to respect the duties of lawmakers toward the citizenry. If blame for the delay in introducing adequate provisions for contraceptive facilities is to be apportioned, it rests with "the faintheartedness of Irish politicians," as one journalist noted (Whyte 1980, 412–413). In the end, a 1973 judgment of the Supreme Court supporting a married couple's access to contraceptives effectively changed the law followed by parliamentary regulation of the position in 1979 and a further liberalization in 1985.[4] Although the 1979 law on contraception was passed amid allegations that the government had come to an arrangement with the church hierarchy, little hard evidence supports this contention. By 1995, non-medical contraceptives were widely available without restrictions (Galligan 1998a, 142–160).

Reforming the contraceptives laws is claimed as a success by feminists, but credit for the passage of the 1979 and 1985 acts is equally due to the persistence of liberal politicians. As in all studies of policy, pinpointing one particular group as deserving of all the credit for significant policy change is difficult. Yet, Irish feminists have been quite influential in shaping public policy on the status of women. They have succeeded in doing this through developing a strong framework for the advocacy of women's rights.

Central to the strategic success of women's groups in influencing public policy has been a willingness to work together within existing political structures while maintaining a strong sense of feminist identity. The older women's groups of the 1960s and the radical feminists of the 1970s quickly came together in the early 1970s to form a coalition of women's organizations in the Council for the Status of Women, with the general aim of improving the status of women in Ireland (Fitzsimons 1991, 37–51). Membership of this umbrella body, now known as the National Women's Council of Ireland (NWCI), stood at 124 groups in 1997. The NWCI is recognized as an official representative of women's interests by government and is consulted on a diverse range of policy issues with a potential impact on women. Importantly, too, the NWCI is given representation on the boards of state agencies such as the Employment Equality Agency and on social partnership committees such as the National Economic and Social Forum in recognition of its special position as women's rights advocate. Since 1997, the NWCI, together with other voluntary groups and NGOs, has formed the community and voluntary "pillar" in national economic negotiations. This brings the NWCI into the ambit of the quasi-corporatist decision-making structure which has developed in Ireland since the 1970s.

The NWCI does not merely react to government initiatives. Since its inception, the body has sought to articulate the consensus view of its members, has initiated many political campaigns for women's rights and has sought to influence the government agenda in this regard. Although the organization has experienced internal tensions in coming to a consensus position on many issues, it has been successful on two occasions in bringing about the establishment of two commissions on the status of women, one in 1972, the second in 1992. Both commission reports have been hailed in their time as blueprints for women's rights in Ireland. In advance of the Beijing Conference, the NCWI published an independent report on the situation of women in Ireland in each of the twelve areas of action identified for discussion in Beijing. The report outlined an extensive range of measures that required implementation by the Irish government in order to meet the strategic objectives set out in the United Nations Draft Platform for Action.

Although the NWCI can be seen as the most representative of women's NGOs in Ireland, other feminist organizations have made their mark on specific policy areas. The Rape Crisis Centre groups have made a significant contribution to reforms in the law on sexual violence and in raising public and political consciousness on this issue. In recent years, Women's Aid has played a similar role in relation to domestic violence and abuse. AIM (Action, Information, Motivation), another offshoot of the women's liberation movement, has made family law its area of special expertise and over a period of twenty five years has exerted a critical influence on policy reforms in this area (Galligan, 1998a). Cherish, initially established in the early 1970s as a support group for single mothers, has consistently campaigned for an end to discrimination against lone parents in the social welfare code and for equal rights for all children.

For many years, campaigns on women's rights have been characterized by single-issue group activity, with little evidence of coalition-building at a political level. This may be attributed in part to lack of material and human resources and in part to the unreceptiveness of the Irish sociopolitical climate to feminist alliances. By the 1990s, women's group leaders had amassed extensive political and media experience, had built up satisfactory working relationships with government and the bureaucracy, had put their respective organizations on a relatively sound financial footing, and, often through the NCWI, had developed links with other feminist advocates. In the mid-1990s, the tendency of the more visible women's representatives to work alone began to modify. Recent signs of cooperation are evident in the 1996 report on violence against women and children and judicial process for crimes of violence against women and children (Report 1996). This report was the result of a joint venture between the Rape Crisis Centre, Women's Aid, the NWCI, the Irish Council for Civil Liberties and the Irish Countrywomen's Association (ICA). As a matter of historical note, it was the ICA that first brought the issue of domestic violence to light in a survey of its members in 1968. While government acceptance of the report was immediate, the real task facing women's groups is to keep such issues on the agenda of government.

Elite feminist groups, with a national profile and a focus on government lobbying, often obtain media attention at the expense of smaller, more localized, and less high-profile women's groups and organizations. Irish women in the 1990s have become actively involved at the local level, often with the needs of their children as a catalyst for action (for instance, the provision of recreational activities and resources for younger children and the employment and training needs of teenagers and young adults.) Women also have assessed their own needs and have developed a range of support groups and services at the local level, with the Inner City Organizations Network (ICON) Women's Group in the northeast inner city of Dublin, the North Letrim Women's Resource Group, the Western Women's Link, and others providing an opportunity for a wide range of women's civic participation. The mushrooming of adult educa-tion activities and community writing workshops attest to this desire for self-improvement. Women are contributing to their communities through initiatives to solve local unemployment, in campaigning for improved ma-ternity and general health services, and, most recently, in tackling the se-rious drug problem that has ravaged working class families living in inner-city Dublin.

Whether these groups can be seen as part of the women's movement is a difficult question, for, as recent research by O'Donovan and Ward (1999) shows, not all women's groups are comfortable with the identifi-cation of feminist or with an overtly political agenda. The pattern of women's activity, then, is specific and issue-driven. It is seen as an end in itself, not necessarily the start of a broader level of political involvement, as the dearth of women in local politics does not reflect the extent of women's participation in locally based communal activities.

One striking feature about feminist politics in Ireland is the near-in-visibility of the Catholic Church, whether as a reference point or as a rad-ical agency. While the Irish church contains small groupings strongly committed to social justice, their presence in the women's movement is rare. Radical religious thought and action is a feature of a small number of male and female religious in underprivileged urban areas, where they engage in activities designed to enhance the sense of community in areas of economic and social marginalization. Yet, on the basis of the current state of research, their presence has not, to date, been influential in de-veloping a specifically religious feminist vision of Irish society. Irish clerics have not claimed liberation theology as their own in an organized fashion, while the secularizing tendencies in Irish feminism make the development of such a voice more difficult.

FEMINISM WITHIN THE CHURCH

Nevertheless, the church in Ireland has become aware of the need to de-velop an accommodation with feminism and women's rights. Addressing a congregation of bishops in 1987, the leader of the Catholic Church on the island, Cardinal O'Fiach, recognized that "[W]hether we like it or not fem-inism is now a challenge facing the Church. It can no longer be written off as middle-class madness or an American aberration ... it will not be enough henceforth to issue grand statements unless we show progress in ac-tion" (Murphy 1997, 1). By the middle of the 1990s, church leaders were still grappling with the challenge outlined by O'Fiach. In 1994, Bishop Finnegan was moved to observe that "coming to terms (with feminism) is slowly beginning" (Murphy 1997, 2). In 1995, the Jesuit order discussed the unjust treatment and exploitation of women, and concluded that "[we] still have with us the legacy of the systematic discrimination against women. It is embedded within the economic, social, political, religious and even lin-guistic structures of our society" (Society of Jesus 1995, 172).

While the church has attempted to be more sensitive and less offen-sive to women in the liturgy and in religious practices, for many women these measures are considered to be too little and too late. The persis-tence of basic patriarchalism in the church has led it to become an in-creasingly irrelevant institution in women's lives. Many thoughtful women have rejected the Catholic Church in favor of secular feminism.

Feminism, however, is not the exclusive preserve of secular activists. A small yet growing number of feminists seek to build into their lives a specif-ically feminist spiritual dimension, focusing on re-writing and re-interpreting women's role in theology. The growth of small Christian feminist groups has greatly facilitated this challenge of reclamation. The central theme is an ac-knowledgment that patriarchy, politics, and society must be changed through the use of a new discourse that seeks to form an inclusive and em-bracing tradition based on the freedom promised in the gospels. Many de-scribe this vision as a church involved in the issues of the day—justice, human rights, poverty, and violence—a church that can connect at a level of practical spirituality that is sympathetic to the needs and problems that concern women in their everyday lives.

For many women, especially women in religious life, the question of leaving the church does not arise. They see no apparent contradiction in combining radical feminism with a radical approach to Christianity. Many women religious joined church orders because they were committed to a radical stance on social affairs. Vatican II and the events surrounding it was the catalyst that afforded them the freedom to be both feminist and Christian. Although the beginning of the rapid decline in the numbers of people entering the religious life can be traced back to the time of Vati-can II, for many nuns it was a wholly liberating time. For one nun, it meant that "I was no longer confined behind a wall in my convent and constrained by my habit—it enabled me to get back to the source, in every sense" (Interview with Nuala Ryan by Yvonne Galligan. Dublin, Ireland. October 31, 1997). Another nun described the direct link for her between her work as a family therapist, her feminist critique, and Vatican II: "In systems therapy, where individuals are seen in their context, it is assumed that each member of the family is equal. What feminist theory did was to look at the patriarchal structures present in the family. I saw the inequality, the unequal power systems at every level, and I saw patri-archy as the root of this inequality. I linked this with the message of Vat-ican II which not only states that we are all equal, but encourages us to act around issues of poverty and injustice" (Interview with Nuala Ryan by Yvonne Galligan Dublin, Ireland. October 21, 1997).

The Christian feminist movement in Ireland is largely confined to middle-class women and to ecumenical groups. Over the last twenty years, secular feminists and religious feminists have had an uneasy relationship, characterized for the most part by separation from one another. Today, many feminists no longer see a conflict in being active feminists and in drawing on the insights and strengths of religious feminism. The influence of modern feminist scholars and of American feminist theologians has done much to inform Irish women of the scriptural and liturgical injustices done to them over the centuries. One Irish religious feminist has identified many of the new theologies as "theologies attempting to heal the three great divisions in humanity—classism, racism and sexism" (Murphy 1997, 6).

Although the impact of societal critiques informed by feminist spirituality has to date been marginal on the shaping of public policy and practices related to women, the process is well under way. The oversubscription to academic diploma and degree courses in theology indicates a growing interest in Ireland in theology and spiritual development. Vatican II opened the way for Roman Catholic women in Ireland to study scripture in a critical and informed manner. By the 1980s, religious feminists were developing a renewed interest in pre-Christian, ancient Celtic spirituality, which had at its core a vital female, sometimes goddess, presence. This study has gone from strength to strength in the past decade, providing inspiration for religious feminists in their task of reclaiming the liturgy and church practices. In the latter half of the 1990s, this thinking has found a ready audience among ordinary women with few connections to political activism. Yet, it contains the seeds of a profound challenge to policy and practice that goes far beyond that posed by conventional liberal secular feminism.

THE IRISH CHURCH, STATE, WOMEN, AND BEIJING

The extent of the secularization of Irish society and the increased distance between church and state in Ireland was apparent in Beijing, particularly in relation to the debates around health and reproductive rights. The Irish government firmly aligned itself to the position of the European Union (EU) on reproductive rights and Irish government representatives were instrumental in formulating the EU position on the contested sexual rights clause in the Draft Platform for Action (Irish Times 1997). In Beijing, the Irish government further reaffirmed its commitment to maintaining the wording on family planning, reproductive health and sexual health agreed at the 1994 Cairo conference on population and development, but within the constitutional parameters imposed by the ban on abortion. This commitment reflected the limited space for maneuver on abortion in an Irish context. In Beijing, representatives of Irish women's NGOs demonstrated against the government's tardiness in regulating the position on abortion and on other issues (Irish Times 1995). This protest was legitimate, in that successive governments have sought to avoid legislating for abortion, given the extreme levels of conflict any political proposal would generate. Yet, while abortion continues to be the "untouchable" issue in Irish politics, legislators have shown a willingness to press ahead with other initiatives in the area of reproductive health. In 1995, in response to the decisions taken at the Cairo conference, the Irish government had begun to effect a comprehensive family planning service throughout the country and had commissioned a survey of women's health needs in conjunction with the NWCI and the regional health boards.

The issue of abortion, though, continues to cast a long shadow. Political hearings on the issue took place in May and June 2000, and a report from the committee of Parliament investigating the legislative options on abortion is due before the end of the year. Meanwhile, the holding of another abortion referendum is a continuing non-negotiable demand for the four conservative independent members of Parliament supporting a minority coalition administration. On other issues contained in the Platform for Action, the Irish government appeared willing to act to implement the commitments given in Beijing.

The speed of this process, though, is influenced to a large extent by the priority given by government to women's issues. In 1997, a reforming coalition government with a clear commitment to advancing the status of women and other marginal groups in society was defeated in a general election and a new, more conservative coalition took office. One of the first actions of this government was to abolish the ministry responsible for equality policies and place responsibility for equality issues within the brief of the minister for justice. Fears that bureaucratic expertise and interest in gender equality issues would be dissipated have since proved largely unfounded. The equality section of the extended ministry continues to work on an equality agenda—thanks in no small part to the demands of international agencies such as the United Nations for regular government reports on women's rights.

CONCLUSION

The forces of change in Irish society—economic modernization, membership of the EU, shifts in social and cultural attitudes, judicial findings—have acted to counter the hegemony of the Catholic Church that existed until the 1970s. International feminism has influenced successive Irish governments and Irish women's rights campaigners in the form of institutional initiatives such as those sponsored by the United Nations and in the shape of social movement politics. As a result of these influences, a host of woman-centered issues have come onto the national political agenda. A significant gap between the position of the church, the state, and women's organizations on women's rights issues—particularly in the area of reproductive rights, fertility and women's health—continues to exist, with the church espousing a conservative interpretation of women's rights, while the government and women's groups favor a more liberal position.

In Beijing, the Irish government representatives were clearly allied with the representatives from other EU member states, indicating support for a more secular interpretation of the Platform for Action than that of the Catholic Church representatives at the conference. This alliance was maintained at the Beijing Plus Five Conference in New York in June 2000, despite the emergence in Ireland of an organized religious right backlash against the Platform for Action. The extent to which the commitments entered into in Beijing will be fulfilled in the next few years will provide an indicator of the extent to which Irish political life has emerged from the shadow of religious and conservative forces.

NOTES

1. For a full and authoritative account of the politics of the mother and child controversy, see Whyte, 1980, chapters 7 and 8, 196–272.
2. For more extensive discussions on the shaping of women's national identity in Ireland, see Yvonne Galligan 1997; Maryann Gialanella Valiulis 1995; and Margaret Ward 1983.
3. A comprehensive account of the abortion referendums of 1992 is given by Brendan Kennelly and Eilis Ward 1993. The social, political, and ethical context in which the 1992 abortion debate took place is extensively documented in Smyth 1992.
4. The debate on the reform of the contraceptive laws is given extensive treatment in Whyte 1980, Chapter 13, 403–16, and in Galligan 1997b, chapter 7. Solomons (1992) offers the insights of a doctor involved in the campaign for the reform of the contraception laws in Pro Life?, while the views of a feminist active in the campaign are put forward by Anne Speed in Smyth 1992.

REFERENCES

Breen, Richard, Damien F. Hannan, David B. Rottman, and Christopher T. Whelan. 1990. *Understanding Contemporary Ireland: State, Class and Development in the Republic of Ireland*. Basingstoke: Macmillan Press.

Coakley, John. 1993. "Society and Political Culture." In Politics in the Republic of Ireland, eds. John Coakley and Michael Gallagher. Dublin Folens and PSAI Press.

Condren, Mary. 1995. "Sacrifice and Political Legitimation: The Product of a Gendered Social Order." In Irish Women's Voices: Past and Present, eds. Joan Hoff and Moureen Coulter. Journal of Women's History. 6:4/7:1 (Winter/Spring): 160–89.

Connolly, Linda. 1996. "The Women's Movement in Ireland 1970–1995: A Social Movement Analysis." Irish Journal of Feminist Studies. 1:1: 43–77.

Durkan, Joe. 1995. Women in the Labour Force. Dublin: Employment Equality Agency.

Economist. (February 4, 2000) 21.

Fanning, Ronan. 1983. Independent Ireland. Dublin: Helicon Press.

Fitzsimons, Yvonne. 1991. "Women's Interest Representation in the Republic of Ireland: The Council for the Status of Women." Irish Political Studies. 6: 37–51.

Galligan Yvonne. 1997. "Women and National Identity in the Republic of Ireland, or The Plight of the 'Poor Dinnerless Husband.'" Scottish Affairs. 18: 45–53.

———. 1998a. Women and Politics in Contemporary Ireland: From the Margins to the Mainstream. London: Pinter.

———. 1998b. "The Changing Role of Women." In Ireland and the Politics of Change, eds. William Crotty and David E. Schmitt. London: Longman.

Government of Ireland. 1996. First Report on Implementation of the Platform for Action, United Nations Fourth World Conference on Women. Dublin: Stationery Office.[Pn. 3245]

Henley Centre Ireland. 1990. An Equal Future: Policy and Women in the 1990s. Dublin: Henley Centre Ireland.

Inglis, Tom. 1987. Moral Monopoly: The Catholic Church in Modern Irish Society. Dublin: Gill and Macmillan.

Irish Times. March 2, 1991.

———. September 5, 1995.

———. September 9, 1997.

Joint Committee on Women's Rights. 1988. Changing Attitudes to the Role of Women in Ireland: Attitudes Towards the Role and Status of Women 1975–1986. Dublin: Stationery Office.

Kennelly, Brendan, and Eilis Ward. 1993. "The Abortion Referendums." In How Ireland Voted 1992, eds. Michael Gallagher and Michael Laver. Dublin: Folens and PSAI Press.

Kerrigan, Gene. 1997. "No More Cover-ups, Just Answers." Sunday Independent. July 20. 32. 4.

Murphy, Clare. 1997. Women as Church. Dublin: Gill and Macmillan.

National Women's Council of Ireland, 1995. Beijing and Beyond: An Independent Report to the 4th UN World Conference on Women. Dublin: NCWI.

National Woman's Council of Ireland. 1996. Report of the Working Party on the Legal and Judicial Process for Victims of Sexual and Other Crimes of Violence Against Women and Children. Dublin: NWCI.

O'Donovan, Orla, and Eilis Ward. 1999. "Women's Networks and Politics." In *Contesting Politics: Women in Ireland, North and South,* eds. Yvonne Galligan, Eilis Ward, and Rick Wilford. Boulder, Colorado: Westview Press and PSAI Press.

Pollack, Andy. 1996. "Poll Shows Church's Moral Authority in Decline." Irish Times. December 16. 5.

Rumpf, E., and A. C. Hepburn. 1977. *Nationalism and Socialism in Twentieth-Century Ireland.* Liverpool: Liverpool University Press.

Smyth. Ailbhe. ed. 1992. *The Abortion Papers: Ireland.* Dublin: Attic Press.

Society of Jesus. 1995. *Documents of the 34th General Congregation of the Society of Jesus.* St. Louis, Missouri: Society of Jesus.

Solomons, Michael. 1992. *Pro Life?* Dublin: Lilliput Press.

Speed, Anne. 1992. "The Struggle for Reproductive Rights: A Brief History in its Political Context." In *The Abortion Papers: Ireland,* ed. Ailbhe Smyth. Dublin: Attic Press.

Valiulis, Maryann Gialanella. 1995. "Power, Gender and Identity in the Irish Free State." In Irish Women's Voices: Past and Present, eds. Joan Hoff and Moureen Coulter. *Journal of Women's History.* 6:4/7:1.(Winter/Spring) :. 117–36.

Ward, Margaret. 1983. *Unmanageable Revolutionaries: Women and Irish Nationalism.* Dingle: Brandon Books.

Whyte, J. H. 1980. *Church and State in Modern Ireland 1923–1979.* Dublin: Gill and Macmillan. 2nd edition.

Wilcox, Clyde. 1991. "Support for Gender Equality in West Europe—A Longitudinal Analysis." *European Journal of Political Research* 20:2: 127–47.

Women's NGO Beijing Coalition. 2000. *Promises Broken, Beijing + 5 Alternative Report For Ireland.* Dublin: Women's NGO Beijing Coalition.

CHAPTER 5

IMPLEMENTING WOMEN'S
RIGHTS IN SPAIN

CELIA VALIENTE

Spain is a culturally homogeneous Catholic country. After the expulsion of Jews in 1492 and of Muslims in 1502, no significant religious community other than the Catholic community has been openly active in Spain in the last four centuries. During the right-wing authoritarian regime headed by General Franco (who governed the country between the second half of the 1930s and 1975), Catholicism was the official religion of the country and some Catholic doctrines were reflected in state laws. For instance, divorce was prohibited and abortion was criminalized. Spain is the birthplace of the conservative Opus Dei organization, which was founded in 1928 and has been invigorated by Papal favor in the last decades.

In this chapter, I argue that despite the strong influence of the Catholic Church in politics in the past, Spain belongs now to the group of western countries with secularized polities. In Spain, church and state are separate. The Catholic Church runs an important part of the education system but does not control the agenda of government. Gender equality policies are in line with the policies of other European Union member states (with the possible exception of abortion).

I proceed in two steps. First, I provide a general and historical background of Catholicism in Spain and of Franco's regime. Second, I develop the aforementioned argument with the study of four dimensions of the policy area of gender equality: violence against women, abortion, gender equality in employment, and childcare.

CATHOLICISM IN SPAIN
AND THE FRANCOIST REGIME

The overwhelming majority of Spaniards consider themselves Catholic (85 percent in March 2000). Although the number of practicing Catholics is much lower than the number of self-declared Catholics, it is significant. In March 2000, 21 percent of those self-declared Catholics affirmed that they attend religious services (excluding social events such as weddings, first communions, or funerals) almost every Sunday or religious festivity, and around 3 percent attend on various days per week (Centro de Investigaciones Sociológicas 2000). The Catholic Church has an important presence in the education system. For instance, in the so-called MEC territory (ten regions whose education was administered in the 1990s by the Ministry of Education and Culture [MEC] of the central state), in the academic year 1996–7, 29 percent of children and youngsters enrolled in preschool, primary, and secondary education attended a center administered by the Catholic Church (calculated by Celia Valiente from data in Pérez-Díaz, Chuliá, and Álvarez-Miranda 1998, 139).

To suspect that the teachings of the Catholic Church influence the ideas and behaviors of the population is reasonable. Nevertheless, this is true only to a certain point. For instance, the Catholic Church mandates that couples marry in the church. The acceptance of Catholic marriage is high in Spain but not overwhelming. In March 1998, the Spanish adult population was asked, "Which is the best living arrangement for stable partners?" Over half of the respondents (54 percent) chose religious marriages. The remainder preferred other options such as: "living together without getting married" (11 percent); "living together and marrying in the church afterwards" (9 percent); "a civil marriage" (9 percent); and "living together and having a civil marriage afterwards" (8 percent) (Centro de Investigaciones Sociológicas 1998).

Examples of disconnection between official Catholic doctrines and societal views abound. The Catholic Church advocates that married women have as many children as "God sends them," but recently Spain has had one of the lowest fertility rates in the world. In 1998, the synthetic index of fertility in Spain was 1.15 children per woman (Bovagnet 1999, 5; provisional data). In March 1998, the Spanish adult population was asked: "What is the ideal number of children for a family of a similar socioeconomic level as yours?" Only 2 percent chose the answer in line with the official church position: "As many as they come." More than half of the interviewed (58 percent) chose two children, and a quarter (26 percent) chose three children (Centro de Investigaciones Sociológicas, 1998). The Catholic Church affirms that people must be married in church before they have children. In December 1995, however, more than two-thirds of the Spanish adult population (71 percent) agreed with the statement, "A woman can have children without being married" (Centro de Investigaciones Sociológicas 1995). The Catholic Church unequivocally opposes divorce. By contrast, in December 1995, three-quarters of the Spanish adult population agreed with the proposition, "When a couple cannot solve its problems, divorce is the solution" (Centro de Investigaciones Sociológicas 1995). The Catholic Church prohibits homosexual sex. By contrast, in December 1995, two-thirds (65 percent) of the Spanish adult population agreed with the statement, "Homosexuality is a personal option as respectable as heterosexuality" (Centro de Investigaciones Sociológicas 1995). The Catholic Church defines abortion as murder in all circumstances, but in December 1995, slightly over half of the Spanish adult population (56 percent) agreed with the view that, "the decision to have an abortion corresponds only to the woman" (Centro de Investigaciones Sociológicas #2203). As José Casanova (1993, 118) rightly points out: "not only can the church no longer control the public morality of the Spaniards, it can no longer take for granted the control of the private morality of the Catholic faithful."

As for the political arena, the church has no direct representation in the political space, because no Christian Democratic Party or trade union exists (Casanova 1993). The separation of church and the Spanish state is reflected in the constitution. According to Article 16, Spain is a nondenominational state based on religious freedom. Nevertheless, this very same Article also states that "public authorities will take in mind the religious beliefs of the Spanish society" (that is, Catholicism). Article 16 also refers to the desirability of the cooperation between the state and the Catholic Church and the remaining denominations. The Catholic Church accepted the principle of non-confessionality of the Spanish state and the constitutional regulation of state-church relations (Casanova 1993, 117; Linz 1993, 35). The church does not agree with some laws regulating moral matters, such as the laws that legalized divorce (1981) or that liberalized abortion (1985), but it has not made a big effort to reverse them. Resistance by Catholics to these public policies has been more moderate in Spain than in other western countries. The Catholic Church is not involved in the main political controversies of the country (with the possible exception of the nationalist question in the Basque country) but is not silent regarding the matters that the church considers important (education and moral issues such as abortion and sexuality, among others). The church does not explicitly support a political party and does not ask Catholics to vote for any given party. Nevertheless, the Catholic Church sometimes transmits a sense of preference when speaking about its position regarding certain issues. At times, this coincides with the position of specific parties (Linz 1993, 32–48).

The separation of church and state is a characteristic of the democratic regime established after the end of the dictatorship in 1975, but not of the right-wing authoritarian regime headed by Franco.[1] During the first Francoism (between the second part of the 1930s until the late 1950s-early 1960s), the church and the political regime supported each other. Catholicism was the official religion of the country. Freedom of worship was abolished. The state gave the church the prerogative of managing all matters regarding marriage and the separation of married couples. Catholic marriage was mandatory, with very few exceptions (Pérez-Díaz 1987). The state allowed the Catholic Church to control part of the education system: that is an important number of primary and secondary schools—but not most universities, which had been under state control at least since the mid-nineteenth century (McNair 1984, 18–19). In all primary and secondary schools, the state made religious teaching and religious practices mandatory and education had to conform to the teachings of the Catholic Church. The church was given the right to inspect private and public centers (McNair 1984, 28–29). Sex segregated schools were the norm, and boys and girls not only attended different schools but also had different curricula. Divorce was abolished, and the selling and advertising of contraceptives was criminalized. Abortion was defined as a crime punished with prison. The state economically supported the Catholic Church, which was exempted from taxation. In turn, the church supported the authoritarian regime, provided it with legitimacy, and declared the civil war (1936–39) a crusade, that is, a fight, between supporters of Christianity (Franco's followers) and the unfaithful and immoral (the Republicans). Some of the administrative cadres of the Francoist state came from Catholic lay organizations such as the *Asociación Católica Nacional de Propagandistas,* and later the Opus Dei. Catholic hierarchies occupied a salient place in official governmental acts. State authorities ex officio attended religious ceremonies (Casanova 1993, 107–08; Linz 1993, 9–25).

During the first Francoism, economic policies tried to reach the objective of productive autarchy and isolation from the international market. State intervention in the economy increased. Productivity growth remained very low, and unemployment and underemployment remained high. For the majority of the population, the 1940s was a period of scarcity, black market, and economic hardship. Economic difficulties also were present in the 1950s (Anderson 1970; González 1979). Francoist policy makers elaborated pro-natalist policies to stimulate population growth. The ideal family was a hierarchical unit, since it was assumed that authority within it rested with the father, who was supposed to be its sole (or, at worst, its main) supporter. Motherhood was defined not only as the main family duty of women but also as women's main obligation toward the state and society. The role of mothering was perceived as incompatible with other activities, such as waged work. The state took measures to prevent women's labor outside the home. Examples of this were: the so-called marriage bars (prohibitions from working in some companies or sectors of the economy after marriage); the requirement that a married woman obtain her husband's permission before signing a labor contract and engaging in trade; or the prohibition that women perform certain jobs, especially in the field of law. The official female employment rate[2] during the first Francoism was very low, oscillating around 10 percent. The real female employment rate was probably higher (Nash 1991; Valiente 1997, 82–95).

The second Francoism (between the late 1950s- early 1960s and 1975) was economically different from the first Francoist period. Economic policies changed at the end of the 1950s as the economy began to be liberalized and opened to international markets. Export development policies replaced import substitution policies. Economic recovery started in 1961, with the beginning of a period of high economic growth, and the appearance and consolidation of a mass-consumption society. Male unemployment remained very low due to the economic recovery and the emigration of Spanish workers to work in other countries (Anderson 1970; González 1979). At the end of Franco's regime, the female employment rate had increased to a level of around 20 percent. During the 1960s and 1970s, Francoist policy makers approved some liberalization measures related to women's status, such as the abolition of some prohibitions and obstacles regarding paid employment (such as marriage bars, or the prohibition to perform some professions in the field of law). Liberalization, however, did not take place regarding the regulation of sexuality and reproduction (Valiente 1997, 82–95).

Relations between church and state were different in the second Francoism. A part (only a part) of the church distanced itself from the regime, self-criticized the position and actions of the church in the civil war, and even gave protection and support to political dissidents. Catholics became members of groups and parties of all ideological colors in opposition to the dictatorship. Thanks to this progressive distancing of a part of the church from the political regime, when Franco died in 1975, the church could align itself with other political and social forces in the building of a new democratic regime (Casanova 1993, 114–17; Linz 1993, 25–32).

CENTRAL STATE GENDER EQUALITY
POLICIES IN SPAIN AFTER FRANCO

After 1975, democratic policy makers began to dismantle the discriminatory legislation inherited from Franco's time and to promote women's rights and status. The 1978 Constitution explicitly states that women and men are equal before the law, and sex discrimination is prohibited. The selling and advertising of contraceptives was decriminalized in 1978. Divorce for civil marriages was permitted in 1981. Whereas the Franco's regime actively promoted sex-segregated schooling, the post-Franco governments encouraged girls and boys to go to school together. This is currently the norm (with very few exceptions). Spanish policy makers at the central state level have been advocating gender equality policies in line with the policies of other European Union member states. In 1983, partly in response to the United Nations' recommendation that a national policy machinery be established in each member state, Spain created the Instituto de la Mujer (Women's Institute), charged with promoting gender equality for the state (Stetson and Mazur 1995). This governmental agency has been an important force for gender equality policies. Even though the Women's Institute was founded in Spain later than the women's policy machineries of other western countries, the Women's Institute is now comparable to agencies in other advanced industrial societies in terms of goals, budget, and personnel. As is the case in other countries, the Women's Institute has neither the responsibilities nor the budget to define and put into practice all gender equality policies of the country. The goal of the Women's Institute is to persuade other state units to include gender equality in their policy agendas, and to encourage taking gender into consideration in all public policy making (Valiente 1995b).

One way to obtain a sense of the nature of the current Spanish regime and its attitude toward women is to examine specific gender equality policies established by the central state level. The four public policies considered here are (not in order of importance): violence against women, abortion, gender equality in employment, and childcare. These four policies have been chosen because they are linked to four of the dimensions of social life in which women's subordination takes place: sexuality, reproduction, paid employment, and the family. This list is by no means exhaustive, but it gives a fairly extensive (if incomplete) vision of central state intervention in women's lives in Spain. Some of these policies were advocated by a center-right party, the Unión de Centro Democrático, which governed the country until 1982. Although many gender equality policies were installed under the Socialist party government (1982–1996), for the most part, all have been sustained since 1996 when the Conservative party, the Partido Popular, took power.

The Spanish women's movement has also played a role in this change; however, the feminist movement was weaker and its influence less noticeable in Spain than in other western countries for most of the nineteenth century and for much of the twentieth century. The first Second Wave feminist groups appeared in the late 1960s and early 1970s. These first groups were active in the opposition to the dictatorship, where they collaborated with other (often illegal) organizations and political parties. Many feminist groups continue to be close to political parties of the left. The Spanish feminist movement has not managed to develop umbrella organizations that represent most groups. The feminist movement in Spain is not a mass movement. Women's organizations with headquarters in Madrid, Barcelona, and other cities show signs of strength and hold regular national feminist conferences attended by between three thousand and five thousand women (Kaplan 1992, 208–09). In comparison with other western countries, however, the women's movement in Spain has not achieved high visibility in the mass media, organized mass demonstrations, or initiated many public debates. In general, not many Spaniards join voluntary organizations of any sort.

VIOLENCE AGAINST WOMEN

Ever since 1975, Spanish central-state policies against violence against women (AVAW) have mainly been of two types: fairly extensive legal reforms, and quite modest services for victims of violence, for instance, refuges for battered women. The most important AVAW policies in Spain after 1975 are legal reforms. In the Penal Code, the different violent acts perpetrated against women are defined as either misdemeanors (faltas) or offenses (delitos), and each of them is assigned a punishment (pena), which is lower for misdemeanors than for offenses. Legal reforms have expanded the definition of rape, sexual aggression, and domestic violence in order to include more behaviors and punish them accordingly. With respect to rape, before 1983, if the victim "forgave" the perpetrator, no prosecution could take place. In 1983, the Penal Code established that when victims of rape forgive the perpetrators, they should still be punished according to the law. Before 1989, rape was defined in a very restricted way, because it referred only to heterosexual vaginal coitus. The concept of rape has since been expanded to include anal and oral coitus, and penetration with foreign objects. Rape is an offense defined in the laws independently from the marital or professional status of victims, for instance, irrespectively of whether the perpetrator is the husband of the victim, or whether she works as a prostitute. Now, rape is punished in Spain with a period of imprisonment up to twelve years. Gang rape (committed by three or more people) is punished with a higher number of years of prison. Legal porceedings against a rapist can be initiated by a prosecutor. A complaint by the victim is not required. According to provisional data presented by the government to the Low Chamber of Parliament, the number of reported sexual aggressions was 6,527 in 1999. This figure includes rape and sexual attacks (El País 1999, 34). The number of non-reported cases makes the total much higher.

With regard to domestic violence, in 1989 the Penal Code classified repeated physical domestic violence against women perpetrated by husbands or cohabiting partners as an offense, and not as a misdemeanor, as it had been legally defined in the past. Currently, the offense of repeated physical domestic violence is punished with a period of imprisonment that ranges from six months to three years. In 1999, the offense of repeated psychological violence in the domestic sphere was defined in the Penal Code. According to provisional data presented by government to the Low Chamber of Parliament, the number of reported cases of domestic violence was 24,985 in 1999 (El País 1999, 34). Again, the number of non-reported cases of violence against women makes the total much higher.

As the 1990s ended, legal reforms were almost completed on paper. Nevertheless, a huge implementation deficit exists regarding this type of legislation. Services for victims have been established, but these services are still clearly insufficient and less developed than in other countries (Asociación de Mujeres Juristas Themis 1999; Defensor del Pueblo 1998). The best-known services for victims are the battered women's refuges (Scanlon 1990, 99). As in other countries, refuges are mainly temporary safe accommodations for female victims of violence and their children. In addition, women receive in these shelters other services that range from legal advice to psychological support and vocational training with the aim of helping the women to initiate a new life away from perpetrators of violence. In Spain, the first refuges were set up in 1984 (Instituto de la Mujer 1994, 99). By 1997, 129 refuges provided a safe haven for about every 302,000 inhabitants in Spain. This proportion is still lower than the proportion recommended by a Resolution of the European Parliament in 1997: a shelter for every 100,000 inhabitants (Defensor del Pueblo 1998). In 1999, around 3,300 women and 4,000 children stayed in shelters (El País 15 May 2000, 30).

In post-authoritarian Spain, the impact of women's advocates in the policy area of violence against women has been of paramount importance. In the late 1970s and early 1980s, certain feminists "discovered" the problem of violence against women in some cases accidentally (Threlfall 1985,

62–63). Feminists from the Separated and Divorced Women's Association (*Asociación de Mujeres Separadas y Divorciadas*), who provided counseling and legal advice to women who wanted to initiate separation and/or divorce proceedings, found that the main goal of many of their clients was to escape from a situation of high levels of domestic violence. By the same token, some activists who worked in health centers as physicians or psychologists were shocked by the high number of female victims of violence who turn to these centers for help. Feminist activists were able to convert a social problem (attacks against women) into an issue worthy of governmental intervention. Women's advocates have continuously demanded that policy makers intervene in this area, reform the legal system in order effectively to protect women against aggressors, and organize services for the relief and help of the victims. The state often does not provide services for victims of violence directly, but instead subsidizes non-governmental, non-profit women's organizations to do the work. Women's organizations (with the help of state subsidies) have administered battered women's refuges, emergency phone lines for rape victims, psychological support for victims of violence, and training workshops for the police on violence against women.

ABORTION

In Franco's Spain, the Penal Code punished abortion with prison (between six months and six years). Abortion was a crime with no extenuating circumstances for women (Barreiro 1998, 35). Since 1975, the only reform in this policy area has been the 1985 partial decriminalization of abortion.[3] According to Act 9 of July 5, 1985, on the reform of the Article 417 of the Penal Code (hereafter 1985 Abortion Act), abortion is a crime punishable under the Penal Code except on three grounds: when women have been raped; when pregnancy seriously endangers the physical and psychological health of the mother; and when the fetus has malformations.

Abortion has been a unifying demand of most groups of the Spanish feminist movement since the 1970s. Spanish feminists mobilized endlessly in favor of the decriminalization of abortion and were able to influence policy makers and public opinion (Sundman 1999; Trujillo 1999).[4] The impact of the Women's Institute in the policy process regarding the implementation of the Abortion Act can be used as an illustration of the influence of feminist advocates in the policy area of abortion.

The regulation of the implementation of abortion legislation is very important, because this regulation may make easy or difficult the access to induced abortion (Outshoorn 1996, 150). The 1985 Abortion Act does not say anything about the implementation of abortion reform. The material and human means required in clinics for the performance of abortions were established by Ministerial Ordinance of July 31, 1985 from the Ministry of Health and Consumption. These material and human means were more extensive than what is strictly required from a health point of view. A very broad and flexible conscience clause permitting health personnel to refuse to help in abortion cases was established in August 1985.

Abortion was clearly one of the top priorities of the Women's Institute since its establishment. The Women's Institute identified two main problems (among others) in the implementation of the 1985 Abortion Act. First, very few public clinics and no private clinic performed abortions. Second, due to the broad nature of the conscience clause, very few abortions were actually performed in public hospitals (Instituto de la Mujer 1985, 1986a, 1986b; Barreiro 1998, 238–46). The Women's Institute also made recommendations (among others) to increase of the number of authorized centers. After an intricate negotiation process among the Ministry of Health and Consumption, the Women's Institute, and other policy actors, the government approved Royal Decree 2409 of November 21,1986 on the implementation of the 1985 Act, which replaced the aforementioned Ministerial Ordinance of July 31, 1985. The decree made access to abortion easier by requiring that clinics have fewer resources for the performance of "low-risk abortions" (up to 12 weeks of pregnancy).

As expected, because of the lowering of human and material requirements (trained personnel and specific instruments or rooms), private clinics became interested in becoming authorized to perform abortions. Since then, private clinics perform an overwhelming majority of abortions in Spain. In 1998, 53,847 abortions were reported in Spain. The total number of abortions, both reported and not reported, is much higher. In 1998, the reported abortion rate was six abortions per thousand women of reproductive age. Ninety-seven percent of reported abortions were performed in private centers, and the remaining 3 percent in public centers. Almost all (97.32 percent) of reported abortions were performed because of risks for the physical or psychological health of the mother due to pregnancy, 2.27 percent were performed because of presumed malformations of the fetus, 0.03 percent were performed because of rape, and the remaining 0.38 percent for unknown reasons (El País 19 February 2000: 22). Most cases officially registered as abortions performed on the grounds that the psychological health of the mother is in jeopardy are, in reality, performed on socioeconomic grounds, a type of abortion not permitted by law. Thanks to the loose implementation of the 1986 Royal Decree, access to abortion is easier than before, and very often goes beyond what is permitted by the 1985 Act (Barreiro 1998, 248–252).

Access to abortion still has some serious limits in Spain. First, private centers charge fees, while public centers do not. As most abortions take place in private centers, some women cannot afford an abortion. Second, authorized clinics are scarce in some cities, towns, and regions. As a result, abortion rates vary widely among different regions (*El País* 19 February 2000, 22). Third, doctors who perform abortions and women who have them are permanently under the threat of being prosecuted because many abortions that are performed are not permitted by law. This could only be solved by further reform to the 1985 Act (Barreiro 1998, 248–252).

The fact that after the 1980s, no important political party has been mobilized against the partial liberalization of abortion shows how secularized the Spanish polity has become. The main opposition to the 1985 Abortion Act was political. This opposition was led by the conservative party. Nevertheless, in the late 1980s it accepted the abortion settlement. Abortion is not a topic currently being debated in Spain. Although feminists have been continuously mobilized in favor of a further liberalization of abortion policies, they have not succeeded in this battle. On the abortion issue, Spain is different from the United States. Mass demonstrations by pro-life and pro-choice groups have not taken place in Spain.

GENDER EQUALITY IN EMPLOYMENT

The central government in Spain, regardless of the party in power, has initiated three types of public policies for working women since 1975: measures to help women combine their family and professional duties, the revision of labor law in accordance with the constitutional principle of sex equality, and (very few) affirmative actions.[5] Since the dictatorship ended twenty-five years ago, postauthoritarian policy makers have witnessed periods of economic crisis combined with periods of economic recovery. The female activity rate[6] has been constantly increasing during the whole period, reaching the level of 48 percent in 1998 (Franco 1999, 8).

With regard to measures that help women combine family and professional duties, since 1975, political elites have developed these programs, and have allowed men to be the beneficiaries of some of them. Policy makers have extended paid maternity leave. Now, working mothers who have been previously employed and have contributed to the social security system for at least 180 days within the five years previous to childbirth are entitled to sixteen uninterrupted weeks of paid maternity leave at (approximately) full pay. The right to return to one's job is guaranteed. Maternity leave also applies to mothers who adopt children. The father can take up to ten weeks of maternity leave. Nevertheless, the number of fathers who take some weeks of maternity leave is very small. The Spanish

Labor Force Survey provides data segregated by sex of wage earners who are not working during the week when the survey questionnaire is administered. In the fourth quarter of 1998, 97 percent of wage earners who were not working due to maternity leave were women, and the remaining 3 percent were men (calculated by Celia Valiente from data published in Instituto Nacional de Estadística 1999, 204). Working mothers or fathers can take non-paid parental leave for up to three years. The right to a job in the same professional category is guaranteed during the second and third years. The period of leave is counted as effectively worked in terms of seniority.

Discriminatory legislation, inherited from former times, has been modified in accordance with the constitutional principle of sex equality. Women have been allowed to perform some types of work prohibited to them in the past, such as night work, and work in the police, in the army, or in the mining sector. In addition, the concept of wage equality was broadened to include not only the principle of "equal pay for equal work" but also that of "equal pay for work of equal value" (in 1995), and not only the concept of direct but also indirect discrimination. Indirect discrimination includes harmful treatment of either gender due to job requisites that are not necessary for the performance of the job.

Today, the principle of equality of all citizens before the law informs general legislation. The discriminatory clauses that exist are contained in collective agreements negotiated between representatives of employers and workers. Wage discrimination is one of the most common forms of gender discrimination. It occurs with the creation of labor categories that include only or mainly women. These female workers are paid less than workers included in mixed, or male categories.

Affirmative action (or positive action) policies that give preferential treatment to women with respect to men for the purpose of achieving de facto equality between both sexes in the labor market are usually of a pilot nature in Spain and, therefore, affect a very low number of beneficiaries. The state has subsidized and/or managed job training courses for women and has fostered the employment of women in some circumstances, such as: when women are the only economic provider of their families, when women work in sectors of the economy where women are underrepresented, when women are self-employed, and when women create their own companies.

After 1975, equality in paid employment between women and men has been one of the top priorities of feminist activists. Feminist advocates have repeatedly argued that economic independence is a necessary ingredient for women's liberation. Economic autonomy very often means participation in the labor market, because the majority of the population of active age acquires economic autonomy through paid work. Thanks in part to feminist mobilization, these ideas have permeated political parties, trade unions, and state institutions; the main actors in the policy-making process in democratic Spain.

CHILD CARE

After 1975, the main central state childcare policy (for children under the age of six, when mandatory schooling starts) has been the supply of free educational preschool programs for children age three or over administered chiefly by the Ministry of Education and Culture (Ministerio de Educación y Cultura, MEC; before 1996, it was called the Ministry of Education and Science—Ministerio de Educación y Ciencia). In the 1996–97 academic year, the proportion of children who attended public preschool programs was 70 percent of children age four and five, and 43 percent of those age three. The scope of these programs is quite high in comparative terms. Since the private sector also provides pre-school places, school attendance rates of three, four, and five-year old children in public schools are high in Spain in comparative terms (67, 99, and 100 percent, respectively). In contrast, the percentage of Spanish children age two or under cared for in public centers is one of the lowest in the European Union: 2.5 percent. The proportion of children age two or under cared for in private centers is also very small: 3.5 percent—calculated by Celia Valiente from data contained in Ministerio de Educación y Cultura (1999, 79, 132–34).[7]

Public preschool programs cannot be used by parents (or mothers) as perfect substitutes for childcare, because preschool hours are shorter than working hours (sometimes much shorter and interrupted by a break). Preschool holidays are much longer than working holidays. For instance, preschool summer holidays last approximately three months, whereas paid summer holidays for workers last one month. Even though the percentage of women in employment is lower in Spain than in most European Union member states, most Spanish women who work for wages have full-time jobs. In 1998, the Spanish female employment rate (35 percent) was the lowest in the European Union, and much lower than the European Union average (51 percent). Eighty-three percent of female workers worked on a full-time basis in Spain. This figure (together with that of Portugal and Finland) was the third highest in the European Union, after that of Greece (89 percent) and Italy (86 percent), and sixteen points above the European Union average (67 percent) (Franco 1999, 8–9).

In brief, since 1975, a substantial expansion of the supply of public preschool programs (the main child care policy) has taken place in Spain. Public pre-school centers were attended by 347,025 children younger than six in academic year 1975–6. In academic year 1999–2000, the figure was more than double; 758,458 children—calculated by Celia Valiente from data contained in Instituto Nacional de Estadística (1977: 101–02; 1981: 12) and data available on July 17,2000 at http://www.mec.es/estadistica/Cifras/Nac–01.html. Other childcare policies (state regulation of public centers, tax exemptions for childcare expenses, and state scholarships for pupils of private centers) have been less important than the supply of preschool places in public centers. Generally speaking, childcare has been seen as an educational matter by policy makers from all political parties that have governed postauthoritarian Spain. The MEC has been the chief institution in charge of defining the "problem" of childcare for children under six: a shortage of educational programs. This MEC definition has influenced the "solution" provided: an extension of the number of preschool places mainly for children over three in public centers.

I have argued in another place (Valiente 1995a, 254–256) that, in contrast with other countries, Spanish feminist advocates (the feminist movement, the Women's Institute, and women's departments of the main trade unions) have mainly advanced rhetorical demands in the policy area of childcare chiefly for two reasons. First, the Franco regime actively opposed the advancement of women's rights and status. After 1975, feminist activists had to pursue numerous objectives, including equality before the law and reproductive rights. In this situation, it was reasonable for feminists to concentrate on some demands and to leave others aside. Second, in paying considerably less attention to the issues of motherhood and childcare than to other issues, feminists in Spain were rejecting, more than in other countries, a problematic past. After almost forty years of literally being bombarded by authoritarian policy makers with the idea of mothering and caring as the most important task in women's lives, the last thing Spanish feminists wanted to do after 1975 was to pay a lot of attention to the issue of motherhood. Women's liberation was then understood as broadening the range of concerns that define women's lives, such as waged work. This definition carefully avoids considering the place of motherhood and childcare in the life of the newly liberated female Spaniards.

CONCLUSION

Religious mobilization was highly visible at the United Nations Fourth World Conference on Women held at Beijing in 1995 and at the Beijing Plus Five meeting in New York in 2000, confirming the fact that the role of religion in shaping women's lives is far from disappearing. Countries in which the overwhelming majority of citizens are Catholic, however, differ widely among themselves along several dimensions, including: the degree of the separation of church and the state, the existence or absence of Christian democratic parties, and the degree to which Catholicism is part of the national identity and consequently an element of differentiation from other political communities. Differences among Catholic countries are, in some cases, very wide, as the chapters on Spain and Ireland of this book clearly illustrate. The case of Spain illustrates that even when the overwhelming majority of the population declares itself Catholic, this does not necessarily mean that public policies reflect the views of the Catholic Church or that all or even a majority of the people subscribe to and adhere to Catholic doctrines. Spain is a country with a strong Catholic past and tradition that has, in the last twenty-five years, emerged as a secularized polity and anchored itself in the European Union with its state-led policies toward women. In Spain today, contraceptives are legal (since 1978), divorce is available (since 1981), and abortion is permitted on three grounds (since 1985). All these policies reflect views contrary to those supported by the official doctrine of the Catholic Church. Furthermore, in Spain, violence against women is clearly defined as a crime in the Penal Code and, in theory, punished accordingly. State policies encourage women not to endure violent husbands for the sake of the family or of their children. Female and male workers are equal before the law, labor policies do not provide any explicit incentive for women to leave the labor market and stay at home, and public childcare provision is extensive in comparative terms. The impact of feminist activism in the promotion of these and other gender equality policies has been an important contributor to the change. The influence of the Catholic Church remains and should not be underestimated. The school system remains dominated by the church, and the church's position on abortion is perhaps a factor that explains why most (but not all) European Union member states have more liberalized access to induced abortions than has Spain (Outshoorn 1996).

Notes

1. The alliance between the Catholic Church and political powers was not a peculiarity of the Franco regime, but has constantly existed during the last centuries. The main exception to this rule was the Second Republic (1931–6), when political elites approved the separation of state and church, and withdrew many of the privileges of the Catholic Church. For reasons of space, this chapter analyzes Spain since the Francoist period.
2. The female employment rate is the proportion of employed women out of the female population of working age.

3. The description of abortion reform in this chapter follows Barreiro (1998) closely.
4. English-speaking readers interested in feminist activism in Spain concerning abortion can consult the following accounts on the feminist movement: Threlfall (1985, 1996); and Durán and Gallego (1986). Accounts in Spanish include: Borreguero et al. (1986); Folguera (1988); Scanlon (1990); and Escario et al. (1996).
5. The description of gender equality policies in employment since 1975 follows Valiente (1997, 144–153) closely.
6. The female activity rate is the proportion of active women (the employed and the registered unemployed) out of the female population of working age.
7. For preschool attendance rates in Spain and other European Union and Organization for Economic Cooperation and Development (OECD) member states, see: European Commission (1998, 76); and OECD (2000, 135).

REFERENCES

Anderson, Charles. 1970. *The Political Economy of Modern Spain: Policy-Making in an Authoritarian System*. Madison: University of Wisconsin Press.

Asociación de Mujeres Juristas Themis. 1999. *Respuesta Penal a la Violencia Familiar*. Madrid: Asociación de Mujeres Juristas Themis and Consejo de la Mujer de la Comunidad de Madrid.

Barreiro, Belén. 1998. *Democracia y Conflicto Moral: La Política del Aborto en Italia y España*. Madrid: Centro de Estudios Avanzados en Ciencias Sociales del Instituto Juan March de Estudios e Investigaciones.

Bovagnet, François-Carlos. 1999. "Premiers Résultats de la Collecte de Données Démographiques pour 1998 en Europe." *Statistiques en Bref: Population et Conditions Sociales*. Luxembourg: Office for Official Publications of the European Communities.

Borreguero, Concha, Elena Catena, Consuelo De la Gándara, and María Salas. 1986. *La Mujer Española: de la Tradición a la Modernidad (1960–1980)*. Madrid: Tecnos.

Casanova, José. 1993. "Church, State, Nation, and Civil Society in Spain and Poland." In *The Political Dimensions of Religion*, ed. Said Amir Arjomand. Albany : State University of New York Press.

Centro de Investigaciones Sociológicas. 1995. Study Number 2,203, December, data available on March 3, 2000 at http://www.cis.es/boletin/3/est4.html.

———. 1998. Study Number 2,283, March, data available on March 3, 2000 at http://www.cis.es/boletin/17/hijos.html.

———. 2000. Study Number 2,387, March, data available on May 22, 2000 at http://www.cis.es/baros/mar2387.htm.

Defensor del Pueblo. 1998. *Informe sobre la Violencia Doméstica contra las Mujeres*. Unpublished report.

Durán, María A., and María T. Gallego. 1986. "The Women's Movement in Spain and the New Spanish Democracy." In *The New Women's Movement: Feminism and Political Power in Europe and the USA*, ed. Drude Dahlerup. London: Sage.

El País. December 27, 1999, 34.

————. February 19, 2000, 22.

————. May 15, 2000,30.

Escario, Pilar, Inés Alberdi, and Ana I. López-Accotto. 1996. *Lo Personal es Político: El Movimiento Feminista en la Transición*. Madrid: Instituto de la Mujer.

European Commission. 1998. *Social Portrait of Europe*. Luxembourg: Office for Official Publications of the European Communities.

Folguera, Pilar, ed. 1988. *El Feminismo en España: Dos Siglos de Historia*. Madrid: Pablo Iglesias.

Franco, Ana. 1999. "Enquête sur les Forces de Travail: Principaux Résultats 1998." *Statistiques en Bref: Population et Conditions Sociales* 11.

González, Manuel J. 1979. *La Economía Política del Franquismo (1940–1970): Dirigismo, Mercado y Planificación*. Madrid: Tecnos.

Instituto de la Mujer. 1985. "Informe del Instituto de la Mujer sobre Aplicación de la Ley de Interrupción Voluntaria del Embarazo" (Septiembre 1985). In *Seminario sobre el Aborto, 4 de julio de 1989*, ed. Partido Socialista Obrero Español (Secretaría Federal de Participación de la Mujer). Unpublished dossier.

————. 1986a. "Informe del Instituto de la Mujer en Relación al Documento Remitido por el Ministerio de Sanidad sobre Desarrollo de la Ley de Interrupción Voluntaria del Embarazo" (Agosto de 1986). In *Seminario sobre el aborto, 4 de julio de 1989*, ed. Partido Socialista Obrero Español (Secretaría Federal de Participación de la Mujer). Unpublished dossier.

————. 1986b. "Informe sobre la Ampliación de la Ley Orgánica 9/85 Realizado por el Instituto de la Mujer" (Abril de 1986). In *Seminario sobre el Aborto, 4 de Julio de 1989*, ed. Partido Socialista Obrero Español (Secretaría Federal de Participación de la Mujer). Unpublished dossier.

————. 1994. *La Mujer en Cifras: Una Década, 1982–1992*. Madrid: Instituto de la Mujer.

Instituto Nacional de Estadística. 1977. *Estadística de la Enseñanza en España: Curso 1975–76*. Madrid: Instituto Nacional de Estadística.

————. 1981. *Censo de Población, Tomo I, Volumen I, Resultados Nacionales, Características de la Población*. Madrid: Instituto Nacional de Estadística.

————.1999. *Encuesta de Población Activa: Resultados Detallados, Cuarto Trimestre 1998*. Madrid: Instituto Nacional de Estadística.

Kaplan, Gisela. 1992. *Contemporary Western European Feminism*. London: UCL Press and Allen & Unwin.

Linz, Juan J. 1993. "Religión y Política en España." In *Religión y Sociedad en España*, ed. Rafael Díaz-Salazar and Salvador Giner. Madrid: Centro de Investigaciones Sociológicas.

McNair, John M. 1984. *Education for a Changing Spain*. Manchester: Manchester University Press.

Ministerio de Educación y Cultura. 1999. *Estadística de la enseñanza en España 1996/97: Resultados Detallados, Series e Indicadores.* Madrid: Ministerio de Educación y Cultura.

Nash, Mary. 1991. "Pronatalism and Motherhood in Franco's Spain." In *Maternity and Gender Policies: Women and the Rise of the European Welfare States, 1880s–1950s,* ed. Gisela Bock and Pat Thane. London: Routledge.

Organization for Economic Cooperation and Development. 2000. *Education at a Glance: OECD Indicators, 2000 Edition.* Paris: Organization for Economic Cooperation and Development.

Outshoorn, Joyce. 1996. "The Stability of Compromise: Abortion Politics In Western Europe." In *Abortion Politics: Public Policy in Cross-Cultural Perspective,* ed. Marianne Githens and Dorothy McBride Stetson. New York and London: Routledge.

Pérez-Díaz, Víctor. 1987. *El Retorno de la Sociedad Civil.* Madrid: Instituto de Estudios Económicos.

Pérez-Díaz, Víctor, Elisa Chuliá, and Berta Álvarez-Miranda. 1998. *Familia y Sistema de Bienestar: La Experiencia Española con el Paro, las Pensiones, la Sanidad y la Educación.* Madrid: Fundación Argentaria and Visor.

Stetson, Dorothy McBride, and Amy G. Mazur, ed. 1995. *Comparative State Feminism.* Thousand Oaks, Calif.: Sage.

Scanlon, Geraldine M. 1990. "El Movimiento Feminista en España, 1900–1985: Logros y Dificultades." In *Participación Política de las Mujeres,* ed. Judith Astelarra. Madrid: Centro de Investigaciones Sociológicas and Siglo XXI.

Sundman, Kerstin. 1999. *Between the Home and the Institutions: The Feminist Movement in Madrid, Spain.* Gothenburg: Acta Universitatis Gothoburgensis.

Threlfall, Monica. 1985. "The Women's Movement in Spain." *New Left Review.* 151: 44–73.

———. 1996. "Feminist Politics and Social Change in Spain." In *Mapping the Women's Movement: Feminist Politics and Social Transformation in the North,* ed. Monica Threlfall. London and New York: Verso.

———. 1998. "State Feminism or Party Feminism? Feminist Politics and the Spanish Institute of Women." *The European Journal of Women's Studies* 5: 69–93.

Trujillo, Gracia. 1999. "El Movimiento Feminista como Actor Político en España: el Caso de la Aprobación de la Ley de Despenalización del Aborto de 1985." Paper presented at the Meeting of the Spanish Association of Political Science and Public Administration, Grenada (Spain), September 30-October 2.

Valiente, Celia. 1995a. "Children First: Central Government Child Care Policies in Post-Authoritarian Spain (1975–1994)." In *Childhood and Parenthood: Proceedings of ISA Committee for Family Research Conference on Children and Families, 1994,* ed. Julia Brannen and Margaret O'Brien. London: Institute of Education.

———. 1995b. "The Power of Persuasion: the *Instituto de la Mujer* in Spain." In *Comparative State Feminism,* ed. Dorothy McBride Stetson and Amy G. Mazur. Thousand Oaks, Calif.: Sage.

————. 1996. "Partial Achievements of Central-State Public Policies Against Violence Against Women in Post-Authoritarian Spain (1975–1995)." In *Women in a Violent World: Feminist Analyses and Resistance Across Europe*, ed. Chris Corrin. Edinburgh: Edinburgh University Press.

————. 1997. *Políticas Públicas de Género en Perspectiva Comparada: La Mujer Trabajadora en Italia y España (1900–1996)*. Madrid: Universidad Autónoma de Madrid.

CHAPTER SIX

THE POLITICS OF IMPLEMENTING WOMEN'S RIGHTS IN CATHOLIC COUNTRIES OF LATIN AMERICA

LAURA GUZMÁN STEIN

"The Fourth World Conference on Women was the last scenario where delicate mantles of words were weaved to defend the rights of women. The outcome were innovative alliances and conflict resolution strategies. . . . Beijing was the point of arrival of a long path cultivated with encounters and conflicts between development, human rights and women's sexual and reproductive rights. . . ."

—Sonia Montaño (1996, 165).

The Vatican, or Holy See, is an Observer State at the United Nations. Regardless of its limited status, the Vatican played an aggressive role during the preparatory process for the United Nations Fourth World Conference on Women and during the conference itself. Never before had the Vatican been so involved in such a process. Alliances were developed with delegations of fundamentalist Islamic states to fight against proposals threatening the primacy of women's roles as mothers, male control of women's bodies and sexuality, the confinement of sexuality to marriage, and the elimination of legal restrictions limiting women's access to safe birth control and abortions. The Vatican pressured several Latin American governments to influence decision making during the preparatory process and during the conference itself.

The Opus Dei,[1] a lay fundamentalist Catholic organization supported by Pope John Paul II, was called to infiltrate the women's movement in Latin America to generate less radical positions and use its influence with certain political figures to negotiate appointments in official delegations to the regional and world conferences. Asia, Africa, and Latin America held their regional conferences during the preparatory process. In each region, UN member states discussed, negotiated, and approved a Plan of Action. A Plan of Action for Latin America meeting was convened in Mar del Plata, Argentina (September 1994). The Regional Plan of Action addressed substantive issues and actions in eight strategic areas of concern. Argentina, Ecuador, El Salvador, Guatemala, Honduras, Nicaragua, Perú, and the Dominican Republic consistently made reservations on strategic actions dealing with sexual rights of women. The position of these states also was consistent with that held during Cairo's Conference on Population and Development. The hierarchy of the Catholic Church has a strong influence among governments of these eight nations. Argentina, Costa Rica, and Bolivia are confessional states, meaning countries where the Roman Catholic religion is supported by the state in the constitution. Ecuador, Perú, and the Dominican Republic are still strategic strongholds of the Vatican, while the other Central American countries had Catholic presidents with strong traditional views concerning the family, gender, and sexuality. Breaking away from fundamental religious positions on sexual rights meant losing the support of a very important political ally influential in building public opinion.

Why did the Holy See want to influence the content of the Regional Plan of Action and the World Platform? The Vatican became active on these issues at the beginning of the preparatory process to the International Conference on Population and Development (Cairo, 1994), when the women's movement placed sexual rights as human rights on the agenda for the first time. At previous United Nations forums, governments, NGOs, and multilateral agencies debated issues concerning reproductive rights of men and women, including the number and spacing of children, birth control methods, and access to information about birth control methods. Sexual rights had not been part of the official agenda.

For the first time in the history of the United Nations, feminist organizations were demanding international recognition of women's rights to self-determination, including full access to non-prejudiced sexual education, liberty to enjoy and control their own sexual life, elimination of forced motherhood and matrimony, and access to safe abortions. This struggle provided women with the opportunity to control their lives independently of men, culture, religion, and the state. For the Vatican, international recognition of sexual rights implied a transformation of the paradigm guiding social relations between genders and sustaining patriarchal structures within the Roman Catholic Church. The United Nations World Conference on Human Rights in Vienna in 1993 recognized that women of all ages are entitled to human rights in the private sphere, a position that questioned male patriarchal authority and the "holy institution of the family." Feminist organizations from Latin America and the Caribbean were extremely active during the conference and the implementation phase, influencing the approval of international legislation and critical legal reforms at the national level, as well as gender sensitive public policies and programs.

The Roman Catholic Church has been powerful in Latin America since the Spanish and Portuguese Conquest, shaping social structures, legislation, political thought, and cultural identities. However, its authority has taken different expressions and intensities depending on the nature of the historical and cultural processes shaping structures and identities. Latin America represents for the Vatican an important political stronghold. Although a vast majority of nations have constitutional provisions to guarantee religious liberty for all citizens and separation of state and church, the influence of the church is still strong. Approximately 85 percent of the population of this region considers itself Catholic. Catholic values permeate most laws and educational systems and the religious hierarchy of the church is still politically influential in most countries. One might expect that the three confessional states (Argentina, Costa Rica, and Bolivia) would be the strongest supporters of the Vatican position. With the exception of Argentina, this was not the case. Countries such as Costa Rica and Colombia[2] did not include members of the Opus Dei in their delegations, made no reservations to the Plan of Action, and have been implementing gender equity public policies in response to the Beijing commitments. Republics with more advanced constitutions than Costa Rica—such as Guatemala, El Salvador, and Honduras—voiced conservative positions during the conference and have been slow in implementing the Beijing commitments, especially those concerning reproductive and sexual rights.

Other variables help explain the "contradictory" behavior of confessional states and states with progressive liberal constitutions in matters associated with gender equity and sexual and reproductive rights of women. The "power" of the Catholic Church has developed and changed with time, depending on the correlation of political forces, such as government ideologies, ideological penetration, and the control of strategic institutions, such as ministries of education and health and the mass media. Advancement of gender equity policies in countries of Catholic tradition is most likely when the government mechanism (e.g., gender equity or women's office or ministry) is part of the decision making structure of government, has relative financial independence, and has established strong linkages with strategic sectors of the women's movement.

This chapter discusses the participation of the Catholic Church in shaping policy making during the preparatory process for the United Nations Fourth World Conference on Women and the implementation of the World Platform for Action, focusing on reproductive and sexual rights. Special reference will be made to Costa Rica, a confessional state that has been able to distance itself from several of the Vatican's teachings and policies on reproductive and sexual rights. Comparisons with other Latin American countries provide the basis for understanding the role of contextual variables in shaping policy.

CATHOLICISM AND THE ROMAN CATHOLIC CHURCH IN LATIN AMERICA

Religious beliefs influence behavior, norms, language, and daily cultural expressions, as well as social structures and personal interactions. The ideological and cultural significance of five hundred years of Christian Hispanic evangelization is an engrained part of Latin American identity, permeating civil society, art, culture, government, political thought, and public policy. Spanish and Portuguese conquest and colonization in America produced the "mestizo" culture, the foundation of a new order and new subjects—not Indians or Europeans, but hybrids whose birth is marked by an "illegitimate" origin from the perspective of both foundational cultures. The "mestizo" culture embraces a new view of gender relations, spirituality, and social politics. The mother is the only reference to the mestizo's roots, and in many cases the only reproducer of the new family world. The mestizo's father is unknown, its only reference being a member of the conquering class (Montecino 1995).

An adequate understanding of the role and influence of the Catholic religion in the lives of Latin American women requires an understanding of the "mestizo" culture. A significant process of sincretism[3] is the allegory created around the Virgin Mary and the legend of Malinche, as sources of folk explanation of the mestizos' origin and fate, as well as collective ritual. Gender identities take diverse and complex forms, mediated by social constructions of a religious nature that demand appropriate understanding in different historical moments and from the perspective of each social class and ethnic group.

The cultural clash of the Conquest in Central and South America takes a tragic dimension, especially for indigenous women. Marcos (1989) asserts:

La agonía de los viejos dioses y diosas es un proceso traumático que arrastra consigo toda una visión del mundo, de los hombres y mujeres y de sus interrelaciones: la nueva ética, la nueva moral del severo cristianismo español de la Contrarreforma, cuando no es coartada para los explotadores y violadores, resulta amargo veneno que enturbia lo que era el placer erótico. Ni la bondad de sacerdotes individuales como de Las Casas, ni la dulzura inherente al Evangelio bastan para salvar a los americanos de la miseria sexual que será su destino hasta hoy.[4]

The introduction of Catholicism in America[5] was achieved generally through coercive and violent means. Spain's economic exploitation of the continent was supported by the Vatican, since one of the Vatican's main purposes was evangelization of indigenous populations (Marcos 1989, 11–34). In no other region of the world was Catholicism imposed so broadly with so much violence. Some priests and monks (such as the Franciscans, Domicans, Augustines, Jesuits, and Fray Bartolome de Las Casas) were charitable and benevolent toward native populations. However, they were incapable of neutralizing the anger and bloody persecution of others intolerant of religious and symbolic systems they could not understand (Bonfil 1987; Gruzinski 1987). Spanish priests also were narrow-minded about indigenous norms and practices on sexuality, representative of a different social construction of gender, moral and ethical values about the body, motherhood, sexual pleasure, abortion, and marriage[6] (Marcos 1989). The priests considered these native customs indecent, uncivilized, and barbarian. They acted immediately to "save" lost souls by imposing new norms of conduct to repress erotic pleasure and spirituality, and to create westernized images of the feminine.

For indigenous peoples, sexuality was at the center of their religious rituals. Female priestesses were important elements of these ceremonies. Many of their deities incarnating love, eroticism, and fertility were female such as Xochiquetzal, Tlazekteotl, and Ixmucane. In the process, indigenous women lost control over their bodies, sexuality, spirituality, and social position in the name of God, religion, and patriarchy (Quezada 1975; Marcos 1989).

The "mestizaje" of Latin America (or crossing of cultures) made religion one of the prime instruments of women's domination by breaking women's gender identity. Indigenous women had to cover their bodies and behave according to Hispanic law. Many were raped by Spanish conquerors or used sexually, giving birth to children of mixed races or "mestizos," considered second-class citizens. Patriarchal values concerning the family, sexuality, and marriage were part of the legal system by the sixteenth and seventeenth centuries. Marriage was the legal means of

subordinating women and reinforcing notions about procreation and female subjection to male authority (Castro Alvarado 1996).

THE CATHOLIC RELIGION AND THE FORGING OF GENDER IDENTITIES IN THE "MESTIZO" CULTURE: THE LEGEND OF MALINCHE, THE CULT OF THE VIRGIN MARY, AND "MACHISMO"

Montecino (1995) contends that religion is one of the primary elements
organizing social and personal identities in Latin American societies. Religious folk mythology also has been an effective means of controlling
women's lives and position in society. Myths and legends based on sexist
and patriarchal explanations of the conquest and the making of the "new"
society have created an unconscious collective image of women that con-
spires against their self-determination and autonomy. Most of these myths
blame women for all evils in the region. The male mestizo carries the sign
of victory for having fought against the conqueror, while the female is
blamed for the downfall of the native culture because she established an
alliance with the conqueror and betrayed her people. This is the legend
of Malinche, a legend that helps mestizo men justify their own superiority
over women who cannot be trusted. Folk mythology and religious teachings blended, creating a collective image of women serving patriarchy by
incorporating elements of the traditional Catholic perspective. Malinche
is no different from Eve (Palma 1991; Montecino 1995).

"Malinchismo" is a term used to describe female betrayal. Several
Latin American authors such as Octavio Paz (1959) have revisited the
concept to explain the historical tragedy of the mestizo male deceived by
Malinche, the Indian woman given to the conqueror Hernan Cortes as a
token.[7] Patriarchal thought, according to Palma (1991), uses tradition
and history to blame women for the downfall of the indigenous world and
to justify male domination. Raping the mother produced the crossing of
races or "mestizaje." The "mestizo" world, like other patriarchal social organizations, built a culture of rape to perpetuate and justify male superiority, while also creating a problem of cultural identity by denying the
mestizo his indigenous ancestry. Being born of an aboriginal mother dis-
graced him.

The new social organization required taming women's sexuality to enable patriarchal society to be fully established with a particular alliance
between men, conquerors, and "mestizos." Exchange and control of females was the basis of this covenant (Palma 1991). Traditional anthropology has demonstrated how male reciprocity is established with these
exchanges, where women play an important role as tokens or presents.

The conqueror recognized Mestizo men as having authority in the family, control of women's sexuality, and provided appropriate legislation to protect male honor. For example, abortion is penalized by law, but most legislation in Latin America since the colonial periods provides men with pardons when they provide the means for the termination of a pregnancy to defend their family's honor. Similar norms existed until recently in some countries for criminal cases related to a wife's adultery.

The complexity of the "mestizo" world is lived in many ways: instability, dualism, and denial. Its vision of the conquest of the feminine as rape, both from a historical and carnal standpoint, is a devastating female image. Baptism had the power to erase Eve's original sin but not Malinche's fault (Palma 1991). Searching for the perfect mother, "mestizo" culture developed the cult of Mary, the Immaculate Virgin, also known as "Marianismo."

The Marian cult represents much more than a legitimate devotion to the mother of God. It recognizes spiritual female superiority incarnated in the ideal of motherhood and chastity, two ideal states impossible for any woman to accomplish. As a model, the Virgin Mary is mainly a symbol. Sexual intercourse is only permitted within matrimony and for procreation purposes. Females are able to recuperate their honor and be reflected in the image of Mary through motherhood. Motherhood, by way of "Marianismo," provides all women with a state of grace and special powers (Portugal 1989).

Stevens (1977) developed the term "Marianismo" to designate the cult regarding women as morally superior and stronger than men. Marianismo lauds women's spiritual force, women's patience with sinful males, and promotes respect for the sacred image of the mother. A spiritual force of this nature engenders self-denial, along with an infinite inclination for sacrifice and humbleness. Latin American women are socialized to believe that men are not responsible for their faults, because they are unable to control their sexual impulses and are morally like children.

A parallel ideology to male superiority explains why women accept "machismo" in men and their own apparent gender subordination. Fuller (1995) concludes that females believe they have all the power within the domestic sphere and great influence in decision making because the mother has authority over her children and exerts political influence through moral inspiration. These beliefs explain the driving force behind formal education policies targeting girls during the late nineteenth and early twentieth centuries in this region. Undeniably, girls would be the mothers of future political leaders.

"Machismo" as a cultural expression of masculinity and sexist behavior among men, defines the male as irresponsible, undomesticated, and romantic—a person who despises domestic obligations, especially those related to daily household life. It emphasizes independence, impulsiveness, and physical force as the "naturai" way of solving conflicts and treating women. Masculinity rejects any expression of mysticism or religious behavior, unless it becomes part of male traditional cults such as the "Cofradías," especially reserved for males once they marry[8] (Portugal 1989).

Many authors (Montecino, Dussuel, and Wilson 1988; Portugal 1989; Melhus 1990; Palma 1991; Montecino 1995) consider Marianismo and machismo the main symbols of femininity and masculinity in Hispanic America to this day. Fuller (1995) is critical of this view, as the masculine is assimilated to the public, while the feminine to the private sphere. She argues hierarchical organization idiosyncratic of Hispanic colonial societies should be understood contextually, not via opposites representing western European thought.

Latin America is a mosaic of peoples, cultures, ethnic groups, and social classes with a common origin: the Conquest. Indigenous peoples were not eliminated as in the United States, and were not fully assimilated into the dominant culture, developing diverse modes of articulating native views, customs, and rituals with those of the conqueror. Mestizo values and beliefs need to be clearly recognized and differentiated from others to understand contradictions in legislation, public policy, and social behaviors within and between countries. Fuller (1995) argues that a binary perspective on gender requires adjustment, as different communities and groups exhibit a diversity of gender relationships. Alternative explanations of a less contradictory nature should be developed to avoid caricatures of "machismo" and "Marianismo" as cultural phenomena. Both are not static or absolute realities but a way of symbolizing views about masculinity and femininity, male and female sexuality, and expected gender roles.

THE IMPACT OF MODERNIZATION

Currently, Latin American societies are undergoing rapid modernization processes critical of traditional hierarchical systems. These are particularly strong in countries with higher socioeconomic indexes and with small indigenous populations, as in Costa Rica, Chile, and Uruguay. The impact of modernization is stronger among urban communities representative of Mediterranean traditions inspiring the complex "Marianismo-machismo" dichotomy. Fuller (1995) contends that many of these inconsistencies and ambiguities can be explained as part of a holistic rationality prevailing in various traditional systems. The rationality of traditional systems does not operate according to universal dichotomies, because in holistic traditional systems, hierarchy is the principle organizing social life (Dumont 1965). Each group or unit has a predetermined place in a social system in which all elements are linked and need each other. This concept explains a holistic system. Still, hierarchies entail two distinct levels. The superior level integrates or unifies the system, while inferior levels are included in the whole. Each segment can establish different connections without reproducing the whole, although hierarchical reversals do occur. For example, men can be superiors as warriors but inferiors in the domestic sphere where the mother dominates, as in the case of indigenous communities in Central America and Andinian countries. Religious images provide some examples. Jesus Christ represents humanity, although at times he appears beside Mary, since both are patrons of the church. In other instances, Christ might be her inferior as in the case of Baby Jesus.

In some traditional Latin American contexts, women are not tied to the domestic sphere. Women perform as mediators between the sacred and the profane, between political groups and social classes. Mary mediates between God and humans. Public and private spheres are not clearly defined in traditional societies, intersecting at times and unfolding different types of relationships. The feminine can sometimes represent the public, while the masculine can express sexual purity (Fuller 1995).

Anderson (1985) found that among native populations of the Peruvian Amazon, motherhood is less influential in the definition of the feminine than in the rest of Latin America. In contrast, Andinian peasants have developed a deep religious syncretism where the Virgin Mary is not assimilated to the image of the woman-mother but to the Pachamama, the female deity representing fertility and life. The Pachamama symbolizes the mother, not the sexual purity of the Virgin Mary. In traditional Andinian culture, as well as in Central American indigenous cultures, gender roles do not imply separate spheres of action. Women are linked to the domestic but have more mobility in urban spaces as they play a central role in management, distribution, and production in household economy. Women dominate the markets. Both partners cooperate, although the male is the authority figure within the family and in public matters, in spite of the fact that the female expresses opinions and her partner has to negotiate decisions with her.

According to Buxó (1991), the feminine is not associated exclusively with motherhood. Motherhood represents authority and responsibility, while the ideal state for adult men is marriage and fatherhood, so the "machismo" model does not operate among these ethnic groups. In contrast, Montecino (1995) provides multiple examples of practices where behaviors initially condemned as transgression of the norm are accepted in daily life experience (e.g., unwed single mothers, cohabitation).

Whereas Catholic values and practices remain strong and the Catholic Church continues to shape laws, policies, and institutions, rural migrations to urban areas, the mass media, the increase in female-headed households, and increased access to formal education among young women are changing traditional systems. Women are rapidly modifying their views and concerns: Younger generations want to be educated and to work, males are being excluded as heads of household and as economic providers, women have more access to education and reproductive health, and religion is less influential in their lives. Traditions coexist with modern systems guiding legislation, education, the economy, and communications. Challenged by "modern" ideas especially concerning the roles and status of women as well as by other religious denominations—especially Pentacostal—the Catholic Church's influence has been decreasing.

RELIGION AND THE WOMEN'S MOVEMENT IN LATIN AMERICA

The first women's organizations were linked to the Catholic Church, basically groups doing charitable work with the poor and needy, providing religious education to children, and keeping the church's household (e.g., cleaning, cooking for the priest, mending religious clothing). Another important organization was the "Daughters of Mary," which educated girls and young women in the ideals of "Marianismo." Priests exerted strong control over religious organizations and its members, although women always found ways to use these spaces as self-help groups and even to organize political resistance as part of independence movements. Women began mobilizing around other types of needs and interests during the 1970s and 1980s: access to basic services, land reform, reproductive health services, and education. In countries with military regimes and military conflicts, women were active members of human rights organizations and social movements demanding political changes and democratic institutions (Instituto de la Mujer and FLACSO 1995; Caravaca and Guzmán 1996).

Many Catholic feminists in Latin America began as active followers of Liberation Theology, organizing working-class and poor women to fight for better living conditions and opportunities to exercise their human rights in the church and society. They learned that male followers of Liberation Theology were not interested in supporting women's right to birth control, voluntary abortion, a satisfying sexual life, or priesthood. In fact, Liberation Theology showed a profound androcentric bias on issues related to gender equity and equality (Portugal 1989). Ferro and Quiros (1993) argue that socially active Catholic women were not critical, initially, of women's subordinated position within the church and the theological principles supporting male domination: the feminine "nature" of women; their physical, emotional, and spiritual "differences" with men; and the holy mission of women on earth.

During the last decade of the twentieth century, groups of Catholic women and feminists from Latin America began to critique the sexist role of the church and its implications for the lives of millions of women (Ferro and Quiros 1993). They have been very active in the International Women's Health Movement and the Latin American and Caribbean Network for Women's Health. Both organizations have been instrumental in moving forward legal reforms, intersectorial policies, and women's empowerment. Also, feminist members of the organization Catholics for a Free Choice are contributing with alternative interpretations to Catholic teachings on sexuality and abortion from a theological perspective (Portugal 1989; Rance 1991; Ferro and Quiros 1993; Montaño 1996). Their contribution to the debate on abortion and sexual rights has been meaningful, supplying the movement with serious arguments based on sound Catholic theological principles (Católicas por el Derecho a Decidir 1995).

Portugal and Matamala (1993) identified the beginning of the women's health movement in Latin America in 1979. Initial concerns focused on abortion rights and the struggle to eliminate abuses in population control programs. The feminist movement understood abortion rights as a sensitive issue among men and women of all social classes and ethnic groups, political leaders, and the Catholic Church. Women were demanding real access to quality birth control services as a means of preventing unwanted pregnancies and, with it, abortion. Since the late 1980s, the emphasis has been on preventing maternal mortality and unsafe abortions. The women have documented an increase in maternal mortality and shown how these deaths could have been prevented if these women had had access to social, economic, and political conditions needed to exercise their reproductive and sexual rights (Instituto de la Mujer and FLACSO 1995; Montaño 1996). The linkage between abortion and maternal deaths as an issue of human rights and religious ethics associated with the right to life has been very effective.

One of the most significant and surprising achievements of Beijing was the recognition of abortion as a problem of public health and the resolution to revise legislation that punishes women who have illegal abortions. Most Latin American official delegations, including those who made reservations on issues concerning sexual rights, supported this commitment. The role of Catholic feminists during the lobbying process was critical for these results, along with an increasing awareness among policy makers that punitive laws do not decrease the number of unwanted pregnancies, a problem that increasingly is putting enormous pressure on public health systems.

THE UNITED NATIONS FOURTH WORLD CONFERENCE ON WOMEN AND THE DEBATE OVER SEXUAL AND REPRODUCTIVE RIGHTS

World conferences and summits are effective instruments when influencing policy making. The United Nations has convened four world conferences on women since 1975. Each expressed a different level of commitment among governments in recognition of gender inequalities as pervasive social phenomena. In fact, since the first conference in Mexico City, UN member states moved from the adoption of declaratory resolutions to commitments for action with the meeting in Beijing (CMF and MPPE 1996). The need to revise and update international strategies concerning the status of women, resulted from worldwide recognition of obstacles limiting advancement and opportunities to exercise rights (Guzmán and Pacheco 1996).

Several international, regional, and national meetings created a preliminary document on the status of women that preceded the Fourth World Conference on Women (CMF and MPPE 1996; Guzmán and Pacheco 1996). At the national level, governments prepared their reports based on a questionnaire prepared by the Division for the Advancement of Women, the United Nations organ responsible of assessing the status of women. Then, the regional specialized United Nations institutions prepared a Plan for Action for each geographical region, which was discussed and adopted in a preparatory meeting. These regional conferences took place in 1994 in Indonesia (Asia), Austria (Europe), Jordan (Middle East), Senegal (Africa), and Argentina (Latin America and the Caribbean). These five plans provided the foundations for a World Platform for Action discussed in China.[9]

Previously, only NGOs with ECOSOC status (recognized by the Economic and Social Council of the United Nations) could participate, but given the worldwide pressure put forth by the women's movement, other organizations were able to attend (Guzmán and Pacheco 1996). This was a major breakthrough. Direct access to government representatives now made it possible to negotiate resolutions, while gaining awareness of existing contradictions and problems before the Beijing conference.

This step threatened the Vatican's influence with governments, especially in Latin America. During the 1990s, most Latin American countries reformed their laws and their constitutions to advance fundamental civil and political rights for women and other populations. Most of these countries also ratified the Convention for the Elimination of all Forms of Discrimination Against Women (CEDAW) and the Inter-American Convention to Prevent, Sanction, and Eradicate Violence Against Women. These new legal reforms also challenged traditional Catholic values.

THE PREPARATORY STAGE

The Platform for Action approved by the Fourth World Conference on Women includes those actions that had the consensus[10] of all United Nations Member states, although approximately thirty-five governments made "reservations" on specific issues or paragraphs.[11] It acknowledges pending commitments acquired by the Nairobi Conference (1985) and in the adoption of the CEDAW Convention. It also reaffirms commitments adopted in other world conferences and summits and in the Plan of Action for each region[12] (Guzmán and Pacheco 1996; Montaño 1996). The preparatory meeting preceding the Fourth World Conference attempted a consensus on principles and resolutions. The platform's draft was examined for the first time by government delegates during the thirty-ninth meeting of the Commission on the Status of Women, held in New York five months before the Beijing gathering. A second meeting was convened a few weeks before the conference to move forward on more agreements (CMF and MPPE 1996).

The Latin American women's bureaus responsible for advancing gender equity policies and programs met earlier, seeking consensus on issues and strategic actions critical to women in the region. Also, governmental officials discussed their government reports with NGOs and women's organizations in most nations. As the conference drew closer, the Vatican pressured several Latin American governments to include Opus Dei members as official delegates. This move in the latter part of the process made negotiations more difficult. The action also announced the Holy See's political strategy to prevent common consent on critical issues. These were sections concerned with recognition of women's rights as human rights; reproductive and sexual health and rights; and the use of the term "gender" in the text.

The women's movement tried to neutralize the pressure of the Catholic Church in several nations (e.g., confessional states or countries whose governments made reservations to the Regional Plan of Action on sections addressing definitions of "gender," "equality," "equity," and reproductive and sexual rights). The women's movement also strengthened its linkages with the Latin American and Caribbean Network of Government Women's Bureaus and engaged in intensive lobbying with presidents and first ladies, legislators and members of the executive linked to ministries of foreign affairs, health and presidency. Women's movement members engaged in debates with representatives of the Catholic Church, political figures, and social organizations, and made conscious efforts to promote these debates using mass media and other means. They also prepared a contingency strategy to neutralize the Vatican and lobby with strategic delegates during the conference.

RELIGIOUS AND POLITICAL FORCES OPERATING
AT THE CONFERENCE: THE PLAY BEGINS

At the conference in Beijing, discussions on the platform were painstaking during regular sessions and "contact groups" assembled to work on alternative texts where no consensus could be reached. The controversy focused on concepts of family and gender, sexuality, teenage health, recognition of parental rights, reproductive and sexual health, recognition of sexual orientations or preferences, association of national law with universal principles, and the precedence of sociocultural and religious views over human rights. Again, reaching a consensus was extremely difficult given the position of the Holy See, Catholic countries, and Islamic states (CMF and MPPE 1996; Montaño 1996). The ambiguities found in the final text express this balance of forces (Boland, Rau, and Zeidenstein 1994).

In spite of these problems, the Beijing Conference made significant advances toward the recognition of women's reproductive and sexual rights. Sexual health is treated in the platform as a human rights issue, including reproductive health and sexual violence against women (*e.g.*, spousal rape, rape, and other forms of sexual abuse). Reproduction and sexuality are viewed as part of a comprehensive concept of sexual health that goes beyond providing information and services to control fertility and sexually transmitted diseases. Furthermore, states agreed to revise legislation on abortion, and recognized the need to implement strategies to eliminate cultural practices favoring discrimination and violence against women, the precedence of the rights of the child, and the responsibility of states to further women's empowerment on these matters (Montaño 1996).

The political "behavior" of Latin American governments and delegates during the conference are reliable predictors of the levels of government commitment during the implementation phase. The Latin American countries who "reserved" on paragraphs of the platform were Argentina, Peru, Ecuador, Mexico, the Dominican Republic, El Salvador, Nicaragua, Guatemala, and Honduras. Five issues or areas of concern directly related with values strongly sustained by the Catholic Church were consistently reiterated.

- Total opposition to the notion of sexual rights and a comprehensive concept of reproductive health and rights, since it could imply actions leading or supporting abortion. The delegates of Argentina, Ecuador, El Salvador, Guatemala, Honduras, Peru, the Dominican Republic, and Nicaragua explicitly indicated that they had to abide by the Constitution and laws of their countries. These recognize the right to life from conception and abortion as a criminal act. Peru, Nicaragua, Guatemala, El Salvador, Ecuador, and Argentina do not sanction therapeutic abortions.

- Acceptance of the heterosexual family model only, with emphasis on traditional roles, mainly in the sphere of human reproduction. The countries listed above also had reservations on related paragraphs, argued concerns with interpretations "against nature."
- Honduras and the Dominican Republic objected to actions leading to democratic relations within the family, since these could promote or lead to radical changes in traditional gender roles.
- Only Argentina objected to the superior interest of the child concerning sexual and reproductive health and rights.
- Mexico reserved its commitment with ratifying the Inter-American Convention to Prevent, Sanction and Eradicate Violence against Women, arguing that this is the jurisdiction of the Mexican Senate.

Two major factors influenced this result. These states (meaning Mexico, Argentina, Honduras, the Dominican Republic, Ecuador, El Salvador, Guatemala, Honduras, Peru, the Dominican Republic, and Nicaragua) had delegates who were members of conservative religious organizations. In addition, they represented countries with conservative political parties in power where the Catholic Church is extremely influential among the both the political elites and the population. Any transgression on church teaching concerning sexuality, abortion, or "the holy institution of the family" can create the wrath of archbishops—or cardinals[13]—along with losing credibility and votes from Catholic followers. Peru emerged initially as a possible exception because President Fujimori expressed during his official speech, his commitment to advancing the reproductive and sexual rights of women. However, the Chair of the Peruvian delegation, a member of a conservative Catholic organization, reported her government's reservations. Nicaragua was not expected to make reservations either, because its delegation had a progressive stand on critical issues. At the last minute, President Violeta Chamorro instructed delegates to submit objections. The pressure of the Vatican was clear and strong.

Basically, these reservations point to a defense of patriarchal family, women's subordination to male authority, and a concept of sexuality limited to procreation. Heterosexuality, motherhood, and control of female sexuality emerged as ideals requiring protection from the state. A deeper analysis indicates government consistency with previous reservations on the Regional Plan of Action and the plan approved by the Population and Development Conference in Cairo.

IMPLEMENTATION OF THE BEIJING COMMITMENTS; THE CASE OF COSTA RICA, A CONFESSIONAL COUNTRY THAT WENT THE "WRONG" WAY

Argentina, the other confessional Latin American nation, fully acknowledged Vatican requirements. Costa Rica, on the contrary, did not include members of Opus Dei on its delegation and approved the Platform for Action without reservations. This stand clearly sent a message to the Vatican concerning what to expect during the implementation phase. Costa Rica was already putting forth public policies and programs coherent with the areas of concern of the platform (CMF and MPPE 1996). Furthermore, the women's movement was extremely active with government delegates and with strategic members of the executive and congress, to neutralize political pressure from the Vatican and religious authorities.

Costa Rica has generally been supportive of democratic ideals, even though its history has periods of authoritarian rule, dictatorships and civil unrest. Since independence in 1821, its political class has been concerned with advancing education, health, and social conditions of its population. Several authors (Solórzano 1987; Castro Alvarado 1996; Molina 1996) argue that, since colonial times, the inhabitants (including women) of the main centers of population had a tendency to ignore established religious norms, and even civil law. The Central Plateau had a secular and sacred culture shared by peasants and merchants, a culture of deep secular roots that shifted from marriage to sin, from imagery to an attitude toward death, from feast to mysticism.

Costa Rica never had economic and political significance for Spain and was far from the political and religious centers of colonial power. The social gap characterizing most of Hispanic America that separated peasants and other small-scale producers from bureaucrats, hacienda owners, and large-scale merchants did not exist in Costa Rica, with the exception of indigenous peasants and the dwellers of Guanacaste[14] (Molina 1996). The clergy had no riches and many family responsibilities. Also, its educational level was limited aside from the so-called "first letters" (Guzmán 1997). Poverty, seclusion, and marginal political and religious importance of the Province of Costa Rica created the foundations for a more egalitarian society—still patriarchal in its foundations, but open to democratic values and liberties. This was not the case of Argentina and other nations such as Colombia, Peru, and Guatemala, where the power of the Catholic Church was significant and the Vatican had political and economic interests.

The confessional nature of the state in Costa Rica also needs to be placed in perspective to understand its scope and the more informal character of the Catholic Church influence. The Constitution of 1949 establishes the religion of the state as Roman Apostolic Catholic, but grants all citizens religious liberty to practice religious cults that " . . . do not interfere with universal moral values or good practices" (Article 75). The Constitution of Argentina also considers religious liberty as a civil liberty, but determines that "[T]he Federal Government supports the Roman Apostolic Catholic cult" (Article 2). The scope of the mandate is broader in this latter case, while restrictive in the Constitution of Costa Rica. The state adheres to the Roman Catholic faith but not its institutions. For example, the Catholic religion is taught in public schools, but is not compulsory for students who profess other religious beliefs or Catholic children who do not want to attend. Likewise, Catholicism is not required to hold office in government, although the Catholic Church has tried to influence government appointments. Clergymen cannot run for public office or receive appointments as ministers or vice ministers (Electoral Code of the Republic of Costa Rica). Religious liberties have been a part of all constitutions since independence. The struggle to make them effective in spite of clergy resistance was a necessity for a republic exporting to non-Catholic European nations (e.g., England).

Costa Rica, like many other Latin American countries, had liberal governments during the last quarter of the nineteenth century. From 1871 to 1880, relations between the state and the Catholic Church were very tense. The 1880s are characterized by a strengthening of civil power; religious orders were proscribed, although priests could operate individually; education was secular, and the Jesuits were expelled because they engaged in religious proselytism (Guzmán 1997). This also was a period when major legal reforms were introduced, an important number of these affecting the rights of women. In fact, this was a time when women had more rights. This also was a period of significant advancements in social policy (Guzmán 1990).

Social unrest and social reform (e.g., labor legislation, social security, health insurance, and child protective services) characterized the first decades of the twentieth century. The Catholic Church played an active role organizing workers and negotiating legislation and policy. It also openly opposed legislation granting political and civil rights to women. The clergy used the pulpits to contest women's right to vote and be elected, arguing that it defied nature and would lead to social chaos. This right for women was finally recognized in the Constitution of 1949, in spite of the opposition of the church. The church pressured congressmen to include articles protecting the right to life from conception, the patriarchal family, and the subordinate role of women in the family and public life (Guzmán 1990).

During the 1950s and 1960s, the state emphasized basic infrastructure, public health, and education, continuing with its interventionist role established in different laws since the beginning of the century ("responsible for the general welfare of the population"). Since the early 1970s, both the state and civil society organizations put forth legal reforms, new laws, and public policies to implement the principle of gender equality and commitments acquired internationally on gender equity. This process was relatively slow until the end of the 1980s, even though Costa Rica had ratified the Convention to Eliminate All Forms of Discrimination Against Women (CEDAW) in 1984 (PRIEG/UCR, 1998). With the strengthening of the women's movement at different levels, the passing of gender-sensitive legislation along with a consolidation of the Institutional Government Mechanism for Gender Equity, and the implementation of strategic public policies, Costa Rica was able to advance with several commitments acquired at the different world conferences. The Catholic Church has not been able to influence policy making as strongly as it did at the beginning of the century, although androcentric and sexist religious values still prevail among the population, mainly concerning abortion, motherhood, and sexuality.

Making Reproductive Health a Public Policy.   Costa Rica was one of the first nations in Latin America to implement family planning and birth control policies and programs. In 1968, the government established the National Committee on Population (CONAPO) with support of the International Family Planning Federation (IPPF) and participation of public institutions and NGOs. Between 1967 and 1971, a university research center in population studies was created, along with programs in family planning and sexual education within government agencies and NGOs linked to the Episcopalian and Catholic churches (Flansburg 1998).

González Gómez (1985) identified three "forces" advancing the first group of family planning policies and making contraceptives legal:

- International organizations associating fertility control with economic development and better living conditions for the poor.[15]
- The U.S. Department of Social Services urging legalization of birth control methods to increase social development.
- Commercial pressure from Shering Pharmaceutical, a transnational interested in selling contraceptives to governments in the region.

During the 1970s, organizations of socialist orientation and the Catholic Church were very active in protesting population control activities in the country—in particular against United States funding and influence in government—including a massive sterilization campaign. The Costa Rican Congress investigated these charges concerning a U.S. backed sterilization campaign, but never corroborated them (Flansburg 1998). Costa Rica did impose restrictions on sterilization procedures, requiring authorization by a physician and a spouse, when married. These policies, as the Constitutional Court ruled years after, were discriminatory, violating fundamental human rights protected by the constitution and international treaties ratified by congress (Gobierno de la República de Costa Rica, 1999). In spite of this interpretation, it was not until mid-1999 that the president eliminated the requirement with the opposition of the church and medical profession. Sterilization has doubled since.

After the investigation from congress, the government decided to continue implementing population policies without being as open and public, mainly providing contraceptives through public health institutions and working directly with USAID instead of using NGOs as intermediaries (González Gómez 1985). The state spends per capita in birth control more than any other Latin American and Caribbean country (US$1.00 per year), while citizens spend more on the average (US$1.50). In Costa Rica and Cuba, a major percentage of its population (75 percent) of reproductive age uses some type of birth control method (Achio, Devries, and Garcia.1994; Population Action International 1994). This behavior indicates a relatively low level of influence of the Catholic Church on contraceptive use, in spite of the position of the Pope on these matters.

Fertility rates in Costa Rica have dropped significantly, from an average of seven births at the beginning of the 1950s to 2.8 births in 1996. Nevertheless, women are still marrying and having children at early ages: 60 percent between twenty and twenty-nine years and 17 percent in the fifteen-to-nineteen age group. This trend explains why the demographic structure is still young (United Nations Population Fund 1995). Women expect to become mothers, even though most females do not desire large families and have babies early on to "get the job done" prematurely. The 1993 Survey on Reproductive Health found that fertility trends vary according to socioeconomic groups. The General Fertility Rate was 2.2 births for the higher strata, 4.2 for women of the lower strata. The average number of daughters also dropped from 2.2 in 1969 to 1.3 in 1996, resulting in one of the lowest rates in Latin America. These changes in demographics, along with other social, economic, and political factors, have generated significant changes in family structures, and in the expectations and values not only among women, but also within society in general.

THE BEIJING PLATFORM FOR ACTION
FIVE YEARS LATER: ACHIEVEMENTS,
INNOVATIVE EXPERIENCES, AND LESSONS LEARNED

CEDAW requires establishing a "national mechanism for the advancement of women" or women's bureau within government structure. In 1994, most Latin American countries had created this mechanism in the executive. Mexico and Colombia were the last two nations to install this body, in 1996 and 1995, respectively (República de Nicaragua, 1998). Their rank and scope, institutional structure, political influence, resources, and technical qualifications vary. Some were founded during the UN Women´s Decade or as initiatives of first ladies, and the rest as part of the struggles of the women's movement (Instituto de la Mujer and FLACSO 1995; República de Nicaragua 1998). Their standing within government is a major factor influencing implementation of international and national commitments. Legislatures created some, executive decrees created others. These differences express degrees of political and social legitimacy, access to permanent funding, autonomy in decision making, and opportunities for mainstreaming public policy on gender equity. Political vulnerability is higher when these bureaus or mechanisms are dependent on the presidency or a ministry, because appointments, policies, and funding are mediated by party politics. Political legitimacy is enhanced when these are autonomous institutions or their heads rank as ministers. Reservations on sections of the platform addressing reproductive and sexual rights came from states with weak institutional mechanisms. For example, the National Council of Women in Argentina was part of the presidency of the republic; El Salvador had a Secretary of the Family at the Ministry of the Presidency; Honduras established a small Women´s Office coordinated by the vice-president.

The dominant government strategy to advance women's rights has been short term, disconnected, welfare-oriented activities targeting sectors of women often labeled "at risk": the poor, single mothers and other groups. Public policies for gender equity have been marginal and a responsibility of institutional mechanisms. During the past decade, more governments formulated comprehensive policies and strengthened these bureaus. Only a few countries, Costa Rica among them, began taking the first steps toward mainstreaming gender equity in national public policies, in an effort to reach the population as a whole—not only women or specific groups—to become state policies.

This process has not been easy. The Plan for Gender Equity among Women and Men (PIOMH) is the policy instrument articulating government actions in eight platform areas: legislation, family, education, health, culture and communications, work, environment, and decision making. It also includes participation of NGOs and grassroots women's organizations. Ministries and public institutions are responsible for implementation and monitoring, while the National Institute for Women—the institutional mechanism—facilitates processes.

On December 12, 1999, the National Institute on Women convened a meeting with women's organizations to assess government compliance with Beijing commitments. Five years after the Beijing conference, the country has made significant advancements in legal and institutional reform, implementation of gender-sensitive public policies, empowerment of women's organizations, and raising national awareness about gender discrimination. The obstacles faced are many and several strategic goals in different areas are not yet a reality.

The Beijing Platform for Action insists on providing women with comprehensive, quality, and low-cost health services, including but not limited to reproductive and sexual health. The need to establish a gender perspective in health prevention and treatment has stimulated implementation of innovative models, several of which are community based and use local resources. The Ministry of Health is developing gender-sensitive guidelines to be applied at all levels of the health system. However, implementation is difficult because health professionals still resist alternative views about women and their gender needs and interests. Gender biases are profoundly engrained, along with androcentric notions about women's bodies, sexuality, and social roles (INAMU 1999).

The National Cervix and Breast Cancer Program and the recent creation of the Hospital for Women respond to women's specific gender needs. Women's access to sterilization is a step in the right direction in protecting reproductive and sexual rights of all persons. Specific legal norms protect women's right to receive information and services concerning health, reproduction, and family planning, as well as sexual and reproductive health education (Flansburg 1998; INAMU 1999). Several women's organizations have worked closely with INAMU and the Office of the First Lady, developing sound technical and religious arguments to use strategically with representatives of the Catholic Church, political authorities, and public health officials.

Abortion remains a sensitive issue where many inequalities exist. Only therapeutic abortions are possible. The law provides for judicial pardon (suppression of penalty) when the woman or a relative terminates a pregnancy to protect her "honor,"[16] a discriminatory norm based on sexist double standards. Maternal deaths resulting from unsafe abortions are a serious public health problem, especially among low-income women who cannot pay for a safe abortion in a private or public hospital. The Catholic

Church insistently demands from the pulpit and in mass media programs that women and young girls conform to the image of the Virgin Mary.[17] It also condemns abortion, divorce, out-of-wedlock births, and other "non-Christian" behaviors. The reality is that, in Costa Rica, 50 percent of births are out of wedlock and a significant proportion involve adolescent mothers. This behavior involves both men and women and prevention requires strong educational programs leading to changes in views about sexuality and gender relations.

In 1998, ten public institutions, the Office of the First Lady, and several NGOs formulated a national policy on sexual education for children and teenagers, seeking to educate for autonomous and responsible use of their sexuality, equitable gender relations, and the full exercise of their rights. When implementation of these programs began in the school system with teachers and students, the Catholic Church reacted violently. The educational system has always been the stronghold of the Catholic Church, a major socialization agent along with the family and mass media. Teachers have propagated Catholic values, moral ethics, and concepts on sexuality, gender relations, the family and women's sexual rights. Intense negotiations were held between government officials, the first lady, and the hierarchy of the Catholic Church until an agreement was reached.

These programs also face constraints coming from public officers in the Ministry of Education, parents, and community leaders who hold strong views on parental authority concerning sexual education, children's rights, and sexuality. As long as androcentric images and concepts prevail in public policy and government, it will be difficult for women to influence decision making and gain political legitimacy. Stronger efforts are required to articulate strategic alliances between the national mechanism, the women's movement, women in politics, the media, and sensitive policy makers. National public policies for gender equity need to reach the general population and women's organizations to guarantee support and commitments (INAMU 1999).

During the 1990s, feminists were able to access strategic political and technical positions in government such as vice-presidents, ministers, legislators, and technical staff. Assessment of this experience indicates difficulties among feminists in public office and social organizations in understanding relationships between the political and the technical. Competencies in this sphere are needed to influence policy makers, civil society organizations, mass media, and the church. Technical plans are important, but large doses of political maneuvering are necessary for successful implementation. This includes the general population and the Catholic Church. Religious values and norms on sexuality and gender relations are deeply engrained in both men and women. Changing these is not an easy task or a short-term project.

Experience has shown that the concerted participation of civil society is crucial to identifying and sustaining women's needs and rights. Women's organizations and the government mechanism should develop intense activities with women, institutions, and grassroots organizations at the local level to facilitate appropriate environments for gender equity strategies to permeate all institutional levels and increase their scope. Local work with priests, nuns, and the lay community can become a facilitating agent for change. Feminists should be skilled in debating the social doctrine of the Catholic Church and theological arguments on reproductive and sexual rights, including abortion and sexual orientation. Including the human rights perspective to the debate was definitely a step in the right direction in overcoming limited perspectives based on family planning and population control. National policies now provide for investment in women's health, for women's empowerment, and for the protection of women's human rights. States now are expected to take the necessary steps to provide women with equitable opportunities to fully exercise their rights as persons, not as mothers, wives, or family caretakers. Access to reproductive and sexual rights is not a problem of individual liberties, it is a collective drama that needs to be tackled collectively through state public policies. Women's sexual and reproductive rights—from a feminist and human rights perspective—are an integral part of the right to liberty, security, and physical integrity, and are associated with decision making on sexuality, motherhood, and the rejection of any type of coercion. Advancing these rights will only be possible if strategic linkages between the government mechanism, the women's movement, civil society organizations, and women in government are strengthened and legitimacy is built around an alternative paradigm based on democratic values and recognition of gender equity as the leading force. The path is open to change and change is taking new forms and paths.

NOTES

1. The Spanish Catholic priest Escrivá de Balaguer founded this lay organization. It targets middle- and upper-class men and women linked to the political class and private entrepreneurial sector as multipliers of traditional religious values concerning family and marriage, gender roles, birth control and abortion, and the role of the state. Opus Dei has been defined by some sectors of the Catholic Church as a fundamentalist sect.

2. The Constitution of this country prohibits religious discrimination, establishing the right to freely exercise religious beliefs and practices (Article 19). However, a covenant between the state and the Pope ("El

Concordato") is still in place, providing the hierarchy of the Catholic Church with formal power in certain areas.

3. Religious syncretism is the process that unfolds with the fusion of religions or spiritual practices and values, where the main components of both are maintained. For example, saints of the Catholic Church represent significant deities of the native spirituality. Native rituals continue to take place inside the Catholic temple.

4. Translation: The agony of the old gods and goddesses is a traumatic process carrying a vision of the world, of men and women and their relationships: the new ethics, the new moral of the severe Spanish Counterreform Christianism, when not restrained for exploiters and rapers, bitterly poisoned what had to be erotic pleasure. Neither the kindness of individual priests like de Las Casas or the sweetness of the Gospel are enough to save the Americans from the sexual misery of their present destiny.

5. Throughout this chapter, America refers to the continent as it should, and not the United States of America, a common ethnocentric bias.

6. Premarital sexual activity was viewed as "natural" for both men and women, marital alliances were not indissoluble, women could leave their partners at any time, remarriage was possible, and punishment for sexual crimes was equivalent for both sexes. Gruzinski (1987) found, in records written by Spanish priests during the sixteenth and seventeenth centuries, constant references to the sin of lust among the Indians. Profuse questionnaires were applied during Confession.

7. It was a common practice among indigenous groups to provide important visitors with presents that included precious metals and stones, women, and food. This suggests that the indigenous cultures prior to the Spanish invasion also had patriarchal gender relationships.

8. These male societies have a more social nature than confessional.

9. The draft of the World Plan for Action was discussed months before the official conference in Beijing by the Commission on Legal and Social Status of Women (CSW), the UN organism that formulates world policies and recommendations for the advancement of women. The Commission performed a Preparatory Committee (PREPCOM) for the World Conference.

10. Consensus is the method used by the United Nations to approve declarations, plans, or other documents produced by international conferences or summits.

11. Reservations imply that the government of the state does not acquire a commitment to implement a particular resolution, will do so partially, or has a different interpretation.

12. The Regional Plan of Action adopted for Latin America and the Caribbean is more specific and progressive than the World Platform for Action (e.g., violence against women, women's participation in decision making and power in public and private life, shared family responsibilities).

13. Very few Latin American countries have cardinals. We should note, however, that member states with appointed cardinals made reservations to the

Platform for Action. Appointment of cardinals is a political move by the Vatican, used to recognize the political importance of that country within the interests of the Holy See. One particular example is Nicaragua, a small nation in a region—Central America—with limited political interest for the church, until local priests, nuns, and influential political leaders were part of a social and political movement critical of the traditional teachings of the Catholic Church. When this movement was in control of the executive and legislature, the threat of another Cuba was real.

14. Guanacaste is the province located in the northern part of the country.

15. During the 1950s and 1960s, Costa Rica had one of the highest birthrates in the world.

16. Most Latin American countries still include norms favoring "honorable abortions," seeking to protect not the woman, but the reputation or "good name" of the family and the men behind it. Similar norms existed that protected men who killed their adulterous wives when discovered with their lovers.

17. Television and radio stations provide the Catholic Church with prime time to develop different programs. Additionally, the Catholic Church or Catholic organizations own several religious TV and radio stations. These programs are an effective means of religious proselytizing among large audiences.

REFERENCES

Achio, M., H. DeVries, and C. García. 1994. *Fecundidad y formación de la familia: Encuesta Nacional de Salud Reproductiva 1993* [Fertility and Family. National Study on Reproductive Health. 1993]. San José, Costa Rica: Caja Costarricense de Seguro Social.

Anderson, Janine. 1985. "Los Sistemas de Género y el Desarrollo en la Selva" [Gender Systems and Development in the Jungle]. *Shapuhui: Revista Latinoamericana de Análisis y Actualidad.* Iquitos, Perú: Centro de Análisis y Actualidad Perunas.

Boland, R., S. Rau, and G. Zeidenstein. 1994. "Honoring Human Rights Population Policies: From Declaration to Action." In *Population Policies Reconsidered,* ed. G. Sen, A. Germain and L. Chen. Cambridge, Mass.: Harvard University Press.

Bonfil, G. 1987. *México Profundo* [Deep Mexico]. México: SEP-Ciesas.

Buxó, M. J. 1991. "Vitrinas, Cristales y Espejos: dos Modelos de Identidad en la Cultura Urbana en las Sociedades Quiché de Quetzaltenango" [Showcases, Crystals and Mirrors: Two Models of Identity Among Urban Quiche Societies of Quetzaltenango]. In *Mujeres y Sociedad: Nuevos Enfoques Teóricos y Metodológicos.* [Women and Society: New Theoretical and Methodological Perspectives], ed. Seminario Interdisciplinar Mujer y Sociedad. Barcelona, Spain: Universidad de Barcelona.

Caravaca, A., and L. Guzmán. 1996. *Violencia de Género, Derechos Humanos y Democratización: La Perspectiva de las Mujeres. Tomo IV.* [Gender Violence, Human

Rights and Democracy: Women's Experience. Volume IV]. San José, Costa Rica: Programa de las Naciones Unidas para el Desarrollo (UNDP).

Castro Alvarado, D. M. 1996. *La Mujer ante el Juzgado Eclesiástico en la Costa Rica del Siglo XVIII* [Women at the Eclesiastical Court in the XVIII Century Costa Rica]. San José, Costa Rica: Editorial Mirambell.

Católicas por el Derechos a Decidir. 1995. "La Educación Sexual de los Jóvenes" [Sexual Education of the Young]. *Conciencia Latinoamericana*. Vol. VII, No. 4. October-November. Montevideo, Uruguay: Edinor-Comunidad del Sur.

CMF (Centro Mujer y Familia) and MPPE (Ministerio Planificación y Política Económica). 1996. *Cuarta Conferencia Mundial sobre la Mujer: Información General y Selección de Documentos* [Fourth World Conference on Women: General Information and Main Documentos]. Series Documents No. 10. San José, Costa Rica: El Centro.

Dumont, L. 1965. *Homo Hierarchicus: The Caste System and its Implications.* Chicago: University of Chicago Press.

Ferro, Cora, and Ana María Quieros. 1993. *Mujer, realidad religiosa y comunicación* [Women, religious reality and communication]. San José, Costa Rica: Editorial EDUCA.

Flansburg, S. 1998. *Los Derechos Reproductivos y Sexuales de las Mujeres: Concepciones de las Mujeres Costarricenses sobre sus Derechos, Salud Reproductiva y Sexual y sus Necesidades de Atención* [The Reproductive and Sexual Rights of Women: Views of Women in Costa Rica about their Rights, Reproductive and Sexual Health and Needs]. San José, Costa Rica: Master Program in Women's Studies, University of Costa Rica.

Fuller, N. 1995. "En Torno a la Polaridad Marianismo-Machismo" [On Marianismo-Machismo]. In *Género e Identidad: Ensayos sobre lo Femenino y lo Masculino* [Gender and Identity: Essays on Femininity and Masculinity], ed. L. G. Arango, M. León and M. Viveros. Bogotá, Colombia: Tercer Mundo, S. A., Ediciones Uniandes, Programa de Estudios Género, Mujer y Desarrollo.

Gobierno de la República de Costa Rica. 1999. *Primer Informe sobre el Cumplimiento de la República de Costa Rica de la Convención sobre la Eliminación de Todas las Formas de Discriminación contra la Mujer* [Compliance with the Convention on the Elimination of All Forms of Discrimination Against Women: First Report of the Republic of Costa Rica]. Report presented by the Ministry of Foreign Affairs to the CEDAW Committee. March.

González Gómez, M. L. 1985. "Planificación Familiar y el Estado: el Caso de Costa Rica" [Family Planning and the State: The Case of Costa Rica]. Licenciatura thesis in Political Science. University of Costa Rica.

Gruzinski, S. 1987. "Confesión, Alinza y Sexualidad entre los Indios de Nueva España: Introducción al Estudio de los Confesionarios en Lenguas Indígenas" [Confession, Alliance and Sexuality among the Indians of New Spain: Introduction to the Study of Confessions in Indigenous Languages]. In *El Placer de Pecar y el Afán de Normar* [The Pleasure of Sinning and the Desire to Norm], ed. Joaquin Mortiz. Mexico: Instituto Nacional de Anthropología e Historia.

Guzmán, L. 1990. *Women's Labor Rights in Costa Rica 1821–1985*. San José, Costa Rica: Universidad de Costa Rica.

Guzmán, L., and G. Pacheco. 1996. "La IV Conferencia Mundial sobre la Mujer: Interrogantes, Respuestas, Nudos y Desafíos sobre el Adelanto de las Mujeres en un Contexto de Cambio" [The IV World Conference on Women: Questions, Answers, Critical Issues and Challenges on the Advancement of Women in a Changing Context]. In *Estudios Básicos en Derechos Humanos Tomo IV* [Basic Studies in Human Rights Volume IV], eds. L. Guzmán and G. Pacheco. San José, Costa Rica: Instituto Interamericano de Derechos Humanos.

Guzmán, M. (1997). *La Costa Rica de la Colonia* [Colonial Costa Rica]. San José, Costa Rica: Universidad de Costa Rica.

INAMU Instituto Nacional de las Mujeres. 1999. "Plataforma de Acción de Beijing: Cinco Años Después"[Beijing Platform for Action: Five Years After]. Working paper for the Meeting Beijing +5: Dec. 12. San José, Costa Rica: INAMU.

Instituto de Mujer and FLACSO 1995. *Mujeres Latinoamericanas en Cifra: Volumen Comparativo* [Latin American Women in Statistics: Comparative Volume]. Santiago, Chile: Instituto de la Mujer.

Marcos, S. 1989. "Curas, Diosas y Erotism: El Catolicismo Frente a los Indios" [Priests, Goddesses and Erotism: Catholicism and the Indians]. In *Mujer e Iglesia: Sexualidad y Aborto en América Latina* [Women and Church: Sexuality and Abortion in Latin America], ed. Ana María Portugal. Mexico: Catholics for a Free Choice-Distribuciones Fontamara, S.A.

Melhus, M. 1990. "Una Verguenza para el Honor, una Verguenza para el Sufrimiento" [A Shame to Honor, a Shame to Suffer]. In *Simbólica de la Feminidad* [Symbol of Femininity], ed. M. Palma. Colección 500 Años, No. 23. Quito, Ecuador: Abya-Yala.

Miguel, M. de. 1972. *La Mujer en la Vida y Doctrina de la Iglesia* [Women in the Life and Doctrine of the Church]. Mexico: Editorial Orion.

Molina, I. 1996. *Costa Rica (1800–1850): El Legado Colonial y la Génesis del Capitalismo* [Costa Rica (1800–1850): The Colonial Legacy and Origins of Capitalism]. San José, Costa Rica: Editorial Costa Rica.

Montaño, S. 1996. "Los Derechos Reproductivos de la Mujer" [Women's Reproductive Rights]. In *Estudios Básicos en Derechos Humanos Tomo IV* [Basic Studies in Human Rights Volume IV], ed. L. Guzmán and G. Pacheco. San José, Costa Rica: Instituto Interamericano de Derechos Humanos.

Montecino, S. 1995. "Identidades de Género en América Latina: Mestizajes, Sacrificios y Simultaneidades" [Gender Identities in Latin America: The Crossing of Races, Sacrifices and Simultaneities]. In *Género e Identidad: Ensayos sobre lo Femenino y lo Masculino* [Gender and Identity: Essays on Femininity and Masculinity], ed. L. G. Arango, M. León, and M. Viveros. Bogotá, Colombia: Tercer Mundo, S.A., Ediciones Uniandes, Programa de Estudios Género, Mujer y Desarrollo.

Montecino, S., M. Dussuel, and A. Wilson. 1988. "Identidad Femenina y Modelo Mariano en Chile" [Female Identity and Marian Model in Chile]. In *Mundo de*

Mujer, Continuidad y Cambio [Women's World, Continuity and Change], ed. Sonia Montecino. Santiago, Chile: Ediciones CEM.

Palma, M. 1991. "Malinche, el Malinchismo o el Lado Femenino de la Sociedad Mestiza" [Malinche, 'Malinchismo' or the Feminine Side of Mestizo Society]. In *Género, Clase y Raza en América Latina* [Gender, Class, and Race in Latin America], ed. Lola G. Luna. Barcelona, Spain: Promociones y Publicaciones Universitarias.

Paz, O. 1959. *El Laberinto de la Soledad* [The Laberinth of Solitude]. Mexico: Fondo Cultura Económica.

Population Action International. 1994. *Fondos Para el Futuro: Cómo Satisfacer la Demanda de Planificación Familiar* [Funds for the Future: How to Satisfy the Demand for Family Planning]. Washington, D.C.: Population Action International.

Portugal, A. M. 1989. "Introduccion." In *Mujer e Iglesia: Sexualidad y Aborto en América Latina* [Women and Church: Sexuality and Abortion in Latin America], ed. Ana María Portugal. Mexico: Catholics for a Free Choice—Distribuciones Fontamara, S.A.

Portugal, A. M., and M. I. Matamala.1993. "Movimiento de Salud de las Mujeres: Una Visión de la Década" [The Women's Health Movement: A View of the Decade]. In *Género, Mujer y Salud en las Américas* [Gender, Women, and Health in the Americas], ed. Elsa Gómez. Scientific Publication no. 541. Washington, D.C. Pan American Health Organization and World Health Organization.

PRIEG/UCR Programa Interdisciplinario de Estudios de Género/Universidad de Costa Rica. 1998. *La Situación de las Mujeres en Costa Rica: Una Evaluación desde la Convención sobre la Elminación de Todas las Formas de Discriminación Contra la Mujer* [The Status of Women in Costa Rica: An Assessment based on the Convention for the Elimination of all Forms of Discrimination Against Women]. San José, Costa Rica: Universidad de Costa Rica.

Quezada, N. 1975. *Amor y Magia Amorosa Entre los Aztecas* [Love and Loving Magic among the Aztecs]. México: Universidad Ncional Autónoma de México/Instituto de Investigaciones ed Antropología.

Rance, S. 1991. *Fecundidad: Entre el Miedo y el Antiimperialismo* [Fertility: Amid Fear and Anti-imperialism]. La Paz, Bolivia: Ultima Hora.

República de Nicaragua. 1998. *Informes sobre el Tema 18 Compromisos de la Cumbre de las Américas: México, Guatemala, El Salvador, Honduras, Nicaragua, Costa Rica, Panamá, Colombia, Ecuador, Perú, Chile, Paraguay, Argentina* [Reports on Theme 18 Commitments of the Summit of the Americas]. Managua, Nicaragua: República de Nicaragua.

Solórzano, J. C. 1987. "Comercio y Regiones Económicas en Costa Rica Colonial" [Commerce and Economic Regions in Costa Rica]. Geoistmo. 1: no. 1. 15–17.

Stevens, E. 1977. "El Marianismo" [Marianism]. In *Hembra y Macho en Latinoamérica* [Female and Male in Latin America], ed. Ana María Portugal. Mexico: Editorial Diana.

United Nations 1995. *Plataforma de Acción Mundial 1996–2001* [World Platform for Action 1996–2001]. IV World Conference on Women, Beijing, Peoples Republic of China, September 8–15.

United Nations Population Fund. 1995. *Estadisticass de Género* [Gendered Statistics]. San José, Costa Rica: Ministry of Planning and Economic Policy and Center on Women and Family.

Valdes, A. 1990. "Mujeres Entre Culturas en América Latina" [Women Between Cultures in Latin America]. *Crítica Cultural* 1: no. 1. May, 7–14.

CHAPTER 7

THE POLITICS OF IMPLEMENTING WOMEN'S RIGHTS IN TURKEY

Ayşe Güneş-Ayata

Since the founding of the Republic in 1923, the most important movement in Turkey has been toward westernization. The content of westernization has not only been economic and political, but also cultural, where the role of women within the society has assumed significance as a symbol of progress toward this endeavour. The reforms involving women's rights were some of the most important, if not the most important attempts to break away from the Muslim world and turn toward the West. The major reforms that led to full citizenship for women, abolition of polygamy, equal rights in divorce and inheritance, and the granting of all civic equalities including political rights to women, were recognized as major accomplishments. Despite efforts by the state and the westernizing middle classes that adopted this new western ideal, the majority of the people retained their traditional lifestyles and perspectives. Throughout the twentieth century, westernized life styles infiltrated large sections of the population. Improved economic prosperity and increasing relations with the western world led to higher levels of education and a tendency to emulate the middle class. Equally significant sections of the population did not accept these western ideals of modernization and democratization, however. Some groups resisted and organized to oppose westernization. This conflict escalated and became more visible in the last few decades of the twentieth century, due to domestic and international pressures on the state from various groups. In this process, the state has become more contradictory in terms of its ideals, pronouncements, and policies, being squeezed between the progressive demands coming from pro-western women's rights groups, the standards imposed by the international institutions including the United Nations and the European Union, and popular electoral reactions opposed to the westernization movement.

This chapter discusses the struggle between the modern West and the traditional in Turkey during the last two decades of the twentieth century. Those resisting westernization have increasingly focused on women as a significant symbol of their political agenda. To complete this story, this chapter will discuss the activities of the women's movement in this environment and the interactions between the women's movement and the state apparatus.

DEVELOPMENT OF THE WOMEN'S MOVEMENT

SECULAR LIBERAL AND RADICAL RESPONSES

Until the 1980s, Turkish women were very proud of the republican reforms which gave women egalitarian rights. Equality before the law, the ultimate achievement, was expected to lead to social equality as women acquired the will and determination to exercise these rights (İnan 1968; Taşkıran 1975). Until the 1980s, women did little to improve their status in the society. Scientific research on women was limited to a few studies either on rural women (Kandiyoti 1974) who were seen as the "oppressed women" to be awakened by republican rights, or concentrated on women in professional life and their achievements (Çulpan 1977; Öncü 1979). Some quasi-political papers sought to propagate the achievements of the Republic rather than to discuss the deep-rooted patriarchy within the society (Abadan 1952; Sönmez 1975).

A very similar attitude prevailed in the women's rights associations that existed throughout the Republican Period. An educated middle class dominated these organizations, whose main activities were charity and representation abroad. The republican reforms benefited these women the most. These women assumed that they enjoyed almost absolute equality with men, and they proved this claim with an unusually high ratio of women in professional occupations (Özkaya 1985). They argued that whatever inequality existed in the rest of the society was due to the lack of education and ignorance concerning women's existing rights among the poor, provincial, traditional, and uneducated. The remedy was "progress," to be achieved by economic development and social-cultural westernization for those in the disadvantaged sections of society. They did not question the inequalities in their own private lives, taking the gendered division of labor in the family as a given. Patriarchy was something to be experienced mainly in the villages and expressed in the form of novels. The women's associations saw it as their duty to inform women about their rights; however, usually they were too elitist and removed from the masses even to accomplish that.

This stance has lost its saliency since the 1980s. A new group of feminists began advocating the idea that patriarchy is a diffused, encompassing ideology which infiltrates private as well as public life, an ideology which extends beyond class boundaries (Sirman 1989). Sirin Tekeli in her pioneering work (Tekeli 1982), made this into an explicitly political issue by noting that the percentage of women in parliament was continually decreasing. She indicated that in the Republic's ideology, women's position in political leadership is a product of tokenism. Women have no real representation nor do they have power. This study was pioneering in two ways. First, it challenged the middle class women's assumptions of equality. Tekeli argued that inequalities were not only in the villages amongst the poor and the uneducated but also in public life, at the heart of the system. These inequalities prevented women from using their political rights. Secondly, Tekeli held that existing women's rights were not necessarily granted to improve women's status in the society, but to serve as showpieces of the ideological commitment of Turkey to westernization and democratization (Tekeli 1982).

The feminist critique of Turkish society and politics began in 1980 mixed with the leftist critique of the existing military regime. Paradoxically, the military itself was not necessarily traditionalist. They also promoted the "progress through women" ideology of the 1920s and took a major step forward to advance the feminist cause by legalizing abortion. In 1981, Turkey became the only Muslim country where abortion was legal on request.

The 1980s brought the introduction of Second Wave feminism to Turkey with its new questioning of public/private dichotomies, new interpretations of the existing inequalities, and new perspectives toward policy formulations. At that time, the Turkish feminist movement split into two components: the women's rights organizations which held their deep-rooted trust within the Kemalist secular ideology, and the "new feminists," whose more radical questioning of patriarchy was bringing new criticisms and perspectives imported from Europe and the United States. They were interested especially in areas such as personal life, the body, and sexual liberties. They also introduced new forms of participation including consciousness-raising groups, street protests, and large media campaigns denouncing violations of women's human rights.

The Kemalist feminists and radical feminists differed from each other in age and in ideological and sociological terms but not in class terms.

Both were composed of urban, middle-class, university educated, professional women, although they differed in age and in their receptivity of the international ideological currents and political ideology. The Kemalists were older and/or representatives of an older generation. They were more sensitive to how things were done within society and family, trying not to raise unnecessary worries within the society that might present a threat to the state. They were generally content with their personal achievements in life even though this was deeply challenged in later years. The radical feminists were younger. They questioned almost everything regarding the establishment from community and family life to the state and its institutions. Significant numbers of younger women, especially their leaders, had knowledge of foreign languages. They were open to international currents, adopting more universal discourses. The new feminists claimed that women and men were neither socially nor legally equal. They argued that the "protective clauses of law" were patriarchal in conception. Citing as examples the clauses of the Civil Code that envisaged husbands as the main breadwinners or gave the final word to the father in decisions involving children, they questioned modern nuclear family relationships, arguing that the modern nuclear family holds its "inequalities hidden under roofs" in the same way as the traditional family, an institution sharply criticized by the modernists. They also introduced other issues such as domestic violence, rape, and sexual liberation into the public discourse, issues that had long been ignored.

Rather than passively advocating more education for women and economic development—as did the Kemalists—the radical feminist groups adopted activist political tactics. They were present on the streets with protest marches, they tried the unusual by invading male-dominated coffee shops, and they organized campaigns against sexual harassment and violence using shock tactics. For the first time, Turkish women were doing things to attract attention, to compete in male spaces, and to criticize male forms. This brought them significant media coverage, but did not necessarily lead to major tangible achievements for women.

ISLAMIC RELIGIOUS RESPONSES:

A picture of the Turkish women's movement in the last two decades of the twentieth century would be incomplete without bringing in the dimension of Islamic reaction. The perspectives of Islamist women are by no means undifferentiated. They range from mild conservatism to radical militarism. Even though Islamic women try to appeal to women from different sections of the society, mostly they appeal to urban women and women with at least a minimal education, usually more than bare literacy.

Islamic women attracted the attention of scholars after 1980 when, for the first time, some young students claimed the right to cover their heads in the university to express their public identity as "Muslim" (Arat 1990). They demanded to be integrated into public life with that specific identity. Turkey, which is 99 percent Muslim, had Muslim women of all levels of education, class background, wealth, and origin prior to 1980. Claiming a Muslim public identity, however, was believed to be confined to the provincial, peripheral parts of the country and considered to be traditional, transient in historical perspective, and, in some cases, reactionary. The majority of women in Turkey until then, covered their heads; however, educated, working, urban, New Muslim women assumed western dress in public. These "New Muslim" women were not only "the other" of the westernized women who sought success in public life through education and work and claimed to be equal to men, but also they were a contrast to the women who traditionally accepted their Muslim identities as given. The "New Muslim" women were an end-product of the Islamic fundamentalist movement in Turkey. They were deliberately fighting for a new order, an elaborate ideologization of Islam. They attacked not only the western world, present-day westernized Turkey, and the Kemalist Reforms, but they also tried to dissociate themselves from traditional Islam.

Magazines published by New Muslim groups give primacy to women's place in the home. None encourage women to work for a wage or salary, which they believe should only be done in cases of financial need (Acar 1990). Careers and promotions are definitely not on their list of concerns. Sex segregation and seclusion—both in work and education—are absolute musts. The total covering of the head and body with a loose fitting material is recommended and wearing black gloves and a face covering is part of the agenda for some. They argue that Islam is the only ideology and religion that elevates women to their proper and high status, which requires a total obedience to the Muslim rules. How this obedience is to be achieved varies. Some argue that obedience to the Muslim order is the answer, others argue that the family is the source of happiness. Still others seek active participation and suffering in the political struggle of Islam. The new Muslim groups also realize the need for professional women, especially since professional women are necessary for segregated lives. Women can be educated to become doctors, nurses, and teachers to serve women and girls. All of these magazines portray westernized women as unhappy, overworked, and exploited both economically and sexually. The Muslim women, in contrast, are not necessarily weak, passive, or frail, but lead dignified lives as mothers, wives, and/or militants (Acar 1990; Özdalga 1997).

The Islamic women have been active primarily in and around the Welfare Party. Women's auxiliaries in the Welfare Party were well known for their networks, efficiency, and organizational capacity. The women's auxiliaries of the Welfare Party maintained very close personal ties with women voters. They entered their homes, brought gifts (including food), and shared their moments of sorrow and joy. They attended funerals and weddings, provided religious services and most important of all, they created a warm atmosphere of solidarity and understanding.

Even though women had a very significant role within the party, the Welfare Party has been reluctant to run them as candidates. Before the 1995 elections, a number of women became candidates for the primaries in the party, although none was listed. This created uneasiness among women in the party ranks and attracted criticism from the secular press. When questioned, the leader of the Welfare Party, Erbakan, said, "The women of our party are working for God, not to become an MP." He added, "The rewards for these activities are written (in heaven) in the records of the deeds of our women."

INTERNATIONAL NORMS
AND NATIONAL MACHINERY

One of the well-known outcomes of Second Wave feminism has been the internationalization of women's problems on the intergovernmental level. As a result, the Convention for Elimination of All Forms of Discrimination against Women (CEDAW) has been adopted, making women's rights a significant part of human rights. The Turkish Parliament ratified the United Nations sponsored CEDAW in 1989 with a few reservations. Even though Turkey took a few years to ratify the convention, this was because of political instability that came with the 1980 coup in Turkey rather than any significant opposition to the convention. CEDAW requires a national machinery within the state apparatus to record the problems of women, to enhance women's rights, and to ensure equality. Following the ratification of CEDAW, the Turkish national machinery (understood as a bureaucratic governmental coordinating agency that monitors the initiation and implementation of policies regarding women's rights) was created as a governmental agency, first as a part of the ministry of Social Security and Labor, and later as a part of the Prime Ministry, tied to a minister without a portfolio. The resulting Department General for the Problems and Status of Women (DGPSW) has very limited resources and does not have a significant position within the cabinet. Initially, international funds were available. Over time, the funds diminished and the department currently is in financial difficulty (Acar 1999).

Most of the ministers in charge of the DGPSW have been women, even though twice men were appointed to this position. Since members of parliament, whether male or female, prefer to be appointed to ministries with more power and resources, and this position is not perceived as an honor, candidates are always reluctant to accept. Only those in marginal political positions saw this as a chance for promotion. Those who did take the position not only resented the appointment but were neither aware of women's problems nor sensitive to them. This ministerial position has served as a learning experience. Soon after appointment, Ministers of DGPSW realize that they have become a media attraction, which increases their interest in the subject. In this learning process they rely on the help of women's groups. Some learn more than others, but eventually most—especially the women ministers—begin to understand the problems, start to speak up, and some even become ardent supporters and spokespersons for the feminist movement.

Recognizing the limited availability of expertise in the area of women's affairs, international fund managers directed monies to training programs. Using these resources, universities initiated gender studies programs. By this time, some universities already had some academics interested in the subject who had attended graduate school in Europe and the United States during the peak of Second Wave feminism. These newly developing gender studies departments within the universities, and different groups active within the feminist movement were fruitful sources of information and ideas. The small number of experts within the existing bureaucracy provided a pool of advisers for the ministry. As an outcome of this interaction between the feminists, experts, and academics, DGPSW eventually became a unit circulating ideas and demands from the women's movement in accordance with international standards, but the agency has had very limited influence over other state departments and ministries.

On the legal side, court decisions have been more effective than legislation in parliament. Parliament passed two laws that were directly and indirectly influenced by the CEDAW demands. The first concerned the right of a woman to retain her maiden family names together with her husband's surnames on marriage. The second was the family protection law that protects women against intrafamilial violence (TBMM Report 1998). No change occurred in the Civil Code, however, despite significant demands from the women's groups.

In contrast, the constitutional court twice annulled laws that hindered egalitarian relations for women. The first case annulled the right of the husband to prevent his wife's professional activity (1990). The second case (1996) annulled the articles in the penal code that claimed adultery to be a crime and called for unequal punishment for husband and wife. Despite the limited influence of the state ministry in charge of women's affairs in both of the events, the minister cheered the decisions and saw it as a major step toward equality.

The foundation of the national machinery for coordinating women's affairs has increased the interaction between the women's movement and the state and its ideology in a lopsided way that favors the state. In return for funding from international resources controlled by the women's ministry, the ministry became a readily available source of ideas, advice, and, probably most important of all, a source of political support. Using these readily available groups as think tanks and as political supporters, ministers could easily mobilize petitions, street demonstrations, lobbies in the parliament, and other political support.

In most cases, the national machinery kept the Islamist women's movement at a distance. The Islamic women rarely participated in the meetings, and were almost never a part of the policy formulation process within the ministry. The secular women had a closer relationship to the ministry but they were not used to being an opposition movement. They actively tried to influence the ministers but were not critical of state activities.

Only some radical feminists influenced by European Second Wave feminism tried to keep a distance between themselves and the state. They continued with their own actions, consciousness-raising groups, and alternative organizations. The momentum of radicalism in the mid-90s began to fade, however, leading to the primacy of the mainstream Kemalist women women for the political and ideological reason that will be discussed later.

TURKEY IN BEIJING

Women's associations and NGOs were very excited about the Beijing meeting. Turkey prepared the country report with wide participation from various women's organizations in an attempt to bring together a variety of perspectives. The state minister who led the country's delegation was a social democrat who sincerely believed in promotion of women's rights. She was eager to include her party's position in the report and also was eager to promote the Turkey's contribution to the whole event. The report itself had two significant foci (Country Report 1995). The first was the self-confident attitude of Turkey toward westernization, integration with the rest of the world towards more egalitarian relations with gender groups, and compliance with CEDAW standards. This state minister's self-confident attitude was a result of her membership in the Republican People's Party, the party that originally introduced egalitarian rights for women in the Turkish Republic. Pride in the republic's achievements and in Turkey's disassociation from the rest of the Muslim world in granting women rights of equal inheritance, divorce, and suffrage are underlying themes throughout the report. The report also highlights the achievements of Turkish women in the professions which have reached ratios that surpass many western nations.

The second focus, however, was an open and frank self-criticism regarding Turkey's failure to expand women's rights in recent years. The report recognized that, in spite of the state's egalitarian policies, existing traditions, cultures, and economic problems that generate acute inequalities in the poorer sections of the society support traditional gender roles. Maternal death rates at birth and infant mortality rates remained high, 30 percent of the female population remained illiterate, and many girls dropped out of school at eleven years of age, the compulsory schooling age. Turkey recognized these problems and exuded an air of utmost confidence in being able to tackle them. In 1995, the general outlook was that the state recognized, however reluctantly, that women's problems existed and that women were becoming increasingly more conscious and aware of these problems (Country Report 1995).

Both the ministry and the NGOs saw the Beijing conference as a significant opportunity to increase awareness about gender problems and to impose new standards on the state. With this aim in mind, the Turkish government made three commitments to be undertaken by the year 2000:

- To ensure that female literacy attains 100 percent and to impose eight years of compulsory education.
- To decrease maternal death at birth by 50 percent.
- To lift the reservations on CEDAW.

As can be seen from these commitments, Turkey was ready to undertake major ideological steps forward in the international arena. Turkey went to Beijing with a large delegation of fifty people. The government provided US$200,000 to fund the government delegation and NGOs. Many of the chairs of the NGOs preferred to be in the government delegation rather than at the NGO Forum. They saw the delegation as representing women and their demands and they wanted to be close to the power positions and to the bargaining. Probably the only real NGOs at the Beijing conference, in the sense of being unattached to the state and its ideology, were the Islamic groups. They came with their own resources, and were treated as outcasts by most of the other Turkish NGOs. They never approached the Turkish delegation with demands, even though they were present and maintained distant and cordial relations in all the open sessions.

In the United Nations preparatory meetings prior to the Beijing meeting, Turkey's stance was very clear on disputed issues such as abortion rights, inheritance, and women's place in private life. In all of these, the Turkish delegation not only sided with Europe but also was very active. The government delegation and the NGO representatives were jubilant when they returned to Turkey, proud of their achievements, only to discover that the upcoming elections in Turkey would be detrimental for women's rights in Turkey.

As a result of these elections in 1995, the Islamist Welfare party became the largest party and soon formed a coalition with other parties with the Welfare party leader, Mr. Erbakan, becoming the Prime Minister. This led to a totally new experience. The Ministry in charge of women went into the hands of conservative women under an Islamist coalition. Uncertainty prevailed for about a year, activity was minimal, and the Beijing conference was discussed only among the secular women.

Meanwhile, Turkey made its periodic report to CEDAW. This report was a sharp contrast to the country report prepared for Beijing in both process and the content. The problems began with the drafting of the CEDAW report. The ministry called a conference to include NGO participation, in which, for the first time, Islamist women NGOs were included—although, together with experts and academics, the Islamists were a minority. The Islamist women had one agenda; they wanted the ban on headscarves (turbans) for those in the universities and for state employees to be lifted, on the grounds that this would improve women's liberties. During the meeting, the secular women—irrespective of ideological differences—made controlling and opposing the Islamist women's agenda their primary focus. Other issues and problems took a secondary position.

The written report sent to New York showed signs of this chaos as well as the existence of the Islamists in the ruling coalition in the country. It was a major diversion from the Beijing Platform for Action. The report, and especially the presentation by Professor Yakın Ertürk, emphasized the problems encountered by women in Turkey, underlined especially problems related to rural development, but did not mention present-day or past achievements. Except for a defensive speech that Professor Ertürk made at the end of the session on Turkey, the achievements of the country in the area of women's rights, the major source of pride until then, were not recognized (Country Report 1994).

Instead, Turkey took an almost apologetic stance of being separated from its fellow third world (if not Muslim) countries. The new government coalition de-emphasized the former universalist women's human rights approach of Beijing in favor of multiculturalism and cultural specificity. In the report itself, this led to an eclectic approach without a unifying theme. The report was not only a diversion from the past but also had an overall pessimistic outlook. Abandoning the West and universalist norms left Turkey without confidence in the past and also without a vision for the future. The report was a major sign that the country was going through turmoil, with women at the heart of it. The CEDAW Report went unnoticed in Turkey. Both the Turkish press and Turkey's secular NGOs expressed little interest in the sessions in New York. Many women's organizations from late November 1996 to mid-February 1997 were very busy dealing with Islamic fundamentalism and the new coalition government that they saw as a threat to the state as well as to women's rights.

THE ISLAMIST COALITION GOVERNMENT (WELFARE PARTY) AND ITS IMPACT ON WOMEN

An Islamist coalition government was virtually assured after the Welfare Party victory in the 1995 elections. Years before, when the Welfare Party came to power, many professional urban women were concerned that an Islamist group might come to power and reverse the secular reforms of the Republic. Women started many associations in the second half of the 1980s (although not all were for women only) to prepare for such a "danger." As soon as the press reported that both of the right-wing parties, the True Path Party and Motherland Party, were starting talks regarding a coalition with the Welfare Party, women began to protest. They sent thousands of letters, placed black wreaths on party's doorsteps, made fierce speeches, and organized meetings and rallies.

These women were effective in deterring Mr. Yılmaz and the Motherland Party. Ms. Çiller, who was the first woman prime minister of Turkey and the leader of the True Path Party, did not yield to these protests, claiming that she herself was the guarantee of secularism and women's rights. Two out of six women from the True Path Party, however, who were members of Parliament did not give a vote of confidence to the coalition. Immediately after the vote of confidence, thirty-five secular women's organizations filed a court case against Çiller for deceiving women in her election propaganda. They accused her of giving the impression that women were unreliable.

The Welfare Party started its discussion on the role of women in private and public life prior to coming to power. They had two significant goals. Their first target was to enable women to work in government offices and attend schools (especially universities) wearing a headscarf (turban). The second was to limit women's participation in public life, especially in paid employment. They also raised other issues but not with the same insistence. For example, they attempted to change items in the secular civic code, such as legalizing religious marriages and allowing religious functionaries to register civil marriages.1 In another instance, they attempted to close women's shelters, arguing that they threaten family solidarity (*Hürriyet* 1996a.).

The two goals or issues—wearing the headscarf and limiting women's employment—were significant because Welfare Party activists and leadership persistently worked to make them central to mainstream politics. In attempting to limit women working in paid employment, the Welfare Party took two kinds of action. First, the leadership argued that they would rather see women as housewives and mothers and that they wanted to make life more difficult for working women. In some cases, they even used derogatory language for working women and attempted to close down nurseries in municipalities (*Cumhuriyet* 1996b, 17). In other cases, they suggested limiting female employment, but mostly they used existing restrictions on women bureaucrats, forcing some bureaucrats to resign and removing others from office (*Y.Yüzyıl* 1997b, 7). Sometimes they appointed women to jobs such as roadbuilding expecting that they would not accept to create excuses for sacking them from office. (*Cumhuriyet* 1996a, 3). In other cases, they clearly indicated that only women obeying proper dress codes and/or in seclusion would be allowed to work. In one case, they issued a declaration banning the wearing of miniskirts (*Günaydın* 1996, 8). In another instance, they banned lawyers from visiting their clients in prisons in mixed sex situations. On still another occasion, they argued that women should be given a leave of absence during their "periods," as they were too fragile in such days (*Sabah* 1996, 1).

Probably the most significant of these attacks occurred in December 1996, in a meeting organized by the women's auxiliary of the Welfare Party to commemorate the suffrage rights of Turkish women. Mr. Erbakan made a speech arguing that women should work only twice a week, four hours each time. He openly declared that the primary duty of a woman is to care for her children and her husband. Women's work in the outside world, he argued, can only be complementary to that of her husband. In the same meeting, he criticized the United Nations declaration in Beijing for allowing abortions (*Cumhuriyet* 1996d, 19). Women's associations considered this an important proclamation and discussed it for days in the media and among themselves (*Cumhuriyet* 1996e, 1, 19). Many politically sensitive groups saw these words as key to the true intentions of Welfare Party in terms of limiting women in the public sphere (*Melodi* 1996, 1).

The other very important aim of the Welfare Party during this period was to enable women to work in government offices wearing turbans (headscarves). Turkish law has never forbidden women from covering their heads in private life; however, since the 1930s, female state employees have been prohibited from covering their heads in office. This rule holds true also for female students, who can only cover their heads in theological schools when reading the Quran. With the resurgence of fundamentalism in the 1980s, for the first time in republican history some female students in the universities demanded to attend classes with headscarves. Between 1980 and 1998, motions were introduced repeatedly in the parliament to liberalize and/or to restrict this practice. Eventually, the constitutional court took a final decision arguing this is not part of religious liberty, and universities can take action to limit the show of religiosity in a secular country. The European Human Rights Court also supported this decision.

With regard to headscarves, the legal situation was very clear when the Welfare Party came to power. This issue constituted and still constitutes a major cause for the Islamic fundamentalists in Turkey, however, and certainly was one of their main issues during the campaign for 1995 elections. They had argued that they would liberalize the usage of headscarves in all cases. They wanted to change the legal situation to make the law state that "women may uncover their heads in public offices," as if a head cover was the norm and uncovering the head was the unusual. To implement this policy, they took many actions. Soon after they came to power, in the ministries they controlled they announced that female employees could cover their heads, and prepared a new bill to liberalize headscarves in the universities (*Milliyet Daily* 1996c, 13; *Milliyet Daily* 1996d). This became an ongoing struggle with secular NGOs. The secular state institutions, including the army and the higher education council, were on one side, and the Welfare Party was on the other. The other significant facet of this struggle took place in the courts, where the minister of justice wanted to appoint female judges with headscarves and enable female attorneys also to wear them. The bar associations, high council of judges, and the other related legal associations strongly protested this (*Cumhuriyet* 1997a, 4; *Radikal* 1997b, 3; *Cumhuriyet* 1996c, 4, *Hürriyet* 1996b, 24, *Türkiye* 1996c, 19).

The ministry in charge of women's affairs was caught in between these two sides. The conservative press had criticized the ministry for being under the influence of social democratic values and feminist pressures. They continued this criticism arguing that the ministry was protecting "liberal" women as opposed to the family values that reflected the tradition, religion and culture of the Turkish society (*Milliyet Daily* 1996c., 18; *Türkiye* 1996a, 9; *Türkiye* 1996b, 9;, 18). The minister defended herself by arguing that this criticism came from an extreme right wing position, one that annihilated the importance of women in the society. To prove herself both to be conservative but also favorable to women's rights, the minister tried to initiate some reforms that would deflect the pressure coming from the secular feminists demanding that she oppose the Islamists in her own government. The two issues that she championed were legalizing marriage and changing the surname code.

Since 1926, a religious ceremony has not been considered the basis for a legal marriage in Turkey. For many reasons, such as the couple being underage or the relative ease of having a religious marriage, about 10 percent of all marriages (mostly among Kurds) have been religious marriages only. This means that the spouses are not legally married, which means that women do not enjoy inheritance and social security rights from their husbands. The campaign, initiated by the Minister for Women's Affairs, proposed to allow thousands of couples to legalize their marriages in common ceremonies. This legalization involved many advantages for women and was welcomed by most feminists. It also was a gesture towards conservative groups indicating the minister's respect for family life. Such an emphasis on the family, however, also indicated a shift of policy in the ministry from the empowerment of the woman as an individual to her empowerment within the family, the basic philosophy of many right-wing political parties, including the Welfare Party.

The other proposal advanced by the minister was to amend the law for family surnames to enable a woman to retain her maiden family name after marriage together with that of her husband. This issue was brought forward by many feminists as an identity issue. Surprisingly, the Islamists welcomed this, because in many Islamic countries women retain their maiden name on the grounds of patriliny.

Despite the ministry's attempt to avoid controversy, the headscarf issue escalated along with anti-Welfare Party sentiments. The newspapers of this period printed an average of five to six articles per day on the topic. Women's associations took a leading role. Their claims were as follows: The Welfare Party wants to limit democratic rights including women's rights. They want to limit women to the mother role with only a secondary role in public life. They see women as weak and subordinate and they want to revoke the rights established by the Atatürk reforms. The headscarf may be seen as an innocent claim of a right to practice religion, but the underlying demand is much more regressive and should be strongly opposed. Welfare Party spokespersons, however, did not try to assuage this massive fear. Instead, they continued to provide further cause for alarm. On many occasions, Welfare Party spokespersons said that they would prefer to legalize religious marriages. One of them even said that Turkey has 2.5 million prostitutes, implying that all women working outside the home were prostitutes (*Radikal* 1997a, 5; *Hürriyet* 1997a, 24).

They called all fashion shows exhibitionism, and the minister of justice announced that he would encourage the prosecution of offenses (*Cumhuriyet* 1997b, 5).

In mid-January 1997, the unanimity of the government began to falter. First, those in the True Path Party began to feel uneasy. Three of the four women ministers (that is, except Çiller herself) began to express discontent. On January 31, 1997, a small newspaper article hinted that the military was carefully observing the situation, and would not approve the legalization of the headscarf. Shortly thereafter, on February 15, 1997 in Ankara, secular women's organizations, including women's auxiliaries of political parties, staged the biggest women' protest ever called Women Against *sharià*. One hundred thousand women came together to protest the Welfare Party's attack on women in public life. The secularist position, which women's organizations publicized in February and March, found its ultimate expression in the declarations of the President and the National Security Council.

A week later on February 23, the president of the country, Mr. Demirel, gave a speech emphasizing the significance of women in secular society. He said, "They (the Islamists) first want to get rid of women in public life, they want to set them aside, this is the first step toward eliminating the contemporary (western) style of life in Turkey." (*Cumhuriyet* 1997c, 1). About a fortnight later, for the first time in republican history, he issued a message for of March 8 (International Women's Day) celebrations, claiming that women's rights were the banners of the republican reforms; democracy, and secularism. He underlined the role NGOs play in promoting women's status in the economy, society, politics, and cultural life. Not only did this speech create a controversy with the prime minister, who limited the role of women to motherhood, but it also legitimized the women's NGOs rally.

Meanwhile on February 28, 1997, the National Security Council issued a declaration saying that the secularization principle of the republic was being threatened. To counter this threat, they proposed along with other measures, that the compulsory education should be extended to the eighth grade. This was one of the commitments Turkey made at the Beijing Conference, a commitment long desired by the women's rights movement. The declaration of the National Security Council ended most of the discussion on the "headscarf" issue. Soon, Welfare Party leadership claimed that they would limit the liberalization attempts to universities only.

However, a wedge between the Ministry and the government was already in place. The Minister of Women's Affairs felt the increasing pressure from women's groups. The ultimate blow came when the Parliament rejected another progressive law proposal. Since early 1997, the Ministry was preparing a law to prohibit intra family violence against women. The proposed law enabled a public prosecutor to act without a complaint to protect women under violence. It also enabled the judge to expel the violent spouse from the domicile irrespective of house ownership or status as bread winner. Even though women applauded such a proposal, the Islamists within the government and the parliament stopped the proposal from becoming law, arguing that this did not promote "harmonious" family relations but on the contrary, cast husband and wife as enemies of one another. This was the last straw. The Minister resigned from her position and the party (*Milliyet Daily*. 1997; *Hürriyet*. 1997b; *Cumhuriyet*. 1997d, Türkiye, 1997; Y.Yüzyıl, 1997a; Sabah, 1997).

For the secular women's movement, the resignation of the minister was significant but not satisfactory. Their target was the government. In this they saw the army as an important and crucial ally. The army was also recognizing the 'sensitivity' of women to the issue. The give and take relationship continued. The Chief of Staff of the army for the first time organized a briefing for women on the potential threats to secularism. They invited all secular women's NGOs, even those that were not registered officially, gathering together almost 500 women. In a reciprocal move, some women's NGOs began to invite generals to speak at their meetings. On one occasion, the Turkish Mothers' Association (very Kemalist in ideology) gave special awards to army generals.

While the Islamic Welfare Party coalition ruled in Turkey, secularization and threats to secularism became the central theme of the women's movement. Not all secular feminists were happy about this single tracked, anti-Welfare Party oriented feminism. Many argued that while secularism was important, feminism was much more than this and the other problems of women should not be undermined. Some hinted that one of the feminist causes was further democratization of the country, noting that flirtation with the military would raise antidemocratic questions. Yet the fundamentalist threat was so acute that secularism became the overriding issue. No secular woman could openly criticize the fundamentalists. The issue galvanized secular women into a significant political force in the country for the first time.

CONCLUSION

This chapter discusses the relationships between the State, political parties, and the feminist and Islamic movements in Turkey. Secular Turkish feminism has been influential and successful in shaping the State's attitudes towards women. Secular women have been influential in making women an issue in Turkish politics, have drawn attention to women's problems, and have played an important role in shaping both the Directorate General for the Problems and Status of Women and attitudes of

Ministers themselves. They are considered a significant political force. They can mobilize media attention, and even though there are limits, they can be effective on some decisions.

The ongoing threat of Islamic fundamentalism has put women into a paradoxical situation. The women's movement advocates have gained a new momentum as strong supporters of secularism. Feminists have shared their cause with large groups of women and organized countrywide. Women have found very powerful allies within the system, such as the army, the president, and other secular groups. Women's rights in this process have been reemphasized as an integral part of Republican reforms. The women's movement has even improved conditions for women on certain issues. One of these is the imposition of eight years of compulsory schooling, a policy which is expected to change the marriage age. Another is the enactment of the law that tries to prevent intra -family violence. This process of prioritizing the defense against Islamic fundamentalism, however, has limited secular women's capacity to critically question the status of women prior to the 1980s. Other issues have taken secondary positions. This has meant that women have lost the search for new solutions and new alliances.

In the 1920s and the 1930s women were symbols of Westernization. In the 1990s, they became both symbols of secularism and Islamic fundamentalism. In both cases, they have been used by others as symbols of an historical and cultural struggle and have themselves taken an active part in using their symbolic position politically to advance their own interests.

NOTES

1. During this period an increasing number of village novels appeared, most of which describe events indicating the extremes of patriarchy. Some can even be considered cruel. Among the best examples are the novels of Bekir Yıldız, Fakir Baykurt, Yaşar Kemal. However, one must also note that the authors are all men at this period. This by itself can be considered indicative of how disinterested women were in the problems.

2. The Welfare Party was founded in 1983. In the 1995 elections had 21 percent of the vote and became the biggest party in that parliament. In 1996 it formed a coalition government with the True Path Party, of Ms. Çiller, the first woman prime minister in Turkey. Erbakan, the party leader, became the Prime Minister.

3. In the journal of radical feminists *Pazartesi*, articles and interviews often criticized the closeness between mainstream feminists and the state.

4. Two examples of such associations are Çağdaş Yaşamı Destekleme Derneği and Atatürkçü Düşünce Derneği.

5. Mr. Baş, member of parliament from Welfare Party, initiated this law proposal as reported in *Milliyet Daily* (1996a, 1; 1996b, 14).

6. The National Security Council is a constitutional body headed by the president that includes the prime minister, several ministers, the chief of staff and chief commanders of the army, navy and air force. The National Security Council meets regularly monthly and discusses the issues pertaining to the security of the country. Their decisions are advisory in nature to the government, but usually are taken seriously because they indicate the attitudes of the military.

REFERENCES

Abadan, Nermin. 1952. "Kadınlık ve Demokrasi" [Womanhood and Democracy], Dünya 2. 27. 03.
Acar, Feride. 1990. "Türkiye'de İslamcı Hareket ve Kadın" [The Islamist Movement and Woman in Turkey] In 1980'ler Türkiye'sinde Kadın Bakış Açısından Kadınlar [The Women in Turkey during the 1980's from the Woman's Perspective], ed. Şirin Tekeli. İstanbul: İletişim Yayınları. 79–100.
Acar, Feride. 1999. "Impact of CEDAW in Turkey," Working Paper presented to the CEDAW Impact Seminar, New York, 24 January.
Arat, Yeşim. 1990. "Islamic Fundamentalism and Women in Turkey," The Muslim World. 80: 7 January.
Country Report. 1994. The Status of Women in Turkey. The Turkish National Report to the Fourth World Conference on Women. May.
Country Report. 1995. Country Report of Turkey to the Committee On the Elimination of Discrimination Against Women (CEDAW). Turkish Republic Prime Ministry Directorate General on the Status and Problems of Women.
Çulpan, Oya. 1977. Türkiye'de İş ve Meslek Alanında Kadının Durumu ve Üniversite Öğrencilerinin Mesleklerle İlgili Tutumları. [The Condition of Woman in Work and Occupational Sphere in Turkey and The Attitude of Students Towards The Occupations] Amme İdaresi Dergisi. 10:4: 104–120.
Cumhuriyet. 1996a. March 31.
———.1996b. July 17.
———.1996c. November 24.
———.1996d. December 15.
———.1996e. December 21.
———.1997a. January 23.
———.1997b. January 27.
———.1997c. February 23.
_____.1997d. May 18.
Günaydın. 1996. July 12.
Hürriyet. 1996a. May 31.
———.1996b. November 24.
———.1997a. January 16.
———.1997b. May 18.
İnan, Afet. 1968. "Türk Kadın Haklarının Tanınmasının Kültür Devrimindeki Önemi." [The Importance of the Recognition of the Turkish Woman Rights in The Culture Revolution]. Halkevleri Dergisi. 2, 16/17: 25–7.

Kandiyoti, Deniz. 1974. "Social Change and Social Stratification in a Turkish Village." *Journal of Peasant Studies*. 2. 206–219.
Melodi. 1996. December 25.
Milliyet Daily. 1996a. April 1.
———. 1996b. April 14.
———. 1996c. September 5.
———. 1996d. September 14.
———. 1997. May 18.
Öncü, Ayşe. 1979. "*Uzman Mesleklerde Türk Kadını*" [Turkish Woman in The Professional Occupations]. In Türk Toplumunda Kadın [The Woman in Turkish Society], ed. N. Abadan-Unat. Ankara: Sosyal Bilimler Derneği Yayını.
Özdalga, Elizabeth. 1997. "Womanhood, Dignity and Faith: Reflections on an Islamic Woman's Life Story." *European Journal of Women's Studies* 4: 473.
Özkaya, Günseli. 1985. *Tarih İçinde Kadın Hakları* [The Woman's Right in History]. Ankara:TBMM Yayınları.
Radikal. 1997a. January 16.
———.1997b. January 23.
Sabah. 1996. April 20.
———. 1997. May 18.
Sirman, Nükhet. 1989. "Feminism in Turkey: A Short History." *New Perspectives on Turkey*. 3, 1: 259–88.
Sönmez, Emel. 1975. "Kadın Hak ve Hürriyetlerinde Kemalizm," [Kemalism in Woman's Right and Freedom]. (Summary in English) *İstanbul Üniversitesi Atatürk Devrimleri Araştırma Enstitüsü Atatürk Devrimleri Milletlerarası Sempozyumu Bildirileri*, (Istanbul, held in December 10–14, 1973): 378–96.
Taşkıran, Tezer. 1975. "Türkiye'de Kadın Hakları Devrimi." [The Woman Rights Revolution in Turkey], (summary in English). *İstanbul Üniversitesi Atatürk Devrimleri Milletlerarası Sempozyumu Bildirileri*, (I. Istanbul, held in December 10–14, 1973): 409–27.
TBMM. 1998. *Kadın Statüsü ve Sorunlarını Araştırma Komisyonu Raporu* [The Commission Report of The Research of Woman's Status and Problems]. 1998. Ankara: TBMM Yayınları. 1–76.
Tekeli, Şirin. 1982. *Kadınlar ve Siyasal Toplumsal Hayat* [Women and Political, Social Life]. İstanbul: Bırıkım Yayınları.
Tekeli, Şirin ed. 1993. *1980'ler Türkiye'sinde Kadın Bakış Açısından Kadınlar* [The Women in Turkey during the 1980's from the Woman's Perspective]. Istanbul: İletişim Yayınları.
Türkiye. 1996a. September 16.
———. 1996b. September 17.
———. 1996c. November 24.
———. 1997. May 18.
Y.Yüzyıl. 1997a. May 18.
———.1997b. September 16.

CHAPTER 8

WOMEN'S STRATEGIES IN IRAN FROM THE 1979 REVOLUTION TO 1999

MEHRANGUIZ KAR[1]

Contemporary Iran is a society very much in flux. Of its over sixty million people, almost 70 percent are under the age of twenty-five. Most of these people were born and educated under the Islamic theocracy established in 1979. Those that remain in the older generations have lived through the British and Russian presence in Iran from the early 1900s. Many of them have memories of the Mossadegh's nationalistic uprising in 1951 that expelled the British, the 1953 coup aided by Britain and the United States to re-install the monarchy of the Shah, the revolution of 1979 that overthrew the Shah and the subsequent victory of Khomeini who installed a theocratic state, and the devastating eight year Iran-Iraq war of 1981–89. In an attempt to evaluate the current struggle for women's rights in Iran, this chapter will identify and describe the spectrum of opinion and some of the political strategies that the women of Iran are using today. Since 1979, women in Iran can be characterized most generally as conformist or non-conformist. The conformists support the Islamic state's policies toward women, while the non-conformists resist. The variance within and between these positions, as well as the evolutionary convergence of these groups with regard to certain issues, are topics of concern in this chapter.

The boundaries of the debate about women in Iran are difficult to draw, because the debate includes a wide range of traditional and religious beliefs, some of which include equality and some of which do not. Debate within the devoutly Muslim community continues concerning what the "true" Islamic position toward women should be. Meanwhile, many Islamist Iranians identify the equal human rights for women position with the imperialistic West. Until the 1953 coup that re-installed the Shah, the Iranian people perceived Britain and Russia as primarily responsible for the West's treatment of Iran as a colony. Because of the role of the United States in the 1953 coup, the Iranian people added the United States to their list of imperialist enemies. The coup's imposition of the autocratic monarchy of the Shah and the subsequent house arrest of Mossadegh, the leader of Iran's national movement, fuelled anger and resentment against the United States and the West, in general. Throughout the 1960s and 1970s, during the Vietnamese and Cambodian wars, Iranian intellectuals and the print media inside Iran maintained and consolidated these anti-western and anti-imperialist sentiments by expressing sympathy and support for resistance to the United States military invasion of Southeast Asia.

The 1979 Revolution, which toppled the Shah and eventually installed a religious Islamic state headed by Ayatollah Khomeini, mobilized these anti-western sentiments. The radical religiorevolutionary forces backing Khomeini campaigned vigorously to eliminate all western signs, symbols, and institutions. They soon managed to take control over all material and spiritual aspects of the society, monopolize the government, and banish all other forces from the most important and critical centers of power. The hostage crisis in Iran and the eight-year Iran-Iraq war (1981–89) reinforced anti-U.S. attitudes. During the Iran-Iraq war, the extremists declared the West as the real enemy, arguing that Iraq started the war under orders from the West to uproot the revolutionary Iranian Islamic system. They argued that the fight against the West, especially the United States, must continue on two fronts: (1) the Iran-Iraq front, and (2) the cultural front. Fighting on the cultural front meant eliminating all signs and symbols of western culture and western decadence. On the streets of Tehran, women and girls with any sort of western appearance became the first targets of this cultural campaign. A woman wearing a pair of sunglasses, for example, could provoke interrogation, arrest, persecution, and punishment by the vigilantes.

This environment put many highly educated professional Iranian women with cultural exposure to the West in the spotlight as the most visible symbols of western cultural imperialism. As the easiest targets of the anti-western campaign, these women faced a paradox. They had fought for the revolution against the dictatorship of the Shah. They cherished the revolution. Yet, this revolution was now persecuting them by regulating every aspect of their personal behavior. The educated, professional, and uncovered women began to protest the violation of their individual rights. They took to the streets and staged demonstrations against compulsory veiling, the nullification of the Family Protection Law,[2] the removal of women judges,[3] and the ruling that barred women from sitting as judges. These protesting women were the first signs of opposition against the revolutionary religious government. The new regime moved quickly to suppress the uprising before it could develop into an organized and sustainable opposition movement.

The protesting women never were unified, homogeneous, and organized. Throughout the Pahlavi dynasty (1925–79), most Iranian women covered themselves either with a short scarf or a long head-to-toe veil (chador). During the peak of the revolutionary fervor against the Shah, a number of unveiled women suddenly turned into supporters of those seeking to establish a religious state. They adopted the veil voluntarily as a statement of opposition to western imperialism. Once the revolution had occurred, many other women became supporters of the new regime and, at the instigation of the new conservative statesmen, staged rallies and demonstrations against the dissident women. The women acting in support of the state shared two common features. Most of them wore a black chador on top of dark robes, pants, stockings, and short veils (maqnaè), and they were passionate about being present in the public arena, a place where their families would never have allowed them to be during the Pahlavi era. Ironically, opposing the uncovered and educated women opened a new political space for some of the most traditional conformist women.

In contrast, the secular and dissident women found the overall social space for their own presence narrowing and becoming increasingly unbearable. Some of these women left Iran. Others retreated into their homes. Many secular women, however, either stayed in their jobs under difficult conditions or switched to new jobs during the "cleansing" process (purges).[4]

GROWING DISSENT AND DISILLUSIONMENT AMONG ISLAMIST WOMEN

Two decades after the revolution, the most striking development among women is the growing opposition among the traditional, conformist women to the violation of their rights. Emphasizing religious and revolutionary principles, these women have begun to object to government policies by raising questions about policies toward women. These questions usually relate to divorce, child custody, and alimony laws. Even the most traditional conformist women have begun to investigate and challenge the present order. Women in Iran still lack independent and effective organizations to bring pressure on the state, but during the Iraq-Iran war, some women's protest strategies met with success.

One example involved the guardianship of children whose fathers were killed in the war and are, thereby, known as war martyrs. Under Khomeini's regime, the martyr's father (swordside or paternal grandfather) became the guardian of the martyr's children and also received childcare payments from the Martyr Foundation (*Bonyad-e Shahid*). Faced with losing their children (and the payments), the martyrs' widows organized and protested this decree, especially in Khuzestan,[5] by frequent and often massive petitions to the Martyr Foundation. The authorities finally intervened and managed to obtain a permit from Khomeini to satisfy the martyrs' widows' requests. On July 28, 1985, the Majlis (Islamic parliament), passed a bill transferring the rights of guardianship and tutorship for the minor or retarded children of men killed in war to their mothers.[6] Seven years after the revolution then, this bill limited the automatic guardianship rights of the paternal grandfather. The strategic impact of this decree among Iranian women was that it reduced the opportunity for secular non-conformist women to join with traditional conformist women against the regime, because it removed a major source of common discontent. However, the political activity and success of the martyrs' wives who were predominantly conservative conformist women gradually encouraged other traditional conformist women to expand their discussions and questioning about women's rights. Here we will focus on the strategies adopted by various groups of religious women.

STRATEGIES OF RELIGIOUS WOMEN

The growing discontent with the Islamic state's gender policy has affected even the religious and traditional sectors of women, resulting in a split among the traditional thinkers over women's rights. A growing number of religious women have gradually adopted a critical and opposing view toward the conservative and traditional thinking about women's role. A group of religious women tied with the ruling conservative faction, however, has retained either a completely conformist and conservative position or has offered mild critique of the predominant gender policies. First, we will discuss the conservative women's views and strategies.

THE CONSERVATIVE RELIGIOUS WOMEN

Some of the women in the religious spectrum belong to the conservative camp, a number of whom are elite women holding high seats of political power. They have remained loyal to the traditional interpretations of religion, but also have realized that the present laws and regulations concerning women do not reflect the promising slogans of the revolution in the realm of the family, politics, and society. These conservative women avoid expressing any clearly opposing views that may go against the wishes of the men in the ruling conservative camp. Ordinary conservative religious women, through their contacts with the family courts, learn about the unfairness of the present laws. The demands and grievances of the ordinary religious women are occasionally covered in the national press, but the female elite, whose political power is based on the ruling traditional right wing, fails to respond to the satisfaction of these aggrieved constituents. To safeguard their power position, the conservative women in power do not go beyond some vague, rhetorical, and general statements about women's issues. As a result, the ordinary conservative religious women have been moving away from conservative politicians. Under the reform-oriented government of Mr. Khatami, the conservative Islamist women elite have still retained their cultural bases within a portion of the media (including some of the women's press), within legislative and judiciary ministries, and within the Cultural and Social Council of Women tied to the High Council of Cultural Revolution.[7]

Conservative women do not directly object to items such as article #1133 of Iran's civil law, which holds that a husband can divorce his wife whenever he likes. Neither do they directly object to article #1169, which holds that a mother can keep custody of her male child only until the age of two, and her female child only to the age of seven. Thereafter, the father assumes custody. As the following cases demonstrate, however, they have chosen a special strategy to pass some laws and regulations that have modified the severity and impact of both of these articles.

The amendment of the divorce law sanctioned in 1992, for instance, states that if a man decides to divorce his wife without her being guilty of any misdeed, he must pay not only her dowry (mahr) and a hundred days' expenses, but also her wages for what she has done (housework and childcare) during their married life according to the court's judgment. The substance of article #1133 of the civil law remains intact with regard to the inequality of men and women. The fair equivalent remuneration amendment, however, makes the outcome less harsh for women.

Similarly, with the amendment of article #1173 of the civil law, the custody rights of fathers have been slightly curtailed. In cases where a father is addicted or has a reputation for corruption, is suffering from mental illness, or abuses his child beyond the defined limits, the father can lose custody of his child. Again, the unequal substance of article #1169 of the civil law regarding custody rights remains with the exception of certain special circumstances. Furthermore, confirming a father's incompetence remains very difficult.

The conformist conservative women believe that articles #1133 and #1169 of the civil law are divinely inspired, fixed, and unobjectionable. Occasionally, this group of women will undertake some projects sanctioned by right-wing traditionalists such as the chastity project, which was passed in 1997. This law emphasized the necessity of rigorous enforcement in dealing with incompletely covered (*bad hijab*) women for the purpose of anticolonialist campaigns. (Western dress for women is associated with colonization by the West.) The incessant struggle of these right-wing women resulted in two laws that were sanctioned by the Majlis in 1998. One of these involved adding a clause and a note to article #6 of the fourth chapter of the press law. This clause states that using either men or women in pictures and texts in such a way as to belittle or insult women, advertising illegal luxuries, defending women's rights illegitimately, or raising subjects that will create dissention between men and women is to be prohibited.[8] Violation of this clause is subject to punishments articulated in article #698 of the Islamic penal law.[9] Cases of repeated violation are subject to even harsher punishment and the revocation of the license to publish. Because of the ambiguity of this law, enforcers can interpret and define violations at will. They can prevent the publication of women's pictures even with complete Islamic cover, and prohibit any objections to discriminatory laws. Furthermore, they can punish anything they deem to be "violations."

The second legislative project of the conservative women resulted in a law passed in March 1998, which holds that male and female patients must be medically treated by individuals of the same sex and that men and women should use therapeutic centers at separate times. After some modification, this legislative measure passed the Majlis, but was vetoed by the Guardian Council.

Perhaps the best representative statement of the conservative women's point of view is the one stated in the preface of the *Zan-e Ruz* (*Today's Woman*) weekly issue of January 10, 1998. *Zan-e Ruz* declares that the principles published in this preface are drawn from the text of a lecture given by the supreme Leader, Ayatollah Khamenei, on the occasion of Woman's Day in 1997. Here are the principles:

1. The spiritual, mental, and scientific rank of Fatima Zahra (daughter of Prophet) should be regarded as equal to that of prophets and saints.
2. The women of our nation have found their way through learning from the life of Fatima.
3. It is necessary to do cultural work about the woman question and women's rights and eliminate women's oppression.

4. The purpose of the vindication of women's rights is not to generate animosity, separation, and rivalry between women and men, but it is for women to reach their perfect selves.

5. The slogan of women's freedom is not a proper one for the women's campaign, because this kind of freedom implies freedom from the family restrictions and boundaries and giving up marriage and childraising.

6. If we defend women for the purpose of not falling behind Westerners and for preventing them from holding bad or negative views of us, we will go wrong.

7. The gender of a woman or a man does not matter in Islam. What matters is the advancement of humane morality, expression of talents, and also duties of each individual for which the woman and man's nature ought to be understood.

8. The issue in Islam is not equality but equilibrium, which is the observation of pure justice among human beings, including females and males.

9. Islam would determine the method and strategy of our fight for women's rights. Muslims would also like and accept any reasonable and prudent method but not an imitation of the West.

10. Up to very recent times, a woman in the West used to be seen as the second sex or the secondary Creation, while this has not been the case in our country. In the old western culture, man was considered the master of woman.

11. Based on the western attitudes toward women, they were not allowed to own property. It was in this milieu and to counter this extremist view in the West that the feminist movement emerged as a hasty, illogical, and foolish reaction that disregarded the innate nature of woman and man and ignored the divine traditions.

12. In the West, women's freedom has resulted in widespread corruption and license that has damaged women's lives and the institution of the family.

13. The vindication of women's rights in our society must be based on Islam and Islamic goals.

14. In our society, women are suffering from oppression and barriers imposed on them, barriers in terms of opportunities in the fields of science and education, civil and moral development, and expression of talents. These barriers must be overcome.

15. If the Islamic society can succeed in training women in an Islamic pattern by using Zahra and Zeinab (granddaughter of Prophet) as role models, they will become great women, awesome women,

women who can impress the world and history. It is then that women will have achieved their truly lofty position.

16. If a family happened to raise their daughter in this way, this girl would be a great human being. We have such women in Iran and in our own era.

17. The intention of Islam is to defend women's rights in a way that frees women from oppression and prevents men from seeing themselves as women's masters.

18. The true Islam has designated the rights of women and men in the family in a strictly balanced and equitable way. We are not defending what is wrong and wrongly attributed to Islam.

19. The most important thing a human being needs is peace and tranquility that can be provided to both women and men within the family.

20. It is within the milieu of the natural family that the divine nature of woman and men can create love and affection between them.

21. The problem for a woman is not that she does not have a big and booming career. The main issue for her is a sense of peace and security, an opportunity for developing her talents and being free from oppressive society and family, whether in the father's or the husband's home.

22. In defending women, one should not be distracted by useless discussions and debates.

23. Women should be defended legally and morally especially within the family. Legal defense is done by changing and reforming the laws. Moral defense is done by confronting individuals who do not understand the law properly and who keep viewing and treating a housewife as an oppressed servant of the husband.

24. In any action or movement in defense of women, the main principle to be preserved is the chastity of women. It is the chastity of a woman that brings her character and honor.

25. Parents should allow their daughters to study, to become familiar with religious studies and humanities, and to strengthen their brains.

26. Society should harshly confront individuals who believe that assaulting women is their prerogative.

27. Any state that manages to educate women on the basis of Islamic principles and knowledge will achieve double progress and a high degree of development.

28. Any field touched by responsible women will progress in manifold ways.

The conservative and conformist Islamist women's strategy as indicated in the above principles is very vague and rhetorical. It appears to be benevolent in its attempt to woo women. Within the conservative camp dissention also occurs. For instance, the weekly *Zan-e Ruz*, which is a cultural forum for these women, has occasionally criticized the lack of women's rights more explicitly and in stronger language. *Zan-e Ruz* sometimes publishes the views and interpretations of more moderate clerics such as Ayatollah Bojnurdi.

One should not conclude that the conservative Islamist women always take up positions on a specific side of a defined border in present-day Iran. One occasionally may find some bright and encouragingly progressive points in conservative women's publications, but the barrage of conservative slogans that usually accompany them diminishes their significance. In any case, the conservative Islamist women are not homogenous and many will inevitably have to choose the path of transformation in the foundations and interpretations of religion. While insisting on the primacy of women's domestic roles as mothers and housewives, the High Council of Cultural Revolution (HCCR) has passed certain bills to allow women to enter the labor market. The HCCR's message is that women can work outside the home as long as they do not neglect their domestic roles. The content of the bill passed on August 11, 1992 in the 288th session of the HCCR, for instance, is reflective of the contradictory nature of the gender strategy of the ruling conservative Islamist faction and its women. In short, the gender critique of many of these religious women does not oppose the principles of the Islamic Republic.

THE REFORMIST RELIGIOUS WOMEN

A main argument of the Islamic feminists[10] is that women should have equal but not the same rights that men have. Men and women are not the same, their rights and duties are not the same. The Islamic system, however, should reflect the fact that men and women are equal in creation and in human virtues and they would be considered equivalent beings with regard to their perception and understanding. Both men and women carry equal burdens of responsibility on their shoulders and enjoy equal blessings. An articulate example of such a position is Ms. Azem Taleqani. She was a member of the Majlis (the Islamic parliament) at the beginning of the revolution and soon realized the need to acquire appropriate methods to reform the situation. She founded the Islamic Institute of Iranian Women and continues to serve as its director. Through a periodical, *Payam-e Hajar* (Hajar's Message), she has promoted the idea that religious interpretation of texts (*ijtihad*) can be the basis for revising the present laws and providing for Muslim women's everyday needs. In response to a question about the implementation of the Nairobi's Forward Looking Strategies in regard to women in Iran, Ms. Taleqani replied: "[O]f course a movement has taken place in Iran and women are gradually waking up to the facts. They should try to gain equal rights, but of course, not the same rights with men. Equal opportunities must be available for women to use whenever they wish so" (*Payem-e Emrooz* 1996).

Generally one of the major theological sources from which many Islamic feminists draw their arguments is the writings of Ayatollah Morteza Motahhari, who was murdered in the earliest years of the revolution. He believed that:

> In Islamic doctrine, man and woman are both human beings and enjoy equal rights, but what matters to Islam is that since man and woman are not by creation or nature the same, they also vary in regard to some rights, duties, and punishments. Today the western world is trying to make men and women equal with regard to all rules, regulations, rights and duties disregarding the innate and natural differences between them. Therefore, the dispute in our country between those who support Islamic rights on the one hand and those who are for western systems on the other, is over the uniformity and similarity of the social roles of women and men rather than women's rights. And the phrase "equal rights" is a deceitful term which has been chosen to suggest the parity of roles in society. (Motahhari 1975, 15)

While many Islamic feminists believe in different social roles for men and women and try to meet current needs through reinterpretation of the scriptures, they oppose political repression and criticize those who restrict freedom of speech and political parties. They insist on women's political participation and the presence of women in the state's high political positions. Islamic feminists even argue that women as well as men can attain the degree of *ijtihad* (authority to interpret the Quran), issue decrees, and become *mojtahid* (interpreter). Islamic feminists have been under attack by the traditionalists and conservative clerics whose Islam is rigid and sexist. For instance, in most of its issues, *Payam-e Hajar* is compelled to respond to such attacks arguing that:

> Ninety percent of our women are living their religious beliefs and would on no account turn laic, but some of their beliefs are rooted in superstition and outmoded traditional religious teachings. Unintentionally, they have mixed their religious lives with superstition. (*Payem-e Hajar* 1998)

Those who are concerned about the emergence of a feminist movement in Iran should revise all laws that oppress people, particularly those that oppress women and children. . . . Due to our relationship with the world systems, we have accepted revisions and transformations in our economic laws, politics and societal affairs. Why cannot we accept revision of laws in regard to women? . . . To prevent the western feminist movement from replacing Islamic laws, it is necessary to reinterpret and revise the existing laws. This will definitely please God and God's messengers. Of course this reinterpretation should never be done arbitrarily without preservation of the principles. (*Payem-e Hajar* 1997b)

In general, Islamic feminists believe that by reinterpreting Islamic jurisprudence, changes can occur in accord with the times and new realities without abandoning Islamic principles. (*Payem-e Hajar* 1997a)

Besides *Payam-e Hajar,* the journal *Farzaneh,* devoted specifically to women's studies and research, also makes the same suggestion, insisting that Islam can actively and dynamically stand up before secular value systems that claim to defend women's rights. In a recent issue, *Farzaneh* defends women's studies programs:

In the last couple of decades, the academic centers of the world have been witnessing the appearance and widespread growth of a new and important interdisciplinary field by the name of "women's studies." . . . This field is based on the idea that women have suffered serious human, familial, and social deprivations due to centuries of negative views and oppressive treatment of women. Women's Studies brings together experts in various fields to seek solutions to women's problems and to bring a gendered view to governmental policies. In his speech and practice Imam Khomeini skillfully and intelligently has presented the principles of women's rights and the improvement of women's situation as an essential strategy of the Islamic revolution and one of the highways of return to the genuine Mohammedan Islam. This attention along with Imam Khomeini's farsightedness has caused the Islamic Revolution to advance Islam's legal and value systems for women over the secular and laic value systems. Without adequate academic and practical support, this movement cannot be sustained. (*Farzaneh* 1996)

Ms. Faezeh Hashemi, daughter of Hashemi Rafsanjani (Iran's former president and present head of the Expediency Council) has been trying for years to obtain more sports facilities for women. Ms. Hashemi, currently a representative in the Majlis, always opposes the traditional rightist conservative women and men who try to pass bills against the improvement of women's rights. Ms. Hashemi supervises the daily newspaper *Zan* (*Woman*). Each issue of *Zan* devotes one page to discussion of Muslim women's rights.

Her sister, Ms. Fatemeh Hashemi, founded the Association of Women's Global Alliance (AWGA). Organized by AWGA, a group of lawyers and religious researchers hold periodic meetings to discuss and interpret Islamic law with regard to women's rights in civil law. They publish these suggested reinterpretations and revisions supportive of women's rights through the national media. The AWGA has presented its suggestions for revision of the civil law to the presidential office on three occasions, March 2, 1996, May 10, 1997, and June 1, 1997. These suggestions contained an amendment of civil law concerning age of puberty, which currently is nine years for girls and fifteen years for boys. They also demanded abrogation of civil law article #1042, according to which the marriage of a virgin daughter of any age depends on the permission of her father or paternal grandfather. Instead, the AWGA suggested that puberty age for both boys and girls be decided by physical changes and that the age of adulthood be eighteen years for both sexes. The conservative fundamentalists have objected to these demanded reforms arguing that:

> Removal of the specific age condition for the puberty of girls and boys will bring about a lot of social troubles. For example, if girls who do not believe in *hijab* (veil) appeared in public without *hijab* and even in a provocative fashion, no one will have the right to regulate their misdeeds because they can claim that they are minors, hence not breaking any laws. Thus the barriers against contact between boys and girls will disappear. Boys over fifteen could also claim themselves as minors. (*Sobh* 1997, 44–45)[11]

Another publication known as Islamic feminist is the monthly magazine, *Zanan* (*Women*). It was founded in 1991 by a group of Islamist women and men who have over time developed a viewpoint known as religious intellectualism, a view that has come into conflict with the conservative clerics. *Zanan* speaks out frankly and clearly about women's concerns and daily problems, while analyzing their causes. Drawing on contributions from the modern religious intellectuals and even secular women writers from Iran and other countries, including the West, *Zanan* argues for the unconditional elimination of discrimination against women. From *Zanan*'s point of view, reform in one article or change in one or two legal codes without revision in the entire legal system cannot solve the problem. The theoretical framework of Zanan is based on the scriptural (Quranic) decrees that hold that God created woman and man equally and gave equal value and virtue to both. *Zanan* also holds that the main purpose of religious decrees is to implement justice. *Zanan's* position emphasizes that every verse of the Quran is not necessarily applicable to all times and circumstances. Some of the verses or injunctions are reflective of customs and norms of the people at the time and location of their revelations. Therefore, they should be re-evaluated and adjusted to the modern times. *Zanan* insists on temporality or secularity (*asri shodan*) of religion.

Since Zanan has acknowledged the diversity of Iranian society and presented the views of both religious intellectuals and secular (*laic*) writers, it has managed to communicate with both secular and religious women. Religious women have been showing increasing interest in what modernized religious women write. The writings of *laic* women about women's rights are of less interest because they sometimes disregard, ridicule, or harshly disparage Islam and the 1979 revolution altogether. The most significant and unique accomplishment of *Zanan* is that it has been able to bring modernized religious women together with secular non-conformist women. The following extract from an article in *Zanan* related to the Beijing conference illustrates this inclusive strategy. In its report on the Fourth United Nations World Congress on Women in Beijing, *Zanan* deplored the fact that

> Iran's delegation had failed to take a progressive position and instead allied Iran with retrogressive states such as Sudan, Honduras, Guatemala, and the Vatican, underscoring, more than ever before, Iran in a position of being supportive of sexual apartheid. . . . Even Ms. Shahla Habibi who headed Iran's official delegation to Beijing admitted that during the last ten years, Iran's government ignored the substance of the United Nation's Third World Conference on Women in Nairobi and made very few preparations for the Fourth one in Beijing. The Iranian women's delegation to Beijing (selected by the government) did not contribute positively but rather promoted the Iranian government's official position and repeated propagandistic cliches.[12]

Another example of courageous reporting by *Zanan* is on the issue of love. In a report titled "This is the Forbidden Love Street," the magazine interviewed young girls and boys and criticized the policy of repression against love, affirming the creative and normal feelings associated with love rather than shame and sin (*Zanan* 1998, 4–10). In another issue, *Zanan* questioned why Iranian women wear black (the veil), concluding that wearing black is not a religious act nor a religious requirement but a reaction to the fearful atmosphere that dominated women's daily lives for too many years under the Islamic Republic.

Zanan has continuously been evolving toward modernity and secularity. The growing division of state powers into supporters of the right-wing traditional view of Islam and supporters of the leftist modern view of Islam has pushed many Islamic feminists, including *Zanan* toward the modern left movement.[13] They believe the modern Islamic left is more capable of responding to women's present needs. It was under such an assumption that during the May 1997 presidential elections, the majority of women voted for the reform-minded Khatami.

A PERSONAL STORY

As a way of explaining the changing roles of different kinds of women in Iran, I will describe my background as a secular non-conformist Iranian woman and try to explain how I have become attached to religious intellectuals and the modernization of traditional revolutionary women.

I was born in 1944 into a middle-class family in the city of Ahwaz, which is the center of the oil-rich Khuzestan province in the south of Iran. I am the third child of the family. My family members, father, mother, grandmother, and grandfather, were faithful Muslims who did not impose their views on others, not even their children. My mother wore a chador all her life, but was infinitely curious about the West and its achievements. Since the British were active in the South because of the oil companies, the children of my generation were impressed by the manifestations of western culture. Both of my parents were eager to see me (the sole daughter in the family) continue my studies and put no value on training that prepared women only for a traditional marriage.

My father, an illiterate man, wanted me to be different and distinct among others. He did not do anything in this regard, but left my mother completely free to shape my education and training. My two older brothers became active as cultured intellectuals when they reached adulthood. At eighteen, my eldest brother became recognized as a talented poet. He became involved in the literary movement founded by the great Iranian poet, Nima Yushij, and left Ahwaz for Tehran. This enabled the rest of the family to visit Tehran every summer. Being in Tehran (the capital city) and having contact with the political and cultural events of the city impressed me during my childhood and adolescence. After graduating from high school, I took the national entrance exams for Tehran University. There I studied law and political science. At the university, I developed clearer lines of thinking for myself. Thereafter, I married a journalist, who, unlike most Iranian men, wanted his wife to be prominent. My first employment was with the Social Security administration of the government.

At the same time, I began to write articles about different social issues, especially those concerning women.

During the 1969–79 period, I considered myself a reformist. I was not a revolutionary and had no connections or affiliations with any political group or party. I confined myself to broadcasting my views in the national and even state media. The main focus of my writing concerned criticizing the existing situation, especially official corruption. The periodical *Ferdowsi* included one of my articles in every issue. This periodical, usually read by rebellious youth, was very important in the evolution of my thinking. I also worked for other print media such as *Kayhan* and the daily *Rastakhiz*. My writings prior to the 1979 revolution concerned advocating social reforms that would provide social justice. I never used the scriptures to justify my proposals nor did I propose a religious government. My picture, published with some of my articles, showed the face of a young woman with a very short haircut and a completely western appearance. During the last years of the Shah's reign, I was consulted by the Iranian Women's Organization (IWO) about women's rights and then recruited to a program called Learning the Law in Easy Language. The IWO was immediately abolished after the revolution because its leader was the Shah's twin sister.

After the 1979 revolution, I—along with many other famous individuals—was banned from the national press. During the years immediately after the revolution, the advocates of religious government invaded the national press. Soon the religious fundamentalists monopolized all the media. Their initial aim was to return to the living styles of fourteenth-century Arabia. At the beginning of the revolution, these revolutionaries scorned reformists like me. Prior to the revolution, I had obtained a license to be an attorney at the Ministry of Justice. During the first years of the revolution, however, the atmosphere was so anti-attorney and anti-feminist that I made no use of that license and remained homebound. I busied myself by writing personal memoirs and stories not yet publishable in Iran. I hope one day I will be able to publish my writings of those years of deprivation under the title of *Rebel* or *Remember Me.*

In the first decade after the revolution, with a friend, Shahla Lahiji, I wrote a book on the history of Iranian women entitled *Recognition of Iranian Women's Identity.* Up to the end of the Iran-Iraq war in 1989, the political conditions did not allow me to write in the national press. After the war, new periodicals gradually emerged, soon becoming a cultural tribune in opposition to the ruling conservatives. Some of my articles, mostly my travel reports to deprived areas of Iran, were published in these periodicals. I was trying to write about my opinions and feelings under the pretext of reporting on a journey. My cultural activity continued in this vein. Meanwhile, to make a living for my family and myself, I managed to work independently at a law office. When foreign reporters were gradually allowed to visit Iran, I became someone to be interviewed. With great caution, I began to criticize the legal situation of women and children in Iran. Gradually, I was recognized and accepted by the Iranian society as a media commentator and pundit. This further motivated me toward sociopolitical activism. I have been a secular woman raised by a veiled yet western-oriented mother, a reformist before the revolution, and a non-conforming dissident after the revolution. After the revolution, in some of my writings I quoted from religious authorities and I made suggestions that involved reinterpreting religious decrees to develop new jurisprudence; however, these Islamic feminist strategies should be interpreted more as strategies rather than as my personal beliefs.

On February 2, 1992, some activist youngsters from the School of Law at the University of Beheshti invited me to present a paper at a seminar on women's social participation held at the Allameh Amini amphitheater in the central library of the university. When I arrived at the amphitheater, these fervid youth that had dared to organize such a seminar after the revolution, and who also dared to let me, a non-conformist dissident not acceptable by the governmental extremists, present my article, met me at the door. They welcomed me and cautioned that since this was the first time that the injustice of Iran's Islamic penal law was being questioned, I should read my paper without emotion or excitement. When I presented my article, I read it quickly and distributed copies to other seminar participants. I then sat down. The next speaker was the head of the seminar and wearing a chador. She gave a speech directly opposing my position. She began with the oft-repeated phrase of "a woman is a woman and a man is a man," which reflects the conservatives' position. She regretted my opposition to aspects of Islamic penal law such as girls' puberty age (nine lunar years), woman's "blood price," which is half of that of a man's, and the procedures that certify the confirmation of a crime (a woman's testimony is inadmissible in some cases and in others, the testimony of two women equals that of one man). She then warned us that the cultural and political spheres of the Islamic Republic are no place to present views that are infected by western ideas. Her position was that the roles of men and women are different. The laws governing the rights of men and women are therefore fixed and immutable and are religiously grounded. She also meant to make those impassioned young organizers of the seminar understand that a woman lawyer like me professing equal rights for men and women should not be allowed to penetrate the cultural jurisdiction of the Islamic Republic. When I left the meeting, I was thinking to myself, "Why is it that women take positions against themselves? Why do those of us who live, work, and contribute to this country, but do not agree with the ruling political and religious regime, have no place in this society? How can anyone believe that a nation of over sixty million people all think the same way and have no opposition to or disagreement with the government's way of thinking?"

The next day, the same four excited youths met me as I entered the hall to attend the second day of the seminar. They apologized for the criticism made against my presentation the previous day and said that we should try to bridle the fanatic, exclusionary, and dangerous mentality of my critics. They also told me that the editor of *Zanan* monthly had asked for a copy of my article and wanted to publish it. I was sure that the article would not be deemed publishable and would be subject to censorship.

A week later, however, *Zanan*'s editor, Shala Sherkat, called my office and asked me to meet her. When I entered *Zanan*'s office, I was not impressed. Three women were crammed into a very small, dull room in a building, all other rooms of which were occupied by men running the *Kiyan* periodical.[14] Only several small flowerpots sitting in the window brightened the room. The women themselves looked and dressed like state employee and conformist women. Soon I realized, however, that, despite their looks, these women were not engaged in supporting the dominant ideological position of the state. Already they had published nine issues of a magazine that had, for the first time, considered the subject of women's rights from the equality position, a position that was at odds with the philosophy and policies of the Islamic Republic.

Ms. Sherkat immediately announced that she intended to publish my article. I was flabbergasted. How could the Islamic Republic in 1992 allow my article to be published when all opposition groups were suppressed, all those who had criticized the Law of Retribution had either left the country or been imprisoned? Putting all these new incidents together, I suddenly realized that something unexpected was happening. It was becoming obvious to me that a split had begun to take place within the ideologues and cultural forces of the ruling system. A new force emerging from within had begun to challenge the status quo.

Soon a young cleric, Hujjat ol-Islam Seyyed Mohsen Saidzadeh, who had come all the way from Qum (a city known for its major seminaries) joined our meeting. Mr. Saidzadeh told me that I could make my article publishable by removing or amending some words and sentences that could prevent my being charged with blasphemy. Ms. Sherkat asked my permission to omit the introductory part, which argued that universal human rights should be the basis of legislation. I consented to both because I realized that this was a historic occasion bringing together people like me with women from a very different and more conformist segment of the society. This collaboration I knew would benefit women and the women's movement. The main ideas of my article, entitled "Women's Position in Iran's Penal Law," did get published in *Zanan*, second volume, number eleven for the two summer months of 1993.

Zanan has now published its forty-sixth issue and since its issue number eleven, I have had an article published in almost every issue about the legal aspects of the necessity of equal rights between women and men. The situation continues to be remarkable and unique because two types of women initially in opposition to each other have now converged: one coming from a religious, traditional, and conformist background and the other from a laic, modern, and non-conformist background. Both have experienced enormous changes, suffered many sorrows and hardships, revised their prejudices repeatedly, and are now working together and expressing their views in one monthly magazine for women. It seems that Iranian women academics living outside Iran, while closely following Iran's cultural and political developments, have been better able to realize the significance of this converging trend and its positive implications for the advancement of reform and the women's movement in Iran than those of us living in Iran.

In conclusion, the strategy of those among the religious and revolutionary women who have come to agree with the equality position and have become modern in their approach is the most effective strategy for changing Iran's cultural, mental and legal orientations. This strategy can be effective because it addresses all Iranian women, whether they are for the religious state or for a secular state. If it proves successful, the generations raised by these cooperating religious and non-sectarian women will be able to dismiss religious superstitions and patriarchal traditions that continually depict women as subordinate and obedient. To understand the importance of stopping the abuse of religion against women, I will present excerpts of an article by the cleric Hujjat ol-Islam Saidzadeh, published in the popular daily *Jameèh* (1998, 7). He criticizes the religious sayings and traditions that rationalize discrimination against women. Following the publication of this article, the ruling conservatives detained its author. Saidzadeh wrote this article in objection to a proposal then under consideration in the Majlis that proposed to sex segregate the hospitals and health care centers. Hujjat ul-Islam Saidzadeh wrote:

> The texts attributed to religion are so versatile that they can justify both the most humane and the most inhumane actions of governments at once. The flexibility of the texts is such that all persons can relate themselves to religion and thereby acquire religious legitimacy. The Taliban, presently rul-

ing over Afghanistan, are drawing upon certain religious texts that are in our hands now, and if Iranians also choose to act based on these traditional texts, they should follow the same route as the Taliban have, and some in Iran have actually done so. One example is the story of some fanatics in Iran who have tried to prevent women from biking which is in the same tradition as that of Taliban's prevention of women from horse riding.

Many of the texts and narratives related to religion currently used in Iran's seminaries contain the same ideology and viewpoints that the Taliban are practicing. Violence and hatred toward women is the distinct feature of these texts as they declare:

1. Women do not have the right to go public and be present in the public arena.
2. Women must stay at home.
3. If women have to leave the house, they should pass by the walls and the sides of the sidewalks quickly.
4. Nobody should see women's faces.
5. Nobody should hear women's voices. If women have to speak, they should not utter more than five words.
6. Women should not go out alone even to public bathhouses.
7. Men should not look at women and if men's eyes catch their sight for a second time, women should hide their faces.
8. Men do not have the right to talk to women or greet them, or invite them for a meal or drink.
9. Women are not allowed to travel.
10. Women are not allowed to ride horses.
11. Women are not allowed to attend a funeral.
12. Women are exempted from presence at mass prayers.
13. Women must whine and cry for their dead.
14. Women are creations of the same rank as horses and houses.
15. Women should be battered.
16. If women die from the kicks and blows of their husbands, their husbands will not be punished.
17. The majority of those who will go to the hell are women.

Each one of the above commands is derived from not only just one recorded narrative, but hundreds of them! . . . With apologies to all my countrywomen and to any noble human being who is reading this article and with apologies before the Islam's sacred legislator, I should say that all this has been done under the name of Islam. . . . These are but a few of the sayings and narratives that have been used as the bases of the law by

fundamentalists. If the law is equivalent to such sayings, decrees, and interpretations presented in these texts, then the law can have different and
even opposite meanings. Everyone can offer his own interpretations and
find acceptable documents and sources to support that interpretation.
Fundamentalism, namely returning to the existing principles and texts,
can never stop. Fundamentalists are basically against people's accepted
and practical humane views. Consequently, it is fitting to criticize the
basic assumptions of their reasoning.[15]

STRATEGIES OF SECULAR AND NON-CONFORMIST WOMEN

The secular and non-conformist spectrum of opinion has never relin-
quished its demand for women's equal human rights. The secular women
who stayed in Iran after the revolution have experienced many hardships,
including war and revolutionary crises. Through dealing with such hardships and challenges, however, secular women have developed remarkable survival skills and effective strategies. They have evolved into
enduring and influential individuals, many of whom have composed the
expert and professional component of the current government. Through
their daily struggles with crises, these women learned that they could not
begin their fight against the ruling theocracy head-on with openly feminist slogans and calls for equal rights. Those who attempted such an open
confrontation incurred a variety of threats and punishments such as slan-
ders and insults at the work place, layoffs, assault and violence, heresy,
and imprisonment.

The non-conformist women who initially expressed objection against
the mandatory veil (hijab), the nullification of the Family Protection Law,
and the removal of women judges were subsequently silenced for several
years. During these years of silence and self-restraint, secular women persisted in preserving their public presence by employing a variety of forms of
resistance. These included occupational and professional activities whenever possible and not complying completely with the strict dress code.

The new generation, daughters of these secular women, are raised not
to bend to the regime's restrictions against their individual freedom. After
the eight-year Iran-Iraq war, some of these women broke their silence and
gradually engaged in a critical dialogue with the ruling traditionalists and
extremist Islamists. Some of them have actively campaigned for women's
rights by publishing poetry, novels, short stories, and articles as a cultural
project. In spite of censorship, their output during the entire postwar period (1989-present) has been considerable. For example, the poem, *Neck-
lace*, by Ms. Simin Behbahani, is a brilliant example of a position

[countercultural positioning against war and mandatory veil—Ed.] by a
secular non-conformist woman:

> Anxious, agitated, sad,
> her face uncovered, her head unveiled,
> not afraid of arrest or policeman,
> oblivious to the order, "Cover! Conceal!"
> Her eyes two grapes plucked from their cluster,
> squeezed by the times to fill a hundred barrels with blood,
> mad, really mad, a stranger to herself and others,
> oblivious to the world, beyond being awakened even by the deluge,
> a particle of dust adrift in the wind, without purpose or
>   destination,
> lost, speechless, bewildered, a corpse without a grave,
> carrying around her neck a necklace of curses and tears,
> a pair of boots tied together belonging to a dead soldier.
> I asked her: what does this mean?
> She smiled: my son, poor child, sitting on my shoulders,
> hasn't taken off his boots yet.[16]

The non-conformist secular women who remained in Iran after the revolution have engaged in educational, artistic, scientific, and academic activities creating a gifted force of lettered and capable women committed
to women's human rights. In recent years, a number of informal groups of
women have been meeting in home circles to study and talk about the position of women. Sometimes they publish and circulate small pamphlets
for consciousness-raising and advocating the improvement of women's
status. Children's rights, family planning, preservation of the environment, and human rights constitute major part of their activities. As experts or pundits, these women participate in all political, social, and legal
debates and discourses ongoing in present-day Iran. They are regular contributors to roundtables, journals, newspapers, and are often interviewed
by international media. Their challenging and effective presence in specific intellectual and women's periodicals have compelled the state and
other ideologues in power to respond.

The effectiveness of such strategies employed by secular women manifested itself during the sixth presidential elections on May 23, 1997. Here,
a limited and far from free election process left people with two choices: one
candidate (Nateq-Nuri) supported the status quo; the other (Khatami)
promised reform, civil society, and criticized extremist policies against
women. The secular non-conformist as well as reform-oriented religious
women, especially the youth, voted for Khatami. An outpouring of support
strong enough to win the election came from many non-conformists, who

had never taken part in previous elections. Thus, both secular and religious women (and men) voted for Khatami, expecting him to pursue more inclusive and democratic policies.

CONCLUSION

Iran currently is a theocratic state, one with an educated population and a vibrant intellectual life. Political parties are not allowed; however, a variety of political positions are articulated in various forums. This article is an attempt to describe some (not all) of the major positions taken by Iranian women in this environment. The traditional Islamist position toward women as compared with the liberal and secular belief in equal human rights for both men and women set the parameters of Iranian women's political positioning. Neither of these polar opposites is a static or well-defined position. Within Islamic thought, determining exactly what the true Islamic position toward women is a continuing source of controversy. Many traditional conservative religious clerics cite religious decrees to legitimate sexist practices toward women, practices that other religious clerics consider superstitions and not true to Islam. In contrast, some Iranians equate the equal human rights position with western cultural imperialism. Within this environment, Iranian women can be categorized roughly into three groups: the conservative religious and conformist (with regard to the Islamic state position); the reform-oriented religious non-conformist; and the reform-oriented secular non-conformist. None of these are homogeneous positions but describe general groupings in the society. Immediately after the Revolution in 1979, the conformist women did not oppose the state's policies against women's freedom of choice including the mandatory veil in public, and many of these women also were about being in public, a stance that traditional conservative practice did not support. During the Iran-Iraq war, these same conformist women took stands against specific practices related to the guardianship of children of war martyrs. More recently, the conformists have split into two camps: the first group, smaller in number, is constituted of the ones who have remained loyal to the patriarchal policies and practices of the ruling conservative Islamists. The second group, growing in number, is known as Islamic feminists, who emphasize religious reinterpretation, reform, dialogue, tolerance, free speech, and greater discussion about women's rights. The Islamic feminists believe that the solution to women's rights lies in the proper interpretation of Islamic texts and decrees. Some of these religious women have been campaigning to change the civil law concerning, for example, marriage, divorce, and puberty age, and adolescence for girls and boys. The more liberal section of the Islamic feminists has been advocating equal rights for women by allowing secular women to publish critical articles about the discrimination that exists in current Islamic law in their journals.

The non-conformist and secular women in Iran are those who stayed after the revolution but who disagree with the regime's stance with regard to women, who object to the dress codes for women, and to other aspects of the law and the society that oppress women. They do not believe that religious interpretation is the correct strategy for women. These women have faced persecution, arrest, interrogation, imprisonment, fear of arrest, and even torture for their resistance. During the immediate period after the 1979 revolution, many of the non-conformist women left Iran. Those who stayed either remained in their old occupations or were forced to find new jobs. During the second period after the Iran-Iraq war, some openings occurred in the society and non-conformist women were able to make contributions as teachers in the schools, in universities, in the press, and as a valuable educated cadre of experts and governmental bureaucrats. In the third stage of the late 1990s, the secular non-conformist women—as well as many religious women—took part in elections, have been active as legal staff in the Islamic courts, and have been publishing scientific articles and social commentaries that criticize Iran's conservative position with regard to women.

The split among the religious women in favor of reform and the convergence of elements of the religious and secular women in their thinking about an increasing number of issues with regard to women, especially in relation to divorce law, custody rights over children, and alimony is encouraging, as is the commitment of the Iranian society to debate, dialogue, and pluralism.

NOTES

1. This article was translated from Persian into English by Mahnaz Tohidi and edited by Nayereh Tohidi and Jane Bayes.
2. The Family Protection Law of 1967 and 1974 contained important points in favor of improving women's legal status in the family, particularly with regard to divorce. According to this law, men, for the first time in Iran's judiciary history, could not divorce their wives without the court's interference. That law also restricted paternal grandfather's custody rights in favor of the mother. That law was nullified right after the revolution.
3. A woman in Iran could become a ruling judge and even preside over the court since 1969. Right after the revolution, however, women judges were barred from their positions and were assigned to do office work in the Ministry of Justice.
4. "Cleansing" (paksazi) is a term used in Iran after the 1979 revolution in reference to the purges of the anti-revolutionary elements from the state

or private offices and enterprises. Purge of most women in this process was due to the issue of hijab and their objection against mandatory hijab.

5. The oil-rich province in southwest Iran neighboring Iraq.

6. According to the article 1181 of the civil law, just like the father, the paternal grandfather has mandatory custody right over the children and can intervene in their financial affairs as they wish.

7. The High Council on Cultural Revolution formed by Khomeini's order can issue commands and rules in regard to cultural policies. For instance, in 1997, this council voted against the ratification of the 1979 UN approved CEDAW (Convention on the Elimination of Discrimination Against Women) and declared it contradictory to Islamic ethics and sharià. One of the divisions of this council is the Cultural and Social Council of Women, constituted of thirteen members, that deals with policies concerning women.

8. This relates to the amendment to Article #1173 of the civil law passed by the Majlis in 1997 (1376/9/11).

9. According to Article #698 passed in 1996, any attempt to harm a person or cause anxiety or distress among the public or officials, either via writing letters of complaints or circulation of statements signed or unsigned, that contain false accusation or defamation will be punished by two months to two years of imprisonment or by up to seventy-four lashes.

10. The term "Islamic feminists" is used here in reference to reform-oriented Muslim women. The choice of this term has not been that of Muslim women in Iran, yet it is used here for the purpose of discussion and it is acknowledged that some (in both conservative and feminist camps) object to the use of this term.

11. Sobh is a monthly representing the traditional right-wing faction in power.

12. For the full report on World Women's Meeting in Beijing, see Zanan, 1995.

13. For further analysis on the views and contribution of the monthly Zanan, see Najmabadi (1998) and Tohidi (2001).

14. Kiyan is a monthly journal dedicated to the new religious intellectuals. It has been an important forum for the reform discourse and debates in Islamic theology and politics in opposition to theocracy (editor's note).

15. Following the publication of this article, Hujjat ol-Islam Saidzadeh was imprisoned for six months. After his release, he was defrocked and prohibited from publishing. For further discussion on Saidzadeh and current gender debates among Shià ulama (clerical scholars) in Iran, see Mir-Hosseini 1999 (editor's note).

16. Translated from the Persian by Milani and Safa (1999, 26).

REFERENCES

Farzaneh. 1996. 3: 8 (Winter 1375): 105–06.
Jameèh. 1998. (77th Khordad 1377/June): 7.

Milani, Farzaneh and Kaveh Safa, eds., and trans. 1999. *A Cup of Sin: Selected Poems/Simin Behbahani*. Syracus University Press.

Mir-Hosseini, Ziba. 1999. *Islam and Gender: The Religious Debate in Contemporary Iran*. Princeton: N.J.: Princeton University Press.

Motahhari, Morteza. 1975. *Nezam-e hoqug-e zan der Islam*. Tehran: Entesharat-e Sadra.

Najmabadi. Afsaneh. 1998. "Feminism in an Islamic Republic: Years of Hardship, Years of Growth." In *Islam, Gender and Social Change*, eds. Yvonne Yazbeck Haddad and John L. Esposito. New York: Oxford University Press.

Payam-e Emrooz. 1996. 15 (Dey 1375/January): 97.

Payam-e Hajar. 1997a. 18: 232 (Bahman ve Esfand 1376/March): 49.

———. 1997b. 18: 230 (Mehr ve Aban 1376/September and October): 3.

———. 1998. 18: 233 (Farvardin ve Ordibehesht 1377/April and May):3.

Sobh. 1997. 76 (Azer 1376/November).

Tohidi, Nayereh. 2001. "The International Connections of the Women's Movement in Iran." In *Iran and the Surrounding World, 1501–2001: Politics of Cultural Exchange*, eds. Nikki Keddie and Rudi Matthi. Seattle: Washington University Press.

Zanan. 1995. 4: 25 (Mordad-Shahrivar 1374/September): 2–8.

———. 1998. 7:43 (Khordad 1377/ June): 4–10.

CHAPTER 9

THE POLITICS OF IMPLEMENTING WOMEN'S RIGHTS IN BANGLADESH

Najma Chowdhury

INTRODUCTION

In Bangladesh, the forces for change in the status of women flow from many sources including the women's movement, grassroots non-governmental organizations (NGOs), and human rights organizations. The impetus for change also comes from sources both in and outside of the government that are concerned with economic development, from international organizations such as the United Nations, donor agencies or "development partners," and from global corporations that bring capital into the country in the form of direct foreign investment, investment that often creates jobs for women. The state faces a situation where its national development goals require that it subscribe to the development discourse that would, for example, seek to educate women, especially the girl child, and provide development inputs for the advancement of women who constitute half of the country's population. At the same time, the state has to exercise caution and not appear to be espousing "equalizing measures" directly promoting women's equality and women's rights too zealously because such measures might displease the conservative, fundamentalist, and patriarchal forces that shape the political contours of the society.

This chapter is a case study of how the United Nations Fourth World Conference on Women, an international event basically designed by forces outside of Bangladesh, has interacted with and influenced the political environment in Bangladesh with regard to the implementation of

women's rights. The first section outlines the constitutional rights and
status of women in Bangladesh and also briefly reviews the society and
culture. The second section describes the existing national machinery for
the advancement of women. The third section defines the Beijing Platform for Action and examines the pre- and post-Beijing actions taken by
the government. In comparison with other member states of the United
Nations, Bangladesh has been remarkably active in taking initiatives during the post-Beijing period. The concluding section explores and attempts
to explain the postures and positions of the government and the women's
movement to two basic issues in the Platform for Action—violence towards women and inheritance—each of which illustrate a different approach to the Women's Question.

SOCIETY, POLITICS, AND CULTURE:
DOMINANT TRENDS

CONSTITUTIONAL AND GOVERNMENTAL ISSUES

Bangladesh is not an Islamic theocratic state, but was created as part of Pakistan in 1947 to satisfy Muslim nationalism as separate and distinct from
"Hindu" India. The eastern part of Pakistan, which in 1971 became
Bangladesh, experienced political and economic domination and exploitation by the western part of Pakistan, which eroded the bond of one Pak-
istani nationhood based on religion. The next two decades witnessed a
surge of cultural nationalism emphasizing the distinctiveness of culture and
ethnicity, which offered the theoretical framework for domination and dissent. The Bangladesh state emerged in December 1971, claiming victory for
secularism in politics. Yet, Bangladesh is a Muslim state by virtue of having
an overwhelming proportion of citizens who are Muslim. Muslims constitute nearly 88 percent of the country's 120 million population, making
Bangladesh the third-largest Muslim populated country in the world. Islam
is the dominant religion of the country and sets the tone of the social and
cultural ethos. Muslim Personal Laws define the status of women in marriage, inheritance, divorce, and custody. In 1988, the Eighth Amendment
of the Constitution was adopted, which included the following article:

> The state religion of the Republic is Islam, but other religions may be prac-
> ticed in peace and harmony in the Republic. (Article 2A)[1]

Although Islam is officially the state religion, the Constitution of the
country stipulates in principle the equality of all citizens, while also recognizing the claims of disadvantaged communities, particularly women,

for special consideration. Article 10 under Fundamental Principles of State Policy enunciates:

> Steps shall be taken to ensure participation of women in all spheres of national life. (Article 10)

The Constitution also takes note of the vulnerability and exploitation of women as the following article illustrates:

> The State shall adopt effective measures to prevent prostitution and gambling. (Article 18:2)

The lofty ideas enumerated in the Fundamental Principles, for example, the promotion of education, rural development, and public health, if implemented are also likely to bring about greater benefits to women, as women are the largest deprived and dispossessed group of people in the community. Parenthetically, the Constitution, in defining the state's obligations, citizens' rights, and the system and processes of governance, retains patriarchal language.[2] Article 19(1), for example, in the official English version of the Constitution of the Peoples' Republic of Bangladesh, states:

> The State shall endeavour to ensure equality of opportunity to all citizens.

As a further elaboration, the Article continues:

> The State shall adopt effective measures to remove social and economic inequality between *man* and *man*. (Article 19:2) (italics added)

The fundamental rights granted by the Constitution contain the following provisions for gender equality.

- All citizens are equal before law and are entitled to equal protection of the law. (Article 27)
- The State shall not discriminate against any citizen on grounds only of religion, race, caste, sex, or place of birth. (Article 28:1)
- Women shall have equal rights with men in all spheres of the State and of public life. (Article 28: 2)
- No citizen shall on grounds only of religion, race, caste, sex, or place of birth be subjected to any disability. (Article 28: 3)
- Nothing in the article shall prevent the State from making special provision in favour of women or children or for the advancement of any backward sections of citizens. (Article 28: 4)

On the whole, the women's movement in Bangladesh often invokes these articles as giving constitutional coverage to affirmative actions to bring about gender equality. As the women's movement rightly points out, however, the Constitution does not guarantee "equality with men in all spheres of private life," that is, in the family. Women's groups and activists maintain that the seeds of inequity are rooted deeply in the many facets of family life and unless measures are taken to eliminate those, women's roles in public life will also remain circumscribed, notwithstanding constitutional guarantees. The patriarchal state, therefore, perpetuates the inequities enshrined in the personal laws. The Constitution grants the rights to freedom of association, assembly, and speech, regarded as basic to citizens' political rights, to every citizen. The Constitution does not make distinctions between men and women with regard to the holding of public office. The eligibility conditions for such offices are the same, but the realities of political operations are very different because of the patriarchal political parties, women's lack of access to avenues that lead to the political arena such as education, occupation, networking, and the negative social factors accruing from the age old custom of *purdah*. *Purdah* is the veiling and segregation of women. Although the custom of veiling is not observed as stringently as in earlier times, the inherent value system prevails, defining women's mobility, dress, and relationships. The dominant patriarchal ideology of subordination of women and their dependence on men, which dictates the custom of *purdah*, re-enforces the division of society into public and private spaces and women are consigned to secluded and stereotyped gender roles in the private, domestic arena. This narrowly defined social space leads to restricted democratic space for women.

The Constitution provides for quotas for women in Parliament. Under Article 65 of the Constitution, women are given dual representation in the 330 member national legislature. They are eligible to contest from three hundred constituencies while thirty are reserved for women. These thirty seats technically represent thirty constituencies (the country is divided into thirty electoral zones) and, as laid down by the Constitution, are elected by members of the three hundred directly elected seats. Past political history of the country shows that these thirty "reserved" seats for women are treated as a bonus for the political party obtaining a majority in the Parliament through a national election. The provision of reservation is due to lapse for the second time in the year 2001, when the term of the present legislature expires. The government contemplated retention of the existing system of reserved seats and accordingly submitted a constitutional amendment—the proposed Fourteenth Amendment Bill seeking to prolong the system of indirect election of the thirty reserved seats for women for another period of ten years (*Daily Star* 1999; *Prothom Alo* 1999).

THE POLITICAL ADVOCACY
OF THE WOMEN'S MOVEMENT

The women's movement has placed increasing the number of reserved seats and direct election high on the agenda and has offered various formulations. Women politicians seem to dislike any system that pits them against male contestants either at the stage of nomination as party candidate or at election at the constituency level, while the movement urges them to face the electorate at the grassroots as a way to political empowerment. Women politicians, with some exceptions, are also reluctant to go for direct election for "reserved" seats, that is, seats for which political parties will nominate only women candidates. These constituency areas would be larger than the constituency areas for the three hundred "general" seats, and therefore require greater efforts at grassroots mobilization and canvassing. These also are areas where women candidates would be competing against each other. Widespread and practically united support existed in the women's movement for an increase in the number of reserved seats for women from the existing thirty to sixty-four. This could have been accomplished by creating sixty-four territorial constituencies demarcated along the sixty-four districts (administrative units) of the country; and by having these seats filled by direct election.[3] The position within the movement changed somewhat over the ensuing months, basically responding to women politicians' apparent reluctance to face large constituencies at the grass roots. Two other formulations gained ground within the women's movement. One propagated increasing the number of reserved constituencies to one hundred, making the Parliament a house of four hundred members. The other formula asked for raising women's reserved seats to 150 with some increase also in the general seats, creating a much larger house, on the grounds of increased population. Tactically, this has exposed a fissure within the women's movement's advocacy role. The major political parties now suggest that the women's movement reach a consensus on number before initiating a political dialogue. The movement's varied and somewhat overblown demand with regard to number overlooked the reality that the decisions at party or state levels are shaped and influenced by entrenched patriarchal values. Those in the women's movement advocating a significantly larger share of political representation also failed to obtain support from party insiders to build the necessary strategic alliances with major political parties. A few women politicians have been vocal and consistent in their support for the women's movements demands, while only some left-leaning political parties have supported devoting a larger number of seats for women's direct representation. From the beginning, women's groups recognized that any scheme of reservation has to move hand-in-hand with a guarantee of a women's quota in the party nominations for general seats. Their demand had varied from 10 percent to 20 percent as a quota for nominations for women candidates at elections. The women's movement's political advocacy role has been successful in spotlighting public and media attention on the issue of women's political empowerment by claiming political representation through democratic means. But it has not been able to translate its demands into tangible political gains. The National Policy for the Advancement of Women announced by the prime minister on March 8, 1997 (Women's Day) is also committed to direct election of women to an increased number of reserved seats in the Parliament following the expiration of the existing system in the year 2001, thereby recognizing this as a strategy for women's political empowerment (Government of Bangladesh, Ministry of Women and Children Affairs 1997).[4] The fact that the government submitted the Fourteenth Constitution Amendment Bill proposing the retention of the earlier system underscores the fragile status of the policy document.

The trends in the national elections held in 1991 and 1996 reveal an increasing turnout of women voters. Perhaps NGO activities have been responsible for creating awareness among the masses to exercise their right to vote at the elections, especially among women. Several NGOs encouraged voters to make personal decisions on the basis of the qualifications of the candidates.[5] This trend of women's increased voting participation augurs well in terms of gaining enhanced political strength. If the present trend of women's voting continues, women are likely to emerge as a major factor in electoral politics. In future national elections, political parties may find it strategically expedient to spotlight women's issues in their election manifestos and will probably seek the women's vote, thereby shifting women's issues from marginal concerns to mainstream issues. The women's movement needs to direct its activities to this end, not only educating the voters but also educating the political parties for commitment to women's development and gender equality. In local elections, the reservation of three directly elected women members to more than 4,400 *union parishads* (Union Council—the lowest tier of local government institution) has the potential to bring a significant number of women to the arena of local level politics and local development processes.

THE INTERPLAY OF ISLAM WITH SOCIOECONOMIC AND CULTURAL VARIABLES

Overall, the political and cultural milieu in Bangladesh reflects traditional Islamic values. Islam is the state religion and Muslim Personal Law prevails in defining the status of women. The practice of *purdah* is not as stringent as in some other Muslim states, but the values implicit in the practice of *purdah* prevail. Education and modernization have contributed to the erosion of *purdah*, as has the dire need to earn a livelihood in the context of poverty and the gradual break-up of joint families. While the traditional system of *purdah* has waned, contact in recent years with the Islamic culture of other countries is noticeable. Women wearing an outer garment and *hijab* are not uncommon sights. The society, in matters of women's dress, generally tends to be guided by a broad and generalized notion of "decency." No strict dress code exists. Yet, certain parts of the women's body—in other words, from head down to the ankles—are to be appropriately covered, at least when in public view or in contact with the category of males with whom *purdah* is to be observed as designated by social mores and custom. The multiple identities of women in the society, however, influence the dress requirements, and how they cover themselves depends on their economic standing, social class, cultural orientation, and religious understanding. A pluralism exists here, although the orthodox Islamic interpretation would sanction an outer garment and *hijab* as essential parts of women's dress.[6]

Certain acts are obligatory for Muslims to perform, which the religion enunciates as the five pillars of Islam. These are: faith in the unity of Allah; prayers five times a day; fasting during the month of *Ramadhan*; pilgrimage to the Holy Mecca, applicable only for those who are financially able; and *zakat*, or alms-giving on the basis of a certain proportion of one's wealth. Muslims in Bangladesh, on the whole, obey these tenets. In fact, they are deeply religious. Because of poverty, a large proportion of them are obviously excluded from having any obligation to perform the last two rites. The tradition of religious learning, generally begun at home, basically constitutes learning to read and recite the Quran in Arabic, to perform the prayers designated for five times a day, and to commit the Holy Book or certain verses to memory. This education is imparted as a kind of informal education by private arrangements at the family level, by tutors (*maulvis*), and also at the mosques. *Madrasahs*, institutions of religious education recognized by the state's education system,[7] offer religious education as a stream of formal education. Also, religious teachings handed down through generations by way of oral narration constitute a source, which may not always be accurate.

Gender specific statistics paint a dismal picture of Bangladeshi women. Women are fewer in number than men, a situation that has persisted historically. According to the population census of 1991, Bangladesh has 57.3 million men and 54.1 million women (Government of Bangladesh, Ministry of Planning, Bureau of Statistics 2000).[8] More women than men live in utter poverty. The bottom 20 to 30 percent of female-headed households are among the poorest in Bangladesh. Some 40 percent of female-headed households are considered "extremely poor," while for male-headed households, the figure stands at 8 percent (United Nations Report 1994). Women have limited access to the resources of the household and to the resources of the state, which limits their opportunities for breaking out of the poverty trap.

The overall literacy rate of the population (seven years and above) in Bangladesh is 32.4 percent (1991 census surveys indicate a significant increase).[9] Adult literacy remains low at around 34 percent, with only 22 percent of women literate, compared with 43 percent of men (Ministry of Social Welfare 2000). The government's claim of substantial reduction of illiteracy is expected to be reflected in the Census Report of 2001. The religious culture prescribes reading the Quran in its original Arabic. Very few people, however, are in a position to read or understand the Arabic text. Those with higher education take recourse to Bangla and English translation, with a view to understanding the message of the Holy Book. Given that a huge proportion of the population is not literate and is at the same time deeply religious, those who are fortunate enough to be learned in Islam satisfy a spiritual need for the community and wield tremendous religious authority in local communities.

The majority of the Muslims, although not well-versed in Islam except in the form of reading and recital, tend to define the role and status of women through a prism that is layered with religious conservatism. The religious tenets, coupled with cultural orientation, prescribe and enforce a subordinate and subservient role for women: a man can marry four times; girls inherit half the share of boys; a man can divorce at will and may only make the utterance thrice to annul the marriage; custody rests with the father after a certain age; women's sexuality is to be restrained; girls are encumbrances whose marriage will require the payment of dowry, girls' "characters" are to be strictly safeguarded; girls are to be trained in domestic work at their parental home. In contrast, sons are assets to their families; sons are future earners and need greater nourishment and better opportunities. A son carries the family lineage and the birth of a boy is to be ensured through the wife's repeated pregnancies. If a woman is unable to deliver a son, a man may contemplate a second—if need be—a third marriage. A patriarchal culture claims domination of men over women, and men's ownership of resources, including women's labor and reproductive role.

Countering these Islamic restrictions, or rather the interpretations of Islamic tradition and theology, on women are trends that are liberating women from hegemonic male control. The movement of poor women in search of livelihood and women's new role as family earner has eased to some extent women's control by and dependence on men. The modernization process has opened up educational opportunities for women and also created newer roles for women, especially in employment. The development initiatives of the government and, in recent decades, of the development-oriented NGOs, promote involvement of women in development activities. The cultivation of arts in forms that are not in total conformity with the perceived dress code of Islam or the concept of segregation also create spaces for women's self-expression. Women are actively involved in the performing arts. Children of middle-class or well-to-do families are encouraged to take up dancing, singing, and playing musical instruments, reflecting Bengali tradition of cultural attainment. Women also participate in games and sports, generally all-girl, and also take part in all athletic events. On the whole, a cultural trend is emerging that stands for liberalization, redefines women's positions, and reappraises gender roles. Many of these changes are the contributions of the women's movement and the development NGOs, as well as due to the changing roles of the state reinforced by interactions with its development partners and the United Nations community.

GLOBALIZATION AND NGOS

Bangladesh's integration into the global market, brought about by globalization and trade liberalization, is largely dependent on the "comparative advantage of a young, flexible, highly expendable and docile female labour force" that the country offers (Hossain et al. 1990; Ahmad and Kabir 1996; Hossain 1996; Rahman 1996). Export-oriented industries have opened up employment opportunities to Bangladeshi women. The garment industry, for example, is concentrated in three major cities and employs over 800,000 women, mostly migrants from rural areas. Sixty-seven percent of the workers employed in the country's two Export Processing Zones are women. These employment opportunities have, to some extent, contributed to women's economic empowerment within the context of their families, enhanced their mobility and visibility, and given them some degree of autonomy, thereby loosening the grip of a patriarchal society. Women face exploitative market conditions, however. The gender-related wage differential is high, jobs are insecure, labor laws are not enforced, and work environments are often hazardous. The women's movement has often expressed solidarity with garment workers and women employed by other multinational or joint ventures for the enforcement of safety regulations and labor laws.

The term NGO in the Bangladesh context refers to non-governmental organizations engaged in development activities. The large-scale emergence of NGOs or, more appropriately, development NGOs is basically a post-liberation phenomenon, organized with a view to undertake relief and rehabilitation activities in a war-ravaged country. By the mid-1970s, the thrust of NGO activities had shifted to community development programs, aimed at improving the quality of life of the rural poor, who constituted the vast majority of the people of Bangladesh. NGOs, in trying to involve people in development processes, also came to target women as agents and beneficiaries of change and development. NGO programs cover areas such as education, legal literacy, skill formation, income generation, health, reproductive health and family planning, credit, and social forestry. In addition to the tangible benefits that the NGO activities bring about, they also contribute to empowering the dispossessed through mobilization, organization, and awareness-raising. The women-specific NGOs as well as those with a major focus on women see themselves as part of, or at least contributing to, the women's movement in Bangladesh. Their contribution to the empowerment of women is immense. The NGOs, mostly donor-funded, have access to resources, which the otherwise voluntary women's organizations do not have. Women's organizations now also solicit donor support for projects, but they are quick to draw the distinction that unlike the NGOs, the service they render is voluntary and not salaried. NGOs, however, have a comparative advantage in reaching the grassroots because of the way they are structured and the way they sustain their activities. The leadership of women-focused NGOs is provided by women, while most of those that have a broader mandate and are larger in terms of activities, organization, and clientele are led by men with women serving at middle and lower levels.[10]

Women's organizations with a tradition of voluntarism constitute the mainstream of the women's movement in Bangladesh. Their approaches to gender concerns and women's issues are shaped by their political and feminist ideology. Women's organizations initially dedicated to "welfare" activities and programs for improving women's lives have gradually shifted to activities leading to skill formation, income generation, and consciousness-raising. Collectively, they have contributed to raising awareness of the society on issues such as violence against women, women's rights, and gender issues through mobilization, demonstration, and organization, and striven to bring women's agendas to the fore (Chowdhury 1994).

STATE MECHANISMS FOR WOMEN'S ADVANCEMENT

Bangladesh was one of the first countries to institute a national machinery for the advancement of women in the late 1970s in the form of a Ministry of Women's Affairs, but the full potential of the ministry remains underutilized. The ministry, renamed as the Ministry of Women and Children Affairs in 1994, is described as the "lead" agency for women's development. The allocation of business of the ministry includes the following: national policy regarding women's development; programs for the welfare and development of women; matters relating to women's legal and social rights; problems and affairs relating to women; programs for improving the condition of women; and matters relating to the Department of Women's Affairs, the Bangladesh Jatiyo Mahila Sangstha (Bangladesh National Women's Organization), the Shishu Academy (Children's Academy), and women's voluntary organizations.[11]

The ministry, however, enjoys little political clout. With rare exceptions, a minister of state has headed the ministry. To date, the (state) ministers have been mostly appointed from among women MPs elected indirectly to the Parliament in the reserve seats. At the time of induction of the present cabinet in 1996, neither of the two women (full) cabinet ministers seemed eager to take on the responsibility of the women's affairs ministry. The ministry has also undergone changes in its organization from time to time which has had an adverse impact on its capacity to fulfill its mandate. The Ministry of Women and Children Affairs does not enjoy the necessary institutional leverage with other ministries. The administrative head of the ministry often is of the rank of additional secretary-in-charge. Consequently, the strategic importance of the ministry as a means of social transformation leading to gender equality is unfulfilled. The ideological position of those heading or occupying important positions in the hierarchy of the women's affairs ministry is of crucial importance in shaping or prioritizing the agenda of the ministry on gender issues.

To promote women's concerns systemwide, Bangladesh has created the position of Women in Development (WID) Focal Points in the various ministries of the government. Unfortunately, the linkages between the focal points and the ministry of women's affairs have been weak. The potential of the WID Focal Point mechanism as a "major means of intersectoral coordination" remains to be fully utilized.[12] Efforts are also underway to strengthen the capacity of the focal points to fulfill their mandate. Until recently, the Focal Points held the position of deputy secretary which is at the periphery of the administrative decision-making hierarchy. Often deputy secretaries did not have enough power to intervene. A recent decision to locate the office of the Focal Points at the rank of Joint Secretary is a welcome move; however, reports indicate that the joint secretaries often cannot give adequate attention to the new responsibility that has been added to their many existing ones. This dilemma illustrates the formidable task of orchestrating the state machinery to implement the goal of gender equality.

The government created a National Council for Women's Development in 1995, comprised of fourteen ministers, secretaries of thirteen ministries, a member of the planning commission, five members of Parliament and up to ten prominent women nominated by the government. The prime minister chairs the council and the women's ministry serves as the secretariat. The council met for the first time in early 1997. The mandate for this high-powered body is to ensure women's participation in socioeconomic development and to coordinate the activities of different ministries, divisions, and agencies regarding these development works. The council met for the first time in early 1997 to approve the National Policy for the Advancement of Women, announced by the prime minister on March 8 to commemorate International Women's Day. The council has met only once since, in July 1999, although two meetings a year were stipulated. The Council faces the prospect of marginalization unless it meets regularly with a well-worked-out agenda and strong secretariat support services provided by the ministry. The membership of the council is rather large for the kind of role envisaged for the body by its term of reference or as defined by the Institutional Review of the WID Capability of the Government of Bangladesh (Government of Bangladesh, Ministry of Women and Children's Affairs. 1998b 2:107–8). Many believe that a smaller working group within the council could make the council more effective.

Within the governmental machinery, the Ministry of Women and Children Affairs, the NCWD, and the Women in Development Focal Points are the most significant actors for the implementation of the National Action Plan.[13] In 1998, the women's affairs ministry started a three-year project, called Policy Leadership and Advocacy for Gender Equality (PLAGE). At the end of the project period, the Policy Leadership and Advocacy Unit (PLAU), which is now donor-funded, will be absorbed in the revenue budget of the government and will become a permanent unit within the ministry. In setting up the unit, the government would be implementing a recommendation of the Institutional Review of WID Capability of the Government of Bangladesh, which had suggested the establishment of a new unit within the ministry "to serve as the 'motor' for initiatives in policy leadership and advocacy," including follow-up to the Beijing process (Government of Bangladesh, Ministry of Women and Children's Affairs 1998a, 20–21).

The government set up an Inter-Ministerial Implementation and Evaluation Committee for Women's Development in 1999, thus putting into effect a recommendation of the National Policy and National Action Plan drawn following the FWCW. The committee, which has a small proportion of NGO membership, is coordinated by the women's affairs ministry and serviced by the PLAGE. The committee has so far met with some regularity. But again its structure and lack of political resources hampers its intended role.

The Bangladesh experience shows that institutional mechanisms, strategic discourses and training, informed dialogues, and documentation of women's development and empowerment constitute important components of development initiatives. A serious mismatch, however, occurs between the mandate and the institutional framework as these exist in laws and rules and the operational realities on the ground. This paradox is difficult to explain. One plausible explanation may be the hegemony of patriarchal ideology that colors the perceptions and goals of gender equality. The mind-set of those entrusted with the formulation and implementation of development policies aimed at gender equality may continue to nurture the values of a patriarchal culture in which they have been socialized. As a consequence, their vision of gender equality may not always encompass the dimension of fundamental restructuring of gender relations that is inherent in the concept of gender equality, but only focus on conventional development goals. To some extent, this may explain why the instruments created for change often fail to produce, although one could argue that conventional development inputs such as education, health, and employment may have a "cascading" effect and lead in the long run to the desired social transformation.

THE UNITED NATIONS FOURTH WORLD CONFERENCE ON WOMEN AND ITS IMPACT

The Beijing Platform for Action contains twelve points that, with some exceptions, reflect a global consensus on the issue of gender equality. Building on the United Nations Third World Conference on Women in Nairobi and its Forward Looking Strategies document, as well as on other United Nations documents and declarations from world conferences on the child, on the environment, on human rights, on social and economic development, and on population held during the 1990s, the preparatory meetings around the world contributed to the Beijing documents which consisted of the Beijing Declaration and the Platform for Action. The Platform for Action calls itself "an agenda for action" and "an agenda for women's empowerment (United Nations 1995b). The Platform for Action draws governments into a timeframe for necessary follow-up initiatives, leading to the formulation of respective national plans of action (United Nations 1995b, 296–7). By raising the issue of monitoring within the envisaged institutional arrangements, the Platform for Action encourages governments to design monitoring tools and measurable targets. A broadbrush global overview reveals small and unique successes but overall, a serious mismatch exists between commitments and actions on the part of the member states of the United Nations who were designated the chief actors in the implementation scheme (APDC 1998; WEDO 1996).

The Platform for Action seeks to bring about fundamental structural changes in existing gender relations "through a full and equal share in economic, social, cultural, and political decision-making." Although the goal of the Platform for Action is envisioned in terms of gender equality in law and in practice, the Beijing document addresses several categories of issues. The states' responses to the platform in terms of follow-up initiatives with regard to implementation are basically shaped by the nature of the issues concerned. For example, the "development" issues, such as noted by the Platform for Action in the global overview and suggested strategies in the case of, say, poverty and education, involve no major shift in the state's ideology. Many developing countries and member states of the United Nations have accepted the women in development approach for more than a decade. Women have been targeted as beneficiaries in development programs and projects, and also identified as active agents of change and development for quite some time.

Certain critical areas of the platform, however, call for the restructuring of gender relations to ensure the equality of women and men and to advocate strategies for empowering women. These issues touch the ideological base of the patriarchal state. Ruling elites may fail to act due to apprehension that the implementation of these measures will upset existing power relations. Government bureaucrats and politicians—those involved with policy formulation and implementation—may continue to regard gender concerns as marginal and not recognize the need for a shift in the development paradigm integrating the concepts of de jure and de facto gender equality.

In countries such as Bangladesh, which nurture and sustain the values of a conservative society, issues of gender equality are likely to be approached with diffidence, lest they create discontent and/or upset the major bases of conservatism. In Muslim countries, Islamic injunctions influence country responses to issues of gender equity. The government of Bangladesh is receptive to development issues and, for example, strongly espouses the promotion of education of women, especially the girl child. While the development discourse stipulates the integration of women in the development paradigm, the policy framers in Bangladesh are cautious about taking visible and strong stands on women's equality and empowerment issues, although these may form part of the political rhetoric. At the political level, both the government and the opposition wish to be seen as conscious of and sympathetic to the issues of women's oppression such as rape and torture, but neither appears as a promoter of women's equal rights in either the public or private spheres as such advocacy could be used to enkindle politically charged debate or enable the manipulation of the religious sentiments of the masses. The ever-present possibility that religious parties might exploit the situation with cries of un-Islamic policies might partly explain why Bangladeshi political leaders, even if they happen to subscribe to such policies, appear to be unwilling to broach such issues for both religious and political reasons.

DEVELOPING AND IMPLEMENTING THE BEIJING PLATFORM FOR ACTION IN BANGLADESH

Pre-Beijing Preparations. As a part of its preparation for the United Nations Fourth World Conference on Women (FWCW) in Beijing, the government formed a National Preparatory Committee in 1994. The committee included a few members from women's groups and NGOs. Experts appointed by the ministry prepared the national report. The draft report was circulated with a very limited time frame for comments and consultation. The non-official members of the preparatory committee served as an informal channel for reflecting the views of the women's movement for dialogue on the report. The official delegations for the ministerial meeting in Jakarta in 1994 and to the FWCW included NGO components.

Diversity and multiplicity characterized the preparations undertaken by the NGOs. A coalition was formed by more than two hundred individuals and organizations representing civil society, in particular, women activists, researchers, professionals, workers, development organizations, grassroots workers, cultural organizations, and human rights groups. The coalition, which called itself Bangladesh National Preparatory Committee towards Beijing, NGO Forum '95 (NGOPC), carried on mobilization and awareness raising activities for nearly eighteen months, promoting activities that also encouraged grassroots participation. The major campaign and mobilization strategies were directed at raising the issues of withdrawal of reservation from the Convention for the Elimination of All Forms of Discrimination Against Women (CEDAW), spotlighting violence against women, promoting open discussion on the question of inheritance, and forging linkages between the women of Bangladesh and women of the world.

Post-Beijing Initiatives by the Government. The post-Beijing scenario was one of enthusiasm, expectation, and hope. Those returning from Beijing after the conference started talking about follow-up initiatives and monitoring mechanisms. Many feared that interest would flag and lapse into inertia unless the momentum created by the preparatory processes both at the NGO and the government levels and by the conference itself could be sustained. On their return, many NGO participants shared information and the experience of Beijing and kept the discussion going so that the Beijing Declaration and the Platform for Action did not experience the same fate as did the Nairobi Forward Looking Strategies. The Beijing Declaration and Platform for Action stipulated a time-bound assessment of needs and prioritization of the national agenda by national governments. The governments were urged to secure the involvement of NGOs in the process.

The government undertook some tentative steps to initiate a follow-up process. On December 31, 1995, the Ministry of Women and Children Affairs organized a half-day workshop on "Beijing Declaration and Bangladesh Perspectives." Two institutional mechanisms, totally unrelated to each other, were established during this time. Later developments bonded them together in what became a unique process of government-NGO collaboration in drawing up a Draft National Action Plan in light of the PFA.

The Ministry of Women and Children Affairs undertook the first of these initiatives by forming a task force in December 1995. The terms of reference for the task force related to matters that concerned the formulation and implementation of a National Action Plan in the light of the Platform for Action adopted at the Fourth World Conference on Women (FWCW). The task force included high-ranking government functionaries and the executive director of the Jatiyo Mahila Shangstha (National Women's Organization). The task force also included two non-government persons, both professors at Dhaka University, one of whom was the chair of the NGO coalition and a member of the national committee set up by the government preparatory to Beijing.[14]

The Department of Women's Affairs under the ministry launched the second initiative by forming a core group in January 1996. The women members of the core group came from a variety of professional backgrounds. In addition to those who served in the department, the membership—drawn from action, advocacy, and research oriented groups—served in universities, NGOs, and multilateral and bilateral donor agencies. All had been closely involved with the preparatory process of the Beijing Conference.[15] The Canadian International Development Agency (CIDA), Danish International Development Assistance (DANIDA), and the United Nations Children's Fund (UNICEF) all supported the government of Bangladesh in its effort to develop a National Action Plan. The rather vaguely defined mandate of the core group referred to implementation of the Beijing Declaration and Platform of Action in Bangladesh. Initially, the core group decided to critique and modify, where necessary, the draft National Action Plan prepared by the joint secretary of the ministry before it was presented to the task force for approval. They also decided to prepare a synthesis document of the extensive pre-Beijing NGO information finding and consultation activities.

Forming the core group gave the ministry and department an opportunity to reclaim leadership in the area of women's issues. NGO representatives used the group to access governmental policy making. Those NGO representatives who also were associated with donor/aid agencies in one capacity or another could use the core group as yet another forum to carry forward the agendas and reinforce their accessibility and acceptability to the government. For all, the core group was an institutional mechanism, with the potential of serving as a conduit for the delivery of the movement's ideology and the thrust of the FWCW to the government and state machinery.

Political developments at the national level in the first week of April 1996 brought about some significant changes in the way the ministry defined its role in the immediate post-Beijing period. A neutral caretaker government replaced the political government, following the passage of the Constitution (Thirteenth Amendment) Act. This neutral temporary government was mandated to assist the election commission in holding peaceful, fair, and neutral elections to the next Parliament. An advisory council headed by the last retired chief justice of the Supreme Court of Bangladesh and ten other appointed members composed the caretaker government. The prime qualification was that all be non-partisan and non-political. The advisory council included one woman who happened to be a member of both the core group and the task force and who had chaired the NGO Coalition for the Forum and the FWCW. She also was a member of the government preparatory committee for Beijing headed by the Minister of State of Women and Children Affairs and who, in the past, had served on many committees established by the ministry. The President of the republic swore in the council on April 3, 1996.

Several important developments with regard to post-Beijing follow-up occurred during this period. The first meeting of the task force convened on April 25, 1996. The task force gave an interministerial umbrella to the post-Beijing initiatives. The core group had the potential to provide the needed expertise to draw up a draft National Action Plan. The core group was to act as the "working arm" of the task force replicating the relationship that existed between the ministry and the department. The task force saw logic in the arrangement. The task force also approved, implicitly, a participatory and consultative process for identifying the needs as well as the goals and strategies for formulation of the National Action Plan.

A process was to be set in motion that would take a holistic view of the question of Beijing follow-up in terms of the ministries concerned. Sectoral Needs Assessment Teams (SNATs) were established for assessing needs and setting priorities as groundwork for formulating the draft National Action Plan to be approved by the task force and adopted by the government. The question of ownership of the document by the government was an important consideration as a basis to generate the necessary commitment for implementation. The methodology adopted was one of direct involvement and participation by each ministry within a consultative framework. Each SNAT was to consist of one member each from the Women and Children Affairs Ministry and the WID Focal Point of Planning cell of the concerned ministry, plus one or two experts. The teams would use multiple methodologies, including review of documents, interviews, consultation meetings, and internal workshops. Core group members would be affiliated with the teams to monitor progress. The working modality involved meeting the administrative head of each ministry as the SNAT moved into the ministry to study the mandate and rules of business, to hold intraministry meetings and workshops involving also the directorates and departments if any existed. On the way out of the ministry, the teams were required to call on the administrative head again and apprise him of the findings and proposed recommendations.

The issue of involvement of the civil society was also an important one, given the overall heightened awareness about the FWCW. To keep the draft National Action Plan from being regarded only as a government document without any contribution from civil society was an objective that dictated the composition of the sectoral needs assessment teams. With this in mind, the National Action Plan noted:

> The sectoral needs assessment exercise represents a fully national effort based on a partnership between government and civil society to elaborate a Bangladeshi version for women's advancement.

The high-ranking officials of the government, secretaries and additional secretaries, were introduced to the process through a half-day debriefing session in May 1996. In the course of the half-day presentations and discussions, the secretaries were informed of the details of the participatory and consultative process envisaged by the ministry in order to draw up a National Action Plan. Two concerns found wide resonance at the meeting. One was the need for ministrywide sectoral review of existing institutions, machineries, policies, and programs in light of the Beijing and Jakarta documents. The other was the identification of sectoral priorities and actions required to implement the commitments made by the government. The Ministry of Women and Children Affairs assumed responsibility for coordination of the entire exercise, thereby reclaiming its position as a catalyst of women's development and equality.

The critical areas of concerns enumerated in the Platform for Action did not all lend themselves neatly or exclusively to individual sectoral ministries. Some overlapped while others gave only partial coverage. Twelve ministries were selected on a priority basis (Ministries of Social Welfare, Education, Home Affairs, Law Justice and Parliamentary Affairs, Industry, Agriculture, Environment and Forestry, Fisheries and Livestock, Labour and Manpower, Local Government, Rural Development and Cooperatives, Health and Family Welfare, and Information). The SNATs began to work in August 1996 and the reports were finalized by February 1997. The draft National Action Plan was already informally in the hands of the relevant officials of the ministry by May 1997. In mid-September 1997, the task force formally received the draft National Action Plan for approval, which it granted and forwarded to the office of the prime minister for her approval.

The National Action Plan envisages linkages and coordination of all actors with responsibilities for policy formulation and implementation. The vision that guides the National Action Plan for the implementation of the Beijing Platform for Action is to build a society that:

- Recognizes women as human beings with fundamental and inalienable rights.
- Provides full equality of opportunity as well as equality of results between women and men as a fundamental concept.
- Eliminates the existing disparities between men and women and creates an environment for bringing out the maximum productive and creative potentials of men and women.
- Puts people—both women and men—at the center of all development processes.
- Promotes greater sharing of work and experience between women and men in the workplace as well as in the household.
- Regards women as essential agents of change and development and creates increased opportunities for women to participate fully and equally in all economic and political fields.
- Values the work and contribution of women in all fields. (National Action Plan 1998, 18–19)

This vision is also broadly reflected in the National Policy for the Advancement of Women, declared by the prime minister on March 8, 1997 commemorating International Women's Day.

Two Basic Issues of Violence
and Inheritance: Differing Approaches

The Issue of Violence Against Women. The Platform for Action identifies violence against women as a critical area of concern. The issue is a
global phenomenon. The issue of inheritance, by contrast, is basically a
concern of Muslim societies and countries. The issue of inheritance appears under the section on the girl child in the Platform for Action.

Statistics and media reporting indicate the incidence of violence
against women to be on the increase. Violence against women has many
faces in Bangladesh: physical and mental torture for reason of dowry, rape,
indecent assault, acid throwing, trafficking in women and children. The
Human Development in South Asia 1999 report shows the incidence of rape
in Bangladesh to be the highest in the region in 1996: ten in every
100,000 women (Mahbub ul Haq Human Development Centre 1999, 7).
Recently religious traditional mediation bodies have been issuing *fatwas*
(religious decrees) based on misinterpretations/misuse of religion, to punish and disempower women—an alarming trend. Traditionally in Islam,
muftis or men of learning in religion, exercised the authority to give *fatwas*
or judgments on civil matters based on interpretation of Islamic laws. Basically, their jurisdiction lay in the legal settlement of disputes outside the
court system. In recent times in Bangladesh, incidents of *fatwa* aimed at
controlling female sexuality and thwarting women's economic independence primarily obtained by involvement in NGO-initiated development
activities have been increasing at an alarming rate (Begum and Ali 1997).
Punishments meted out include throwing stones at the punished—usually
a woman—after making her stand in a newly dug hole in the ground,
lashing 101 times, and death by burning. The women's movement has defined violence against women, including rape by the police and while in
police custody, as state violence. The state is also aware of such crimes
being committed against women.

The women's groups and coalitions stand by the victims whenever an
incident of violence occurs or is brought to public notice. They create and
sustain public opinion against the crime and its perpetrators through rallies, processions, and demonstrations, and also by forging close interaction
with the media, especially the printed media. The women's organizations
also monitor the course of justice and keep their attention focused on the
police and magistracy dealing with the incidents. They also offer legal advice and counseling to victims who are often unaware of the legal recourse
and/or are too poor to initiate legal proceedings. On occasions, the vigi-
lance of the public, largely spearheaded by women's organizations, deters

efforts to hide the crime committed by those with powerful social connections. Some women's organizations also provide homes for victims of violence. Mobilization and advocacy led by the Mahila Parishad, the largest women's organization in Bangladesh, created pressure on the government to enact the Dowry Prohibition Act of 1980 (Jahan 1994, 133). Overall, the efforts of the women's movement are directed at eliminating violence against women, offering succor to distressed women and identifying violence against women as a public agenda issue.

The government has enacted laws and denounced these heinous crimes in public. The Dowry Prohibition Act of 1980, Dowry Prohibition (Amendment) Act 1982, Prevention of Cruelty to Women (Deterrent Punishment) Ordinance 1983, and Women and Children Repression (Special Provision) Act 1995 have been framed by the government with a view to protect women from violence. But the rising trend of violence against women indicates that these legal measures have proved inadequate to curb or eliminate violence against women.[16] The government also operates support systems to provide legal aid and shelter, and to make the law enforcing agencies and magistracy more accessible to victims of violence. Compared to the magnitude of the problem, these support mechanisms that have been put in place serve only a meager and insignificant proportion of victims.

The National Policy for the Advancement of Women takes a strong position on violence against women. The National Action Plan also delineates strategies to strengthen the capacity of the law-enforcing authorities and agencies to deal with crimes of violence against women, including gender sensitization of the police force. Since the FWCW, the ministries of home, and women and children affairs have become more alert and have increased their interaction with the women's movement on the issue of eradication of violence against women. The government has taken initiatives on a regional basis with support by development partners such DANIDA and the Norwegian Development Agency (NORAD) against trafficking of women and children. In this patriarchal fashion, the state is committed to give "protection" to the oppressed women.

The Issue of Inheritance Rights of the Girl Child.   The right to equal inheritance is an "equality" issue for women. A substantial proportion of Bangladeshis have very little to leave behind. The issue is not so much one of material possession as of the principle of subordination and dependence of women within the context of a patriarchal society. Islamic law provides that a girl should inherit half of that which a boy inherits.

Paragraph 274(d) of the Platform for Action of the FWCW in Beijing evoked considerable agitation and lobbying activity especially among the

Muslim countries. This was one of the formulations that appeared in the draft Platform for Action within brackets, signifying that no unanimous or acceptable solutions had been found during and following the meeting of the Commission on the Status of Women held in March 1995. The draft read as follows:

> Enact, as appropriate and enforce legislation that would guarantee *equal succession and inheritance rights of children, regardless of sex.* As appropriate, enact legislation that would guarantee *the succession and inheritance rights of the girl child.* (United Nations 1995a) (emphasis by the author)

The substance of the paragraph contradicts the Islamic law (*sharià*) of inheritance, which states that a girl child inherits half the share of a boy. Some of the Muslim countries, including Bangladesh, felt strongly that the acceptance of the paragraph as formulated in the draft would undermine the sanctity of the Islamic law. Apparently, any concession at Beijing would cause disquiet in some sections at home. The issue of disparity in inheritance was also an issue the women's movement in Bangladesh had put on the platform time and again. Ultimately, a compromise formulation by the contact group was found acceptable at FWCW giving leverage to both the Islamic interpretation and those who propagated equal inheritance rights. The final version adopted was as follows:

> Eliminate the injustice and obstacles in relation to inheritance faced by the girl child so that all children may enjoy their rights without discrimination, by inter alia, enacting as appropriate and enforcing legislation that guarantees *equal right to succession and ensures equal right to inherit, regardless of the sex of the child.* (United Nations 1995b) (emphasis by the author)

The Bangladeshi NGOs, comprised of NGO members in the official delegation and those accredited to the FWCW, studied the implications of the formulation "equal right to inherit" as arrived at by the contact group. Although it fell short of the stated position of the women's movement in the country, i.e., "the right to inherit equally," the NGO members on the whole felt that the formulation of the contact group was more acceptable than the position of the conservative Muslim member states at the FWCW. They lobbied with the official members as well as the leader of their country delegation and found some support. The Minister of State for Women and Children Affairs who led the delegation and was accessible to the NGOs was urged not to register dissent. The fact that the Bangladesh delegation did not put reservation on any of the paragraphs of the Platform for Action at the final adoption of the document underlined the openness with which the Platform for Action was accepted and demonstrated the country's commitment. No country, however, can be held responsible for non-fulfillment of commitment pledged at the forum of the international community. The leadership is often reluctant to negotiate the implementation of such pledges with political constituencies and vital stakeholders in the country for pragmatic considerations, while at the same time finding it politically expedient to reiterate the commitment at subsequent regional and international meets and events. For example, in response to the question as to whether Bangladesh formulated additional goals and strategies reflecting any specific need of the girl child, the Mid-decade Report of Bangladesh at the South Asian Association for Regional Cooperation (SAARC) Plan of Action for the Girl Child 1991–2000 (October, 1996) noted by way of elaboration:

> One of the most debated areas and one of the biggest breakthroughs of the International Conference on Women held in Beijing in September, 1995 was the adoption of the girl child equal right to inherit. Bangladesh adopted the Platform for Action without any reservation, thereby also accepting this principle. (Government of Bangladesh 1996, 2)

The government, however, has yet to make any move toward accepting the interpretation that the women's movement attaches to this paragraph of the Platform for Action, that is, the right to "equal inheritance." The women's movement espouses the cause of women's equal inheritance rights, but takes a broad, comprehensive and holistic approach. The issue of equal inheritance is seen not only as a discriminatory issue for Muslim women but also for those professing other religious faiths. The issue is viewed as only one area of discrimination that is enshrined in the respective personal or family laws. The movement therefore advocates the introduction of a uniform family code but finds limited resonance from the wider community and little appreciation from the government (Mahila Parishad 1993).

The government, when taking steps that reflect a progressive stand on gender issues has refrained from publicity. A case in point is the government's announcement to withdraw reservation from articles 13(a) and 16(1)(f) of the Convention for the Elimination of all Forms of Discrimination Against Women (CEDAW) in July 1997 while presenting the Third and Fourth Combined Periodic Report to the CEDAW Committee. Bangladesh had placed reservations on articles 2, 13(a), 16(1)(c) and (f) when ratifying the convention in late 1984. Article 2 relates to abolition of discriminatory laws and bringing all existing laws in line with the principles of the convention; article 13(a) provides for equal enjoyment of family benefits; article 16(1)(c) grants equal rights and responsibilities in marriage and divorce, and article 16(1)(f) relates to guardianship and custody of children. The women's movement in Bangladesh agitated against, and urged the withdrawal of the reservations. The issue was spotlighted by the NGO coalition (NGOPC) during the Beijing preparatory process. During the period of the Caretaker government (April-June 1996), the Ministry of Women and Children Affairs initiated consultation with the Ministry of Law and Parliamentary Affairs regarding the legal implications of withdrawing reservations once the democratically elected government assumed power.[17] As the time for submission of the Bangladesh report to the CEDAW Committee in 1997 drew closer, the women's movement intensified its lobbying. Minimal publicity accompanied the actual announcement of withdrawal of the reservation made by the minister of state at the seventeenth session of the CEDAW committee in New York. A kind of politics of silence was used to appease forces that might not welcome such inroads into issues which might be seen as ensuing from compromises with the women's movement. However, the two withdrawals reflected the changed realities in Bangladesh in terms of perception and legal decisions. Reports of other member states placed before the CEDAW committee interpreted the relevant section of article 13(1) as state subsidies given to families, and was seen to be in no way connected to the issue of inheritance. In Bangladesh, benefits are offered by the state to families to attract girls to schools and to retain them to higher secondary level. The issue of 16(1)(f), that of guardianship and custody, etc., has been resolved by court decisions that upheld the principle of the best interest of the child in awarding custody.[18]

When addressing the women's constituency, the government or the ruling party, refers to the government's withdrawal of reservations as some of the proactive measures the government has undertaken. However, two of the most important reservations remain, reservations that could impinge upon the personal laws, including inheritance. The National Policy for the Advancement of Women propagates the implementation of women's human rights and fundamental freedoms through such measures as "taking necessary steps to implement CEDAW." Political rhetoric and political realities in Bangladesh have a tradition of being at variance on issues of equality between men and women.

NOTES

1. Women activists reacted sharply to this amendment, claiming that this move was a retrograde one and that it could prove to be regressive in the future. Some women's groups went to the court and challenged the valid-

ity of the amendment. The case rests in the labyrinth of procedural technicalities and is unlikely to move further. The women's groups, whose members had filed the case, as well as their legal advisors chose to let the issue rest. The other section of the amendment, providing for decentralization of the higher judiciary was also appealed and ultimately deleted from the Constitution by the Supreme Court of Bangladesh.

2. The Constitution, for example, uses the third-person singular pronoun, "him," to refer to the citizen body. While providing that all citizens irrespective of class, race, sex, are eligible for all public representative positions in the state, the constitutional provisions use the masculine term "him."

3. During recent months, about twenty women's organizations and NGOs have undertaken concerted activities, involving lobbying political parties, news conferences, and meetings advocating the provision of direct election to sixty-four reserved seats for women in the Parliament. Subsequently increases were demanded in the number of reserved seats.

4. A group of women activists, researchers, and gender specialists who also were involved in the process of formulation of the National Action Plan during 1996–97, made significant contribution to the drafting of the substantive sections of the policy.

5. The Fair Election Monitoring Alliance (FEMA), a non-partisan citizens' coalition of over 180 national and local NGOs and other civil society organizations formed to help ensure free and fair elections in Bangladesh, noted the large turnout of women voters and also observed the presence of women voters in the polling centers with children (FEMA 1996).

6. Leila Ahmed (1992, 55–57) notes that during Prophet Mohammed's lifetime, "the Quranic verses enjoining seclusion applied to (his wives) alone." She further notes, "Throughout Mohammed's lifetime, veiling, like seclusion, was observed only by his wives," and suggests that various reasons, including Prophet Mohammed's wives being taken as models, later led to the general adoption of veiling and seclusion by the Islamic community.

7. Madrasah education concentrates on traditionally Islamic instructions to Muslim boys and girls. The curricula also include science, mathematics, social studies and other subjects (Bangladesh, Ministry of Planning, Bureau of Statistics, 1991 225–26).

8. The population of the country was projected in 1996 to be 122.1 million, 62.7 million male and 59.3 million female (Bangladesh Ministry of Planning, Bureau of Statistics, 2000, 125).

9. For example, 1995 UNICEF data suggest that enrollment for primary education is on the rise for both sexes, although the enrollment rate of girls is marginally lower (79.5 percent) than that of boys (81.6 percent) (Government of Bangladesh, Ministry of Social Welfare. 1996. "The SAARC Plan of Action for the Girl Child, 1991–2000, Mid-Decade Report." October 8. Dhaka, Bangladesh: Ministry of Social Welfare).

10. For kinds of activities undertaken by organizations engaged in women's development, see Centre on Integrated Rural Development for Asia and the Pacific, *Directory of Organizations in Women's Development,* 1994. Also, see, "The Role of the NGOs" in *Report of the Task Forces on Bangladesh Development Strategies for the 1990s: Managing the Development Process,* vol. II.

11. For allocation of business of the Ministry of Women and Children Affairs, see Government of Bangladesh, Ministry of Women and Children Affairs 1998. The review was undertaken by the government of Bangladesh with the support of a number of development partners.

12. There are now forty-seven WID Focal Points, with core and larger ministries having more than one. Associate WID Focal Points have been appointed since 1997, while, under a recent initiative, some ministries also have designated sub-WID Focal Points, with the purpose of integrating gender concerns in all plans, policies, and programs of the government more extensively and effectively.

13. The National Action Plan for Women's Advancement was developed on the basis of government-NGO collaboration following the FWCW.

14. For composition of the task force, see *National Action Plan,* Annex-A (Government of Bangladesh 1998a).

15. For composition of core group for Beijing follow-up, see *National Action Plan,* Annex-B (Government of Bangladesh 1998a).

16. A comprehensive piece of legislation called the Prevention of Women and Children Repression Act has been enacted by the Parliament in 2000.

17. Under the constitutional arrangement, a caretaker government could not make policy decisions "except in the case of necessity" (*Bangladesh Gazette Extraordinary* 1996).

18. For the government's stated positions on these issues, see "Combined Third and Fourth Periodic Report in Accordance with Article 18 of the Convention on the Elimination of All Forms of Discrimination against Women," report presented for consideration of the UN Committee for the Elimination of All Forms of Discrimination Against Women, revised June 1997. Dhaka, Bangladesh: Department of Women's Affairs, Ministry of Women and Children Affairs.

REFERENCES

APDC (Asia and Pacific Development Centre). 1998. *Asia-Pacific Post-Beijing Implementation Monitor,* eds. Vanessa Griffen and Meena Moorthy Shivdas. Kuala Lampur, Malaysia: APDC.

Ahmed, Leila. 1992. *Women and Gender in Islam: Historical Roots of a Modern Debate.* New Haven, Conn: Yale University Press.

Ahmad, Nilufar, and Khushi Kabir. 1996. "Trade Liberalization Policies and Impact on Women Working in the Export Processing Zones (EPZ) in Bangladesh: A Case Study." In *Global Trading Practices and Poverty Alleviation in South Asia: Regional Perspectives on Women and Trade,* eds. Aasha Kapur Mehta and

Camilla Otto. New Delhi, India (Regional Office), United Nations Development Fund for Women (UNIFEM).

Bangladesh Gazette Extraordinary. 1996. March 28 Article 58(D).

Bangladesh Mahila Parishad, *Uniform Family Code.* 1993. Dhaka. Bangladesh Mahila Parishad. [in Bangla]

Begum, Maleka and Khondker Sakhawat Ali, eds. 1997. *Fatwa: 1991–1995.* Dhaka: Shikkha o Sanskriti Charcha Kendra. [in Bangla]

Centre on Integrated Rural Development for Asia and the Pacific (CIRDAP). 1994. *Directory of Organizations in Women's Development.* Dhaka, Bangladesh: CIRDAP.

Chowdhury, Najma. 1994. "Bangladesh: Gender Issues and Politics in a Patriarchy." In *Women and Politics Worldwide,* ed. Barbara J. Nelson and Najma Chowdhury. New Haven, Conn.: Yale University Press.

Daily Star. 1999. October 12: 20.

Fair Election Monitoring Alliance (FEMA). 1996. *The Report of the Fair Election Monitoring Alliance (FEMA), Bangladesh Parliamentary Elections, June 12, 1996 and By-Election to 15 Constituencies Held on September 5, 1996.* Dhaka: Bangladesh: FEMA.

Government of Bangladesh, Ministry of Women and Children Affairs 1997. *National Policy for the Advancement of Women.* Dhaka, Bangladesh: Ministry of Women and Children Affairs.

———. 1997. *Combined Third and Fourth Periodic Report in Accordance with Article 18 of the Convention on the Elimination of All Forms of Discrimination against Women,* Report presented for Consideration of the UN Committee for the Elimination of All Forms of Discrimination against Women, revised June 1997. Dhaka, Bangladesh: Department of Women's Affairs, Ministry of Women and Children Affairs.

———. 1998a. *National Action Plan for Women's Advancement: Implementation of the Beijing Platform for Action (PFA).* Dhaka, Bangladesh: Ministry of Women and Children Affairs.

———. 1998b. *Institutional Review of WID Capability of the Government of Bangladesh. Mainstreaming Women's Development.* Dhaka: Bangladesh: Ministry of Women and Children Affairs.

———. 1998c. *Institutional Review of WID Capability of the Government of Bangladesh National Machinery for Women's Development.* Dhaka: Bangladesh: Ministry of Women and Children Affairs.

Government of Bangladesh, Ministry of Planning, Bureau of Statistics. 1992. *Bangladesh Education in Statistics 1991.* Dhaka, Bangladesh: Ministry of Planning, Bangladesh Bureau of Statistics.

———. 2000. *Statistical Pocketbook Bangladesh 1999.* Dhaka, Bangladesh: Bangladesh Bureau of Statistics.

Government of Bangladesh, Ministry of Social Welfare. 1996. "The SAARC Plan of Action for the Girl Child, 1991–2000, Mid-Decade Report." October. Dhaka, Bangladesh: Ministry of Social Welfare.

———. 2000. *Bangladesh Decade Action Plan for the Girl Child 1991–2000.* Dhaka, Bangladesh: Ministry of Social Welfare.

Hossain, Hameeda, Roushan Jahan, and Salma Sobhan. 1990. *No Better Option? Industrial Women Workers in Bangladesh*. Dhaka: Dhaka University Press.

Hossain, Hameeda. 1996. "Surviving Economic Integration—Can Women Cross the Borders to Security?" In *Global Trading Practices and Poverty Alleviation in South Asia: Regional Perspectives on Women and Trade*, eds. Aasha Kapur Mehta and Camilla Otto. New Delhi, India (Regional Office), United Nations Development Fund for Women (UNIFEM).

Jahan, Roushan. 1994. *Hidden Danger: Women and Family Violence in Bangladesh*. Dhaka: Women For Women: A Research and Study Group.

Mahbub ul Haq Human Development Centre. 1999. *Human Development in South Asia 1999: The Crisis of Governance*. Oxford: Oxford University Press.

Prothom Alo. 1999. October 12, 5.

————. 1999. Editorial. October 16.

Rahman, Atiur. 1996. "Trade Liberalization and its Impact on Women in Bangladesh." In *Global Trading Practices and Poverty Alleviation in South Asia: Regional Perspectives on Women and Trade*. New Delhi, India (Regional Office), United Nations Development Fund for Women (UNIFEM).

Report of the Task Forces on Bangladesh Development Strategies for the 1990s: *Managing the Development Process*. 1991. 2. Dhaka: Dhaka University Press Limited.

United Nations Report. 1994. *A Fork in the Path: Human Development Choices for Bangladesh*. New York: United Nations.

United Nations. 1995a. *Draft Platform for Action for the Fourth United Nations Conference on Women*. New York: United Nations.

United Nations. 1995b. *Platform For Action, Fourth World Conference on Women*. New York: United Nations.

WEDO (Women's Environment and Development Organization). 1996. *Beyond Promises: Governments in Motion—One Year After the Beijing Conference*. New York: WEDO.

CHAPTER 10

THE SILENT AYESHA: AN EGYPTIAN NARRATIVE

Heba Raouf Ezzat

INTRODUCTION

Over a thousand stories have been told about women's public presence in Egypt over the last one hundred years. Many voices have been heard, but sometimes the loudest have been the least representative. Research papers and books, and even theses have been written recently about the social and political presence of Islamist women, but not by these women themselves. I used to disagree with most of what was written on women's issues and the Islamic movement, writings describing the social and political movements we join as extremist or "fundamentalist," or interpreting our decisions to wear the veil as either a symbol of political protest or patriarchal authority. This chapter is an attempt to analyze Egyptian women's strategies as a researcher and document as a Muslim woman who is active in Islamic circles and, even to my own surprise, well-tolerated and sometimes even supported by the Islamist movement.[1]

A CENTURY OF STRUGGLE

Few issues in Islam and Muslim culture have attracted more interest and yet proven so susceptible to stereotyping as issues involving women. Women in Muslim societies have been the subjects of images and generalization from the orientalist look to the harsh feminist critic. The study of women in Islam and Muslim society is complex, reflecting the diverse and varied realities of Muslim women and Muslim societies throughout the ages. Alongside ideals embodied in the Quran and the traditions (*hadiths*) of the Prophet Muhammad, one must look at the actual condition of Muslim women in diverse time periods and sociohistorical contexts. The subject of relations between men and women in Islam is highly controversial among scholars. If some blame Islam for the accumulated ills of Muslim women, others see it as the source of light and reform. Still others insist that the status and role of women in Muslim societies should be attributed more to socioeconomic forces than to the religious belief. Historically, women's role in society was determined as much by social and economic factors as by religious prescriptions. Social custom, poverty, and illiteracy often eroded or subverted Quranic intent.

While Islamic law did provide the parameters for behavior regarding marriage, divorce, and inheritance, the actual rules in practice were the result of local conditions and social class, which often differed from urban to rural, from civic to tribal settings, and from one region to another. Whether or not men took more than one wife, or whether divorce was common, or how modesty expressed itself in terms of women's dress or participation in the work force also varied from one century to another in a non-unilinear mode. Frequently, regional and local traditions overcame in real life the verbally admitted rights of women in Islam. Islamic laws that protected women's right to inherit often were ignored by families who sought to protect the property from division and a woman's right to have an independent economic and financial capacity was limited. The role of women in religious observances and education was similarly restricted.

During the Prophet's time, examples of strong public figures are to be found such as Khadija, Ayesha, and Umm Salama—Mohammed's wives. The last two were a major source of religious knowledge. Ayesha was a transmitter of Prophetic traditions and also took stances that led to confrontation in the battlefield. These women, however, were regarded as "exceptional" personalities.[2] Similarly, while women in the Quran have the same religious duties and are promised the same rewards as men, historically, their religious roles and practices, particularly their access to the mosque, became restricted. In the centuries after the death of Prophet Muhammad, religious scholars increasingly cited a variety of reasons ranging from moral degeneration in society to woman's tendency to be a source of temptation and social discord, to restrict both women's presence in public life and in the mosque.

As in all the world's major religious traditions in premodern societies and cultures, the reassertion of tribal custom and historical interpretations and practice often undermined Quranic reforms. No doubt, women through the centuries had a share in social, intellectual, and economic life. Occasionally, the reader of history might spot a distinguished figure, a scholar, or a prominent character. In rural areas, these women were present in the labor force. Often they donated money to charity and established trusts (awqaf) for all sorts of public and humanitarian services (Al Majd 2000). Yet, women's share or status in reality was never reflective of the role prescribed even in strict Islamic texts.

THE ISLAMIC REVIVAL IN THE LATE NINETEENTH AND EARLY TWENTIETH CENTURIES

During the late nineteenth and early twentieth centuries, governments, intellectuals, and religious leaders responded to the challenge of European colonialism and the impact of the modern West. The object was to resurrect the Islamic community, to restore its strength and vitality through a new Islamic—religious and intellectual—renaissance (tajdid). For many, the hope was that, in time, an Arab or Muslim rebirth would lead to national liberation from European colonial dominance. The challenge existed on all fronts: political, economic, religious, educational, and sociocultural. Approaches to the needed tajdid varied, ranging from a very strict reaction against modernity introduced by the more conservative ulama, to a more progressive one by Islamic modernists who responded positively to the challenges of modernity. Reformers such as Jamal al-Din al-Afghani (1836–97) and Muhammad Abduh (1849–1905) in Egypt were the leading figures of such attempts. They saw Islam as compatible with the pillars of modernity (reason, science, and technology), realizing that the umma (Muslim community) needed to benefit from the technological and modern achievements of the European enlightenment while keeping its Islamic foundations.

In contrast, the ruling elites had no reservations about certain aspects of modernization. They were interested in military, scientific, and economic modernization rather than significant political change. The "modern" political parties, founded to compete in regular elections to enter the parliament, did not represent a real challenge to the ruling class. New schools with western curricula were established, students were sent to the West to be educated, and foreign consultants and advisers were hired. The primary concern remained revitalizing Muslim society and achieving national liberation. Yet, the process of reform inevitably raised questions, and educational reforms affected the status and role(s) of Muslim women and the family. This inaugurated a period of debate and reform that concerned the areas of dress, family relations, education, and employment.

Intellectual Contributions to the Islamic Rebirth and the Islamic Women's Movement. In Egypt, Muhammad Abduh and Refaa Tahtawy represented a vision that supported women's education and social involvement. The former, an Islamic scholar and religious leader, condemned in his writings and *fatwas* (legal opinions) the abuses of polygamy and divorce. He advocated reforms to protect women's rights in marriage, divorce, and education. For Abduh, however, as for other Islamic modernists, women's education was less an inherent right and religious duty than a necessary means to strengthen the family and thereby the Muslim society (Emara 1972).

The disciple of Abduh, Qasim Amin, advocated greater educational opportunities for women arguing that educated wives and mothers would strengthen the Muslim family and thus Muslim society. At the same time, he provided rationales for reforms in Muslim family law, arguing that the Quranic ideal was monogamy, in order to restrict polygamy as well as to restrict a male's right to divorce or repudiate his wife. If males were the advocates for the "emancipation" of women, Muslim women, as individuals and through newly established women's organizations, also pressed for religious, educational, and social reforms (Baron 1994).

Islamic women contributed to the early wave of women's liberation by the end of the nineteenth century, when a women's press developed in the early 1890s in response to increasing interest in women's affairs and a growing (mainly upper- and middle-class) female readership. This was about three decades before the narrative of Egyptian women's modern history and the story of the Egyptian women's movement often begins. The focus has been usually on a few male intellectuals, mainly Qasim Amin. Amin was considered the liberator of women, as were a few females such as Hoda Sharawi. This emphasis on leaders, however, overlooks a wide array of female intellectuals engaged in thinking about women's roles and also male/female relations in Egypt in the decades before and after the turn of the century. Women participated extensively in the literary debate through writings that often were published in the women's press. By the beginning of the twentieth century, active writers such as Malak Hifni Nassef (1886–1918) and Nabaweya Moussa (1886–1951) (Women and Memory Forum 1998–99)[3] were involved in demanding public education for girls. These two maintained an Islamic appearance in contrast to the secular outlook of Hoda Sharawi and her group.

Zainab Al Ghazali (born 1916)[4] was another often ignored but important activist who had a close relationship with Sharawi, yet chose to establish an Islamic association for women and edited a magazine to represent her Islamic ideas. Later, she joined the Muslim Brotherhood and became a figure in the movement. Thousands of "Muslim Sisters" were active within the movement at the time of Hassan Al Banna (1906–49), holding study circles and spreading the call of Islam as a way of life, not merely to perform rituals in mosques. The available material on that period, mainly written by the movement participants in primary sources, indicates that these women were active to the extent of traveling all over Egypt to hold meetings and recruit supporters for the movement (Al Gohary and Hakeem Khayaal 1989). Zainab Al Ghazali is recognized as an Islamist, but rarely considered a leading figure of Islamic women liberation in the sense of defending an active and equal role of women in the Islamic public and political sphere along with their "parental" role in the family.

Ayesha Abdel Rahman (1913–98) is another writer and scholar who has been ignored by those writing the history of the Egyptian women movement. Although not involved in any political movement, Ayesha Abdel Rahman was a distinguished Islamic figure who had an impact on current Islamic thought and who had famous debates with other thinkers who advocated a "modern" and "science-oriented" interpretation of the Quran. Jurists and scholars recognized her as a competent thinker and distinguished scholar. When she died in 1998, the Sheikh of Al Azhar and official figures as well as scholars from different countries attended her funeral. Her central role as a leading Muslim woman has been marginalized in the secular literature. She had no affiliation with the Islamist movements either, and consequently was never recognized by them to be a role model.

The treatment of Rahman reflects the polarized and overpoliticized state of women's issues in Egypt. Only the secular figures gain attention and credit. The literature on Egyptian and Arab women has relied primarily on secular texts and treaties, ignoring the writings of Islamic male and female that have always been available. To reconstruct the lives and ideas of Muslim women who explicitly declared their Islamic identity and also their commitment to the Islamic women's liberation movement is an important project for many Islamic Egyptian women. One might ask: If these Muslim women did not see themselves as engaged in a women liberation struggle, why should they be seen as figures of Islamic women's liberation? The answer is that while they may not be categorized as feminist, according to the Islamic measures of the time, they were active figures in the public domain. Their presence and their activities set a precedent for the recognition of Muslim women as intellectuals, as writers, and as a members of those in the political opposition.

QUESTIONING MODERNITY

Egypt today is not simply witnessing a struggle between tradition and modernity, between rural and urban environments, or between uneducated majority and educated elites, but, rather, between competing definitions of secular modernity, Islamic modernity, and Islamist traditionalism.

Arguments are usually aimed at the new middle class and often focus on the role of women in the society. Influenced by the West and by Islamic modernism, significant changes have occurred in the lives of many Muslim women during the twentieth century. Legal reforms, voting rights, and educational and employment opportunities altered and broadened women's role in society. In addition to being wives and mothers, an increasing percentage of women have entered many areas of public life, ranging from politics to the professions. This varies greatly from one region of the Muslim world to another and often from urban to rural settings. After independence, many emerging Muslim nations pursued paths of modernization and development that were western-inspired or -informed. Implicit were presuppositions that modernization would entail increased separation of religion from public life. The modernization paradigm affected everything from dress, education, and employment to the different aspects of social norms.

While Muslim governments borrowed heavily from the institutions of the West in political, economic, and legal development, Muslim family law generally was not replaced by western civil codes but was reformed through legislation that affected laws of marriage, divorce, custody, and inheritance. Like most of the modernist reforms in "third world" countries where the state took measures to alter the social and judicial system in the name of "nation building," in Egypt, too, the state initiated reforms mobilizing the people with mainly socialist ideas. The change was initiated not from below, as the regimes were in all cases authoritarian, but from above. They did not come from the desires or demands of religious leaders, who were trying to defend what they took for "authentic values and morals," but from political rulers and a minority of modernizing elites who linked modernization to progress and traditions to backwardness. Changes were imposed or "legislated" from above, often rationalized by the belief that the "modern" educated, enlightened few were shaping the future for the more "traditional" or "the ignorant illiterate" masses. Educational reforms opened up new opportunities for women, who then became more visible in public life, in government, and in the professions. As the changes were initiated in the name of modernization (although women's rights were already rooted in sharià), the conflict between Islam and secularization became labeled as one between tradition and modernity.

Starting in the mid-1970s, the "project of modernity" became subject to assault as the nationalist and secular idioms were challenged by the reassertion of Islamic identity. For several decades, much of the Muslim world has experienced a contemporary religious resurgence or revival. The reassertion of Islam in personal and public life has taken many forms, from greater attention to religious practice in public spaces, to the emergence of Islamic organizations, movements, and institutions. Islam visibly has become a significant social and political force beyond organized groups. Islamic activism began to assume a new role as a strong political force in elections, a role that threatened the long-established political regimes in the region. In Egypt, Tunisia, Sudan—and soon Jordan, Algeria, and Morocco—Islamists (those who perceive Islam as a political ideology) gained increasing support. Islamic revivalism has become institutionalized as a social force through its schools, social service agencies, banks, and professional associations. Islamism also has manifested itself politically at the ballot box. Therefore, many have come to fear an Islamic threat and to charge that Islamists are out to ruin the democratic transformation in the Arab world. The call for an Islamic state has put the authority of military political regimes in question and encouraged governments to appeal to Islam to enhance their own legitimacy and mobilize popular support. If many saw a new Islamic order as a solution to almost all problems, others have feared the creation of an Islamic state or the implementation of *sharià* (Islamic law). They have charged that Islamists will turn back the clock, retreat from the gains of modernization in recent decades, and promote extremism and intolerance.

In the 1980s, announced political liberalization and official claims of a shift toward greater democratization have been accompanied by the Arab secularists and feminists warning that Islamists would remove women from public life and restrict their roles solely to that of wife and mother. Secularists declared that segregation, subordination, and second-class citizenship would be the destiny awaiting women if Islamists came to power. The Islamists in Egypt called for a return to *sharià* but failed to introduce an alternative legal system or new codes. When the family code changed in the late 1970s, Egyptian Islamists in parliament in the 1980s attacked what they called a secularist law, but they did not introduce or suggest a more fair or more Islamic solution to the crucial problems facing women, especially with regard to divorce. (Their fellow Muslim brothers in Jordan behaved in the same way in the 1990s.) This put the Islamists in a reactionary position regarding the Islamization of laws.

Islamists stress that Islam empowers women and gives them dignity and full rights. However, they remain skeptical with regard to the secularist discourse of women's liberation in part because of historical figures such as Hoda Sharaawi, an early secular feminist leader who took off her veil as a sign of liberation. Islamists always considered the secular movement of women's liberation to be alien. They referred to it sometimes with harsh descriptions ranging from "Western missionary conspiracy" to "Zionist plotting."[5] Seeing themselves as the counterforce against secularism, the Islamists, on many occasions, opposed any topic on the agenda that the secularists were advocating, stressing women's domestic role to balance the secular/modernist preoccupation with the women's role in public, in politics, and in power positions. This polarized atmosphere hindered the *ijtihad* (reinterpretation of Islam) for women's issues.

In contrast, the secularists dominated the discourse in the name of enlightenment and rationality, portraying the Islamists as a power of "darkness" and "irrationality." They linked reason to secularism, and irrationality and superstition to religious thinking and religious movements (Al Masri 1989; Abdel Wahab 1990; Hamed Abu Zeid 1993). For decades, the secularist discourse did not go through any critical revision and, while accusing the Islamists of stagnation and lack of renovation, secularists themselves hardly revised their ideas and concepts regarding women and family or their conception of the public and the private. During this time, the secular discourse was based on a strong Marxist analysis which, with the demise of the Cold War, has changed to a liberal position. Secularists called the traditional family "patriarchal" and "oppressive." Islamic values were labeled "male dominant" and "stagnant." Secularists considered Islam as a religion to have no liberating potential for women. To obtain a political following, secularists sometimes used the term *ijtihad* for political purposes, to seem as though they advocated a progressive Islam, when in fact they were using *ijtihad* as a screen to mask their own fundamental secularism.[6] In the middle of this conflict between the Islamists and the secularists stood the silent and conservative institution of formal Islam (Al Azhar), and also the silent majority of women, who participate in all aspects of social and economic life and also in political informal activities, but rarely bother to theorize or write about their stances.

When Yvonne Haddad mentions that Islamists remain caught in contradictions, unable to "reconcile recognition of the right of women to determine their futures with the need to redefine the role of men as well as women in society," she was probably looking for language that would openly use the gender approach and terminology, a discourse that Islamists were not likely to use (Haddad 1998, 3–29). Yet, deeds show that women were active in the movement, educated, and career-oriented, while at the same time stressing the importance of the family (Karam 1998). The Islamists' activities were mainly social, focusing on educational, religious, medical, and welfare services in associations, mosques, and syndicates, especially when the movement was politically marginalized. Their *ijtihad* was one of action rather than of theory. The result was that the core of the Islamists' ideas did not appear in books and writings. The Islamists were more reform-oriented in action than they were in explicit doctrinal rhetoric.

Concerning the question of Islam and democracy, some scholars such as Brand (1998) have found that globalization processes often threaten some of the political system's fundamental underlying social structures. Brand argues that a common response has been to secure the home front and focus on the family as a means of protecting the nation, its values, and its youth. She states that Islamist programs often have been directed at reinforcing women's "traditional roles" through means such as encouraging women to withdraw from the workforce, implementing pro-natal population policies, and even launching morality campaigns of various sorts that seek to limit women's "exposure" in the public space outside the home (Brand 1998).

What Brand does not realize is that Islamist women have become politically active "sisters" within the Muslim Brotherhood. They do not stay only in the home, but they have a public presence that has enabled Islamists to win many votes in the elections and, hence, become a force in the parliament. The problem with many secular feminists is that they refuse to recognize that an Islamic women's movement exists and that it might offer women a liberating alternative other than the modernist hostility toward family, religion, and religiosity in the public sphere. Other critics such as Stowasser cite Islamists, for example, Sayyid Qutb, to suggest that "when it comes to its vision of women, Islamism often remains quite similar to establishment Islam, as when Sayyid Qutb, an ideologue of the Egyptian Muslim Brotherhood, reaffirmed that the "guardianship" or "superiority" of men is part of nature (fitna); and thus (western) gender equality would bring societal and cultural destruction" (Stowasser 1998).

Although Stowasser generally recognizes that reformers have engaged (intellectually) in the reinterpretation of sacred scripture to legitimate new Islamic paradigms, and that today, as in the past, the word of God has sustained multiple levels of discourse, she seems to have ignored what happened since the death of Sayyid Qutb on the level of discourse and action within the Islamic movements for almost four full decades.

Still others such as Mervat Hatem correctly realized that contrary to the characterizations of some, Islamists like the Muslim Brotherhood did not seek to retreat to the past, but, in fact, developed a "competing Islamist-modernist discourse" aimed at the new educated middle-class audience of professionals. Their discourse "succeeded in persuading a majority of middle-class college women and working women to adopt the Islamic mode of dress as a visible sign of this attempted synthesis of Islam and modernity" (Hatem 1998, 85–99). Hatem indicates how Islamists redefined the private and public roles of men and women to respond to the realities of the modern nuclear family. She points out that both secularists and Islamists have provided conservative and modern interpretations of gender and that there is more than one interpretation of modernity.

THE SILENT REFORM WITHIN THE
ISLAMIST MOVEMENT OF THE 1990s

If women's involvement and respected position within the Islamist movement was in deeds, the Islamists did not ignore the weight of words in a
religion that is based on the revealed word of Allah. During the 1990s, a
silent reform took place in this arena that was hardly noticed or documented. Many Muslim scholars and some Islamists have boldly struggled
with the relationship of the Quran's eternal nature and the way to implement it in historical and cultural context in relation to women's issues.
For some, a distinction is drawn between the value of the heritage of Islamic jurisprudence (fiqh) and its application to specific sociohistorical
contexts. This enables reformers to distinguish between past theological
and legal doctrines (interpretations and applications) and the need for
fresh formulations or re-formulations of fiqh (jurisprudence) and tafsir (interpretation of the Quran), in which the dynamism and diversity of contemporary Muslim life needs to be taken into consideration.

FOUR REFORMS

Four specific reforms on the level of discourse can be presented as examples of Islamic and Islamist voices that defended women's rights and provided women with strong Islamic support during the controversy that
gained momentum during the International Conference on Population
and Development (ICPD) in Cairo in 1994 and the United Nations
Fourth World Conference for Women in Bejing in 1995. Islamic and Islamist positions are difficult to differentiate here. Contrary to the widely
accepted assumption in the studies on the Islamic resurgence that the Islamic text is outside society, and that the ulama are an entity separated
from the people and from the movements, one finds it sometimes difficult
to sharply separate each from the other. Leading figures within the Islamists were ulama (scholars of Islam) from Al-Azhar—a formal body and
religious institution. The movement, like any other social movement, was
inclusive of different classes and segments of society and bore an influence beyond Egyptian borders.

The First Reform.   The first change happened on the level of jurisprudence (fiqh) and thought within the Islamic movement. Mohamed Al
Ghazali (1917–97) and Yusuf Al Qaradawi (born 1926), as distinguished
scholars and jurists as well as highly influential figures in the Islamic
movement in Egypt and in the Arab and Islamic world, published important literature on the rights of women supporting women's active pres-

ence in the public sphere, ranging from social to political participation. This literature, in contrast to Al Azhar's position that will be mentioned shortly, was published in the early 1990s. These scholars were not influenced by the need to respond to an international event. Their ideas came from a growing authentic awareness of the necessity for reform and change in women's situation from an Islamic perspective. Ghazali called on Islamists to respect the rights given to women in the Quran and *Sunna* and harshly criticized Islamists' conservative attitudes toward women's issues. This was a position that many Islamists did not feel comfortable with, even if they respected Ghazali's other sociopolitical views.

In many parts of his recent books, before passing away a few years ago, Ghazali affirmed the important role of women in all areas of life in the Muslim society. The peak was reached in his book, *Women's Issues Between the Sterile and the Imported Traditions* (1990), referring to the polarization in women's issues between Islamists' and secularists' positions. Ghazali advocated women's participation, referred to women's role all through Islamic history, and defended women's right to access to all domains of life. He returned to the topic in different chapters in the last books he wrote, stressing the importance of revising the dominant approach toward women that is affected by tradition rather than pure Islam. He called for a rational and just interpretation of many *hadiths* that were always used to undermine women and re-read them with a new egalitarian vision.

Although an advocate of an Islamic state himself, Ghazali was aware that some of his fellow Islamists do not like the idea of women being publicly active in it. He expressed a concern that if such voices were to gain credence and power, women would be locked behind closed doors in a future Islamic state. He called on Muslim women to denounce the secular answers to women's questions and establish an Islamic "wise" women's movement on Islamic ground that would play a role in women's liberation globally (Al Ghazali 1989, 1990).

As a jurist, Yusuf Al Qaradawi issued *fatwas* (opinions on Islamic law) confirming that women have the full right to political participation, as well as to many rights in the family and in cases of divorce that have traditionally been denied in the traditional culture and in daily practice. He also criticized the preoccupation of some Islamists with questions of *fitna* and how women's femininity can be a factor of seduction in the public sphere to legitimize segregation. He himself insisted on giving lectures to audiences of both sexes, denouncing an emerging tradition of separate schedules for "brothers" and "sisters" in conferences. He scolded male students who dominated the floor and insisted that queries from female students should be sent to the lecturer in handwriting. He encouraged his female students to speak up and ask questions.

Like Ghazali, Yusuf Al Qaradawi encourages women to stand up for their rights and defend their Islam by reformulating the discourse and action of the women's movement to be rooted in Islam. The "Muslim woman of tomorrow," as he calls her, should be outspoken, active, and reach out to her history and heritage as well as be aware of her era and its challenges in order to play her expected role as an advocate of a global faith (Al Qaradawi 1990, 1991, 1992).

The Second Reform. The second reform took place within the religious establishment of Al Azhar in the 1990s under Sheikh Gad El Haqq, who often was accused of being conservative. During the months before holding the ICPD in Cairo in 1994, Gad El Haqq formed a committee of jurists and scholars to study the situation of women in international conventions, and to prepare an official stance of Al Azhar to be declared during the ICPD. The outcome was a book, with a forward written by Gad El Haqq, stating that Islam gave women all rights within both the private and the public realm. This book included a chapter on women's political rights that allows women to elect and be elected in parliamentary elections, a position that counters a *fatwa* issued three decades earlier by the same institution denying women that right and holding them incompatible with political roles.[7]

The overall position of Al Azhar in 1994 was supportive of women's rights, stating that only explicit anti-Islamic values (especially the radical feminist ideas and the homosexual trend) should be opposed, demanding that the government of Egypt not support any declarations or agreements that go beyond the limits of Islam. Being under attack and facing a campaign by many political forces that shared a moral concern regarding the ICPD draft document, the government did take a middle position by not signing any agreements or supporting any declaration that would be seen as going against Islamic values.

The Third Reform. The third reform took place within the inner circles of the Muslim Brotherhood that in the past used to see writings of Ghazali and Qaradawi as sufficient sign of respect for women's rights. When the time for the ICPD approached and Cairo was expecting the delegates to start arriving, the Muslim Brotherhood felt the need to assert its position to prevent any misrepresentations. They prepared a statement expressing the Muslim Brotherhood's position on the issues of democracy, pluralism, and women. They stressed that women have a dignified position in Islam and the right to be present in the social and political sphere. This is the opposite of what their position had been claimed to be.[8] Because the Muslim Brotherhood has no official presence (it has been banned since Nasser's time), the movement could not be present formally in the NGO forum of the ICPD. Yet, Islamic figures from the middle generation were present as well as delegates from the women's section of the Labor opposition party that had a known political coalition with the Muslim Brotherhood. Muslim Brotherhood members sat on the boards of the medical syndicate, which was also present at the conference with members in the NGOs forum. The medical syndicate hosted some religious and anti-abortionist international delegates to the NGOs forum at a reception to show where it stood.

The Fourth Reform. The fourth reform came during the preparations for the Beijing conference when Sheikh Mohammad Al Khateeb, a leading Muslim Brotherhood figure, issued a *fatwa* contrary to the dominant Islamic jurisprudence (*fiqh*). According to this *fatwa*, women had the right to travel on their own (without a male member of the family) as long as safety measures were taken to guarantee their well-being during travel and a safe accommodation was arranged for them.[9] This *fatwa* was initiated by a question addressed to Khateeb by a group of Muslim "sisters" who wanted to travel to Beijing who explained to him the importance of Islamist contribution and presence in such international women's conferences. Although all the "sisters" who initially traveled to Beijing were accompanied by their husbands, this *fatwa* represents a shift in the conception of the importance of Muslim women's presence in international events and the importance of these events for the Muslim Brotherhood's agenda. The fact that these women were joined by their husbands is a further proof that these husbands were aware of the crucial role their wives played and that they were ready to make the effort (and pay the expenses) to accompany them even if their travel on their own as a group was religiously permitted by the *fatwa* (and far easier and cheaper).

ICPD AND BEIJING:
FROM WOMEN'S LIBERATION TO ARAB FEMINISM

THE IMPACT OF THE CAIRO AND BEIJING WORLD CONFERENCES ON EGYPTIAN WOMEN

With the Islamic resurgence in the late 1970s, many educated women in the Islamic world were rediscovering the liberating potential of their religious traditions. Increasing numbers of them chose—sometimes against the wishes of their own "patriarchal" families—to join the wider Islamic movement. They suffered from restrictions and in some countries from rigid discrimination and violation of their human rights by the political regimes. In the past, Islamic women's voices have gained ground in the religious sphere, which is significant in a religion where God's revealed word is the logos of belief. Their influence has varied from the higher semantic domain pioneered by figures such as Ayesha Abdel Rahman (Bint as-Sahti') and succeeding generations of female professors of Islamic studies at Al Azhar University, to professionals in all domains, and activists in all the different Islamist movements.

While some researchers overlooked the Islamist women's presence in the non-governmental sphere and their efforts to empower women according to the Islamic paradigm,[10] others insisted on classifying them as Islamic feminists, an identity many would be very reluctant to accept.[11] Women's role in the contemporary Islamic resurgence has been analyzed largely within a resistance model. Islamic women are made to appear as the victims of reactionary male fanatics, overlooking the current active female participation in building a self-determined and conscious strengthening of female Muslim identity.

For example, the veil is usually presented as the symbol of women's oppression. Yet, Islamist women have used it as a means of empowerment to get social room to maneuver, to enlarge women's scope of action, and to increase women's independent mobility in the social world outside domestic boundaries, a legitimate strategy within religious authoritative discourse. Women have developed different re-interpretations of Islamic sources, distinguishing between Muslim feminists who stand on secular grounds, and emerging Islamist voices—male and female—stressing the strong liberating potential Islam has for women. Women's religious associations come into existence as local expressions of Islamization, representing women's involvement in Islamist movements. By playing a voluntary active social role in NGOs and grassroots politics, women are carving out legitimate public spaces for themselves within these groups.

In all of these activities, women's involvement results from the personal choices they make to meet their needs and expectations in new modernizing realities. Women through their religious activities have developed positions that push against the fixed traditional dominant forms of gender relationships and roles in different spheres. New dimensions need to be added to the understanding of women within the wider process of Islamization.

While these women have been motivated by Islam, other women in the secular women's movement have been taking a turn toward a more secular frame of reference. In many ways, the discussions and debates over women's status have mirrored the Islamic politics of the Arab world today and the spectrum of positions, from secular to Islamist. The polarized atmosphere resulted in the evolvement of a more radical secular women's discourse motivated primarily by the increasing fear of fundamentalism that drove many governments away from their formerly close relations with and sensitivity to religious values.

It remains important to view the religious, historical, and political factors that contribute to the reconstruction of Islam in Muslim societies and their impact on "gender" (Hijab 1998, 49–52). Factors influencing Arab women's movements have included the presence and input of more progressive North Africans, the growing significance and presence of NGOs as actors in the sociopolitical space, the increased presence of women in the labor force, and also the international women's meetings reflected in recent international conferences such as the United Nations Population and Development Conference in Cairo (September 1994) and the United Nations Fourth World Conference on Women (Beijing, September 1995). The researcher Nadia Hijab observed some significant signs of change, particularly in Arab regional meetings in preparation for the Beijing conference. In contrast to the Nairobi conference of 1985, where women felt a need to place their discussions within the framework of "the heritage of Arab-Islamic civilization," at the Beijing conference of 1995, the framework shifted from "the ethos of the Arab-Islamic heritage to the international arena, and from prescriptions of an Islamic perspective to that of a secular one" (Hijab 1998, 50). This has been due to the wider political atmosphere, as mentioned above. One can argue that this was the moment when the third wave of the Islamic women's movement and discourse became visible, shifting from women's liberation to feminism, and from the second wave's strong link to Arab nationalism in the sixties to a more global agenda that takes the human rights discourse as a frame of reference.

The Islamists became alert only a few months before the ICPD and showed interest in it because the meeting was to take place in Cairo. In the past, similar conferences on women's issues taking place in Latin America and Africa and elsewhere were seen as marginal issues not worth following. The Islamists managed through the syndicates and the opposition press to draw public attention to the conference, an event that had previously been primarily the purview of those within the feminist circles who had prepared well for it. The Islamists were able to mobilize wide opposition to the articles in the draft document of the ICPD declaration related to "reproductive rights," sex education, and similar sensitive issues that were seen as a threat to the Muslim society. Soon, Al Azhar joined Islamists and added to the pressure, resulting in a fairly moderate position as the official Egyptian position insisted that the final document should comply with the *sharià*, otherwise Egypt would not comply with it.

The secular wings of the Egyptian women's movement at the ICPD and in the accompanying NGO forum focused on the notion of equality as an all-encompassing, widely accepted concept. They did not distinguish their goals from those of the dominant international feminist agenda that was earlier considered irrelevant to the Arab Women's Movement. Demands for equality in the economic and political domain were always considered legitimate in Egypt, but in the documents, reports, and position papers of the NGOs there appeared, for example, the concept of "reproductive rights," a concept rarely found in the Arabic literature on women previously. The notion of "human rights" has since become a central concept in the discourse of Egyptian feminism and the formal official discourse, along with the concept of "gender." A diffusion of concepts, or, one can even say, a replacement of the common literary language regarding women took place, in the absence of a counterbalancing Islamic discourse as Islamist women were suffering from the violation of their basic human rights.[12]

At the ICPD, some workshops focused on attacking the widely practiced female genital mutilation (FGM). It became a hot issue in the newspapers after a documentary film appeared on CNN, raising fury in Egypt during the conference. A number of NGOs advocated the criminalization of that practice. Again, the scene was presented as if the "feminists" were against FGM, while the Islamic/Islamist circles were for it, although many Islamists as well as religious leaders declared the practice as traditional rather than Islamic. Although the sexual aspect of the reproductive rights (the women's full authority over her body and sexuality with all its implications) was not publicly asserted in the Arab circles and workshops, parallel issues represented an introduction to that spectrum.

During the ICPD, Islamists regarded the real threat of the West as less one of political, military, or economic hegemony than of a direct attempt to undermine religion and culture. The panels and discussions regarding the North-South relations and the effect of structural adjustment programs (SAPs) on women were not attended by the Islamists, who would not miss the simultaneous sessions on any of the controversial issues.

The Cairo forum of the NGOs witnessed the presence of the Islamists in lectures and discussion, and some of them managed through personal contacts to participate on panels of international NGOs, especially those classified as "religious" and/or conservative (anti-abortionist, more to the right wing). Arab and Islamic NGOs collaborated to form a religious caucus to coordinate Islamic activities in the Forum. This trend was perceived as counternetworking by the feminists who managed after years of well-prepared national, regional, and international efforts to "take over" the responsibility of networking between the Egyptian NGOs and the formal governmental delegations.

POLITICS AT THE BEIJING CONFERENCE OF 1995

The situation at the Beijing conference of 1995 was somewhat different from the one in Cairo. If Islamist men and women as well as many Egyptian NGOs with national and Islamic devotion could attend the ICPD and advocate their views because it was a mile away right in the heart of Cairo, Beijing was quite far to reach and many could not afford the travel expenses. This made the battle an unfair one, as the voices within the secularist women's movement were financially supported by foreign funds, mainly the Beijing Fund that was established by the embassies of Denmark and Holland in Cairo. The few Islamic bodies that applied for funds were turned down. Financial support was given only to the closed circle of secularist feminists or to the NGOs networking with them or carefully selected to be part of the future networking (for reasons of professional fundraising from western donors). In spite of this situation, some Islamic voices managed through self-funding to be present at the Beijing meeting, participating, demonstrating, and networking along with similar Islamic bodies from all over the Muslim world. Some sisters from Egypt borrowed money to go to Beijing and kept paying back the debt for years thereafter simply out of devotion to the cause of Islam that they saw threatened by the international radical feminist agenda.

The power, international links, and access to more funds on the part of secularists influenced the outcome of Beijing. On the international Islamic front, the few networks that were in existence were short of finances and unable to penetrate the iron circles of funding and information regarding women's activities domestically, regionally, and internationally.

NO HAPPY ENDING

The narrative or analysis presented here may lead to the conclusion that the conflict described above is between different sociopolitical forces, yet in a country like Egypt, the state remains the major actor. The development of the postindependence state has embodied a continual redrawing of lines between public and private, between state and civil society, and, in particular, between state, market, and family. The conflict has opened to public debate matters previously confined to privacy, and raised new questions about the relationship between the state and civil society. This was obvious during the Nasser era when the socialist policies and the claim of being a welfare state allowed the state to penetrate domains that for centuries had remained within the hands of the community. The legal "reform" within the Azhar meant that the independent religious body was finally placed under the full control of the state. The laws of *awqaf* (religious endowments) deprived the community of a source of financial independence and a source of power vis-à-vis the state. The laws introduced to modernize society were actually extending the authority of a leviathan state over the society.[13]

With increasing urbanization and the shift to the open market policies in the Sadat era during the 1970s, fundamental changes occurred to the notions of intimacy, domestic ideals, and family. A whole discourse of relativity regarding moral values emerged to stimulate the emergence of an Islamist movement with an alternative value system advocating a moral philosophy. This moral dimension of Islamism that attracted many supporters is a major aspect of Islamist movement often ignored in the "fundamentalist political threat" approach and analysis.

When the different social and political movements had their differences, the legislative body of the state became the judge. Even problems within the family concerning financial matters or issues related to women's position or children's welfare were supposed to be policed and judged by the state authorities. Any social authority (Islamic leaders, active community symbols) was seen as a potential political threat because the main survival strategies were organized by Islamists.[14] The central state was eager to foster its power and saw any form of self-governance on the local socioeconomic level as a threat.

To contextualize Egyptian feminism and understand its history, one has to see its linkage to the history of secularization of the legal system in this country. There has been a prolonged polarization between the supporters of *sharià* laws and the defenders of secularism, and, more recently, feminism. The role of the state has been crucial in the process of changes. The family code has remained the main area of disagreement and struggle. The different political regimes adopted western political, economic, social, and legal institutions and codes, yet family law remained untouched at first, and then it was reformed rather than replaced. Failure to replace family law with western codes was a tacit, if not explicit, recognition of the importance and sensitivity of issues of women and the family in Islamic history and tradition. While other areas of Islamic law were gradually not implemented due to the secularization of law as well as the legal system and court arrangements, the Islamic law of marriage, divorce, and inheritance, as well as the relevant modes of Islamic social habits and norms, remained historically intact.

Modern Muslim family law reforms were initiated then by governments, implemented from the top down, and often rationalized and legitimated in the name of Islam by using (or, as some would charge, manipulating) Islamic principles and legal techniques. While the ulama were generally resistant, at best they were only able to restrict the scope of reform. Supportive "enlightened" ulama were always easy to find within the formal Islamic institutions to label the changes as "complying with *sharià*." The power of authoritarian states and modernizing elites prevailed. The power of classical family law was reflected in the fact that even when modern legislation reformed it, people remained devoted to traditional norms. This situation of a dual frame of reference, one official and formal and the other authoritative, but informal can be found in all Islamic societies. In the Islamic and Arab world, the process of political secularization (the dominance of the state) was not accompanied by the same degree of philosophical secularization, or so-called "rationalization." Yet, the state managed by law and economy to transfer the social functions of the family and the functions of religious institutions into its own realm. Although weakened, the family and religious institutions survived in the public/social sphere. The Islamic practices and the powerful presence of Islamic values prevented the completion of the secularization process on the philosophical and cultural level. Islam has remained a parallel frame of reference, and the source of another legacy on which many opposition groups draw. Yet, the "global era" threatens the remaining forces struggling for any cultural specificity, especially those rooted in religion.

ARAB FEMINISTS AND THE STATE

The legal domain was one of the targeted areas of secularization from the beginning. The women's movements, too, increasingly gave more weight to the legal approach, and the crisis of the family caused by the process of secularization/modernity did not seem to disturb them at all. The high rates of divorce were seen as a legal issue of inequality and feminists advocated women's right to divorce and child custody (a fully accepted principle from the Islamic point of view). Little attention was given to the fact that this was an indicator of a severe social crisis facing the family as a structure and value. How equality can be guaranteed within social structures that are facing increasing poverty and deteriorating basic life conditions under the Structural Adjustment Programs dictated by the IMF and World Bank has been raised as a challenge. But the crucial question of how to face capitalism and its secularist philosophical underpinnings with a non-capitalist yet still secular frame of reference is not addressed by

Arab feminists. The answer would lead to a deeper discussion of the state's social and economic policies, and as these associations and groups are desperate to have the state's approval of their agenda to translate it into legal changes, they would not wish to confront or oppose the regime. The law as a bargaining instrument has been successfully abused by the state as well as by feminists. Despite restrictive political conditions against any legitimate presence of secular feminists, the state and secular feminists have allied against the "fundamentalist" threat.

Brand's argument that vibrant women's organizations may be the most important precursors to more democratic development needs to be revised in the light of the Egyptian case. By the beginning of the 1990s, two changes happened simultaneously. The Islamists, who made good use of the democratization atmosphere, started becoming an influential political power in parties and syndicates, as well as in grassroots politics. In 1992, when Egypt was struck by a strong earthquake, the Islamists were the first to extend relief to the affected poor and homeless, long before the government could start reacting and providing parallel help.

By 1993, the democratization process had slowed and even the presence of the Islamists in syndicates was not tolerated. Soon the government banned Islamist activities and many of their leading figures were shortly subject to unfair trials in front of military courts and sentenced to years in prison. (The last group of the Muslim Brotherhood prominent figures faces the same destiny in mid-2001.) This situation focused the energy of the Islamists on dealing with the regime and diverted their effort away from the issue of women. This allowed the feminist groups to gain strength and appear as the sole actors on the scene. No distinction was made between the "terrorists" attacking innocent civilians and the pacifist civil society advocates and democratic Islamists (mainly the Muslim Brotherhood). The regime decided to put all Islamist groups in the same category and harshly confront them by all available means.

An atmosphere of hostility toward the Islamists prevailed in political and media circles, including the theater, the cinema, and every other effective tool of forming public opinion in Egypt. This has created a golden opportunity for the secularists to attack Islamists harshly on the issue of women, to appear as the supporters of women's rights, and to accuse the Islamists, among other things, of being the major threat to the women's cause. This automatically put the main bulk of secularists and feminist circles on the side of the government, yet the price was that they had to keep silent about the violations of human rights committed by the state in the process. Only a minority could keep defending both, a minority that will suffer marginalization when establishing new formal bodies for women by the beginning of the millennium.

The government has allocated the secularists many positions, especially in the press and media, and rewarded them by consulting them in the preparatory process of formulating the new family code as well as in formulating the law that would regulate the activities of the growing nongovernmental philanthropic sector. During this period that began in 1993 and extends to the present, the two major United Nations conferences, the ICPD and Beijing, took place. After Beijing, the follow up committees were active supervising and networking to implement the gender approach at the grassroots level. Again, Islam was either considered marginal or at best irrelevant to the issue. The ethical code for "the Arab Network of NGOs," a non-governmental body, shows that Islam was not mentioned. Only a very brief reference to the "basics of Arab cultural specificity" (a very ambiguous term), is made. An old campaign to stop FGM was brought to life again, gained momentum, and soon the government responded with a law that prohibited the practice in all public hospitals. The secularists' discourse used religious arguments to confirm that the practice was not Islamic, a fact that some Islamists stressed, too, in the few spaces in the media left for them, especially in the Al Shaab opposition newspaper.

The second campaign was to change the marriage contract and stress its civil nature rather than its religious foundation. The campaign advocated the addition of a section to allow women to add specific conditions in the marriage contract regarding their right to work, travel, or oblige the husband not to take a second wife. Rather than conforming to stereotypical expectations by opposing the project for its support of "women rights," most of the opposing arguments by the ulama concentrated on the philosophy of the advocated changes that would turn the marriage into a long civil contract, stripping from it its confidential, emotional, and passionate nature, and turning it into a one-to-one contract. From a religious point of view, however, the marriage contract should entail a collective agreement between two families that keeps the extended families morally responsible for sorting out any issues of disagreement that might arise. The legal means (state mediation), the ulama argue, should be used as a final resort. Again, the polarization of political views was reflected in the discussion, as actually the marriage contract in Islam is a mixture of both views.

The third issue that the feminists mobilized for was the new family code that has been subject to suggested revisions starting in 1991. Secular legal experts were selected as members of the committee supervising the formulation of changes that were not revealed in the media campaign that took place about a year before the new law was discussed in the people's assembly. Secular legal experts were also those selected to be members of the joint committees responsible for suggesting a new law for the non-governmental sector. This was issued in 1999 (Law 153) and was in its final or approved state a big disappointment for the civil society activists as it put a lot of power in the hands of the authorities regarding the formation, supervision, and dissolution of the NGOs.[15] The subsequent constitutional court ruling that declared the law void only created a judicial vacuum that is still used by the state to continue bargaining with different advocacy groups.

While secularist in its discourse and visions, the feminist movement, in the absence of the public voice of Islamists, started using Islamic statements and concepts and introduced its demands as basic rights of women in *sharià*. The direct attack (critique) of the application of the *sharià* had to be toned down in order not to lose the support of the masses of women who would not tolerate a direct attack on Islam. The revisions introduced were carefully rooted in the *fiqh*'s most moderate views, and delicately given Islamic legacy. Toward the end of 1999, the Egyptian people's assembly agreed to the revisions in the laws covering marriage and divorce, but not without one of the most heated debates that the chambers of parliament have seen in recent years. The bill amending the Personal Status code was presented to the house of *Shura* first and got approval before the end of 1999. The beginning of the new century and millennium witnessed a continuation of the debates in the peoples assembly that mainly revolved around the three most controversial of the proposed revisions: a woman's right to *khol'*), that is, the right to divorce on the condition that she renounces any financial claims; a woman's right to travel without her husband's permission (later approved by a constitutional court decree before the end of the year 2000); and an official recognition of *urfi* marriage that would allow women in such unions (which are non-notarized and often secret) to seek divorce, previously impossible. The bill has been thoroughly examined by the Academy for Islamic Research and approved by thirty-five of its forty (attendant) members, a fact that was used by the opponents to ask for a re-discussion with full attendance of all the members of the Academy. It also received the official approval of Sheikh Tantawi—the current Sheikh of Azhar—who declared that the provisions are in no way contradictory to the *sharià*. Yet, the bill was opposed by a variety of political and social forces starting from members of the ruling party itself (NDP) to the Wafd liberal party and, finally, by many Muslim scholars as well as Islamists. The fear was that these provisions would "break the family" and "allow women to rebel against their husbands." The pressure exerted by the government in this regard has been strong, giving the feminist associations a space in the official mass media. The leading figures advocating the reform of the law were given the opportunity to attend as observers in the hot discussions on it in the peoples assembly, while the opposing "League of the Ualama of Azhar"—an independent (conservative) body of outspoken ulama—was denied the same opportunity.

The above mentioned group of scholars from Al Azhar issued a statement harshly criticizing the bill and calling for a moratorium of three months on the proposal during which time a qualified panel of religious scholars could review and revise the draft in accordance with principles of *sharià*. These scholars did not give the Sheikh of Azhar or the members of the Academy for Islamic Research any recognition, either ignoring their role in approving the draft or implicitly assuming that they represent the state and its official Islam while they (supposedly) represent the conscious of the ulama and the people. Opposition newspapers also were up in arms against the bill as they usually are regarding any issue supported by the NDP.

The bill was ratified by the president as the Law No. 1 for the year 2000. Shortly after that, and just a couple of days after some women in the feminist movement established an Egyptian Women Union, a National Council of Women (NCW) was formed in the beginning of February by a presidential act. The first group declared their newborn union at the head office of the Egyptian Human Rights Association, an association that had had confrontations with the regime during 1998 and 1999. The quick reaction (possibly previously considered) of establishing the NCW and the well chosen names declared as appointed members reveals the previously mentioned allocation of power as a tool of bargaining and rewarding the supporters and allies of the state.

The last example needs further discussion as a blunt example of this game of power and political allocation of institutional resources. As crucial as the role of the state is to an understanding of the politics of women in Egypt, the globalization process is also a major factor in the current changes. International law, the international networking of the NGOs, and their role in North-South relations have become agents of the "new world order." The sad part about the whole story is that the majority of women in Egypt remain excluded from the whole issue because of their lack of presence and representation in Egyptian politics.

Recent socioanthropological studies that western researchers were allowed to resume (while native researchers are usually not permitted to undertake) tried to approach the life of the majority of poor (supposedly oppressed women) and discovered how these women could make their destinies, use their social and kinship ties to survive, and to make a better life for themselves and their children. The importance of the household economy as an informal sector for women to use for their benefit is also under focus in many studies (Singermann 1995; Singermann and

Hoodfar 1996) Yet, the coming years might make the survival strategies of the 1990s ineffective, raising questions about the future of the majority of women, as well as the future of "the political" in Egypt. While the women who advocated the new family law are still celebrating their triumph, and some of them are receiving congratulations for being "nominated" to be in the "official" NWC, the majority of women (and of men) are still wondering about the content as well as the implications of the new family law on the status of family and women in the Egyptian society. The story has no happy ending; it is still unfolding.

NOTES

1. I dedicate this paper to the wonderful sisters of the Muslim Brotherhood in Egypt who consider me one of them and were always keen that I formally join their group. For two decades now—since I first attended their circles and started being active within the wider Islamic movement—they remained persistent, and I remained difficult to discipline. I dedicate this "research/narrative" to them with sincere respect, gratitude, and sisterhood.

2. For a detailed account of the women's situation and presence in all aspects of the early Islamic period during the time of Prophet Mohammad, see Abdul Halim and Abou Shukka 1995.

3. Women and Memory Forum—an Egyptian forum of scholars interested in the history of Egyptian women—held two conferences in 1998 and in 1999 on the writings and life of both figures and re-printed some of their works.

4. She also wrote over almost two decades an interpretation of the Quran that is based on the traditional interpretations, with an introduction written by a distinguished professor of Tafseer at Al Azhar University. They are Zainab Al-Ghazali, 1994a and 1994b. (The latter is a translation of her famous book in Arabic: Days of My Life, narrating her memoir as a political prisoner who had been subject to torture in Nasser's era).

5. Most of the Islamic writings on modern women's liberation use these terms and accuse the movements of being secular, western-inspired or directed. This first undermines the Islamic origins of women's liberation and second ignores the fact that women do face discrimination in reality by all Islamic standards. By blaming it all on the "other," hardly any real addressing of the crucial problems of Muslim women from an Islamic perspective takes place.

6. A rare example of re-reading the text from a secularist stance was Fatima Mernissi's work, and lately Farida Bannani (both from Morocco). See their work: Fatima Mernissi 1994 and Farida Bannani 1998.

7. Al Azhar issued a fatwa in 1952 denying women the right to be elected for parliament. See Resalat Al Islam (formal magazine of Al Azhar), No. 3, Year 4, July 1952. And note the change in the book published in 1995—just before Beijing: Al Azhar and Higher Islamic Academy. Ma' Houkouk Al Maraa Fi Al Isla. Cairo: Al Azhar, (July) 1995.

8. This statement was issued shortly before the ICPD and distributed as a booklet in the NGOs forum of ICPD and attracted the attention of commentators and the written media.

9. The *fatwa* issued by Sheikh Al Khatib was circulated in the circles of the Muslim Brotherhood and hardly raised any discussion within the movement, as it was taken as only concerning the Muslim sisters involved in the matter—a fact that needs further analysis.

10. See "The Case of Egypt," in Nafaà et al. 1999. This reference is an excellent example of the neo-feminists' explicit hostility toward any discourse that links women's issues to family and considers such discourse to be unsatisfactory and hesitant, and accuses it of trying to cope with mainstream culture (that is basically Islamic). Also see as an example of excluding the Islamic presence in women movements' historiography: Amal Abdel Hadi and Nadia Abdel Wahab 1990.

11. This is the term Azza Karam used. See her previously mentioned book.

12. See the report of NGO committee for women empowerment addressed to the ICPD NGO Forum: New Woman Research Center 1994.

13. For a full account on the *awqaf* in Egypt as a model of state-society conflictual relation, see Ibrahim Al Bayoumy Ghanem 1999.

14. Diane Singermann is currently finishing a study that deals with the famous clash in the Imbaba quarter that witnessed, among other marginalized areas, an Islamist presence in the socioeconomic sphere, helping the lay people with survival strategies. The quarter was attacked by the police force in a paramilitary campaign under the claims that the Islamists were running an "independent state of Imbaba." Singerman's study deals with Imababa as an example of the way the Egyptian government deals not with Islamism, but with the marginalized and poor areas usually called "Ashwaeyyat."

15. See an analysis of the process of lawmaking in this case and of the restrictions of the law on NGOs activities in Wahid Abdel Majid 1999.

REFERENCES

Abdel Hadi, Amal, and Nadia Abdel Wahab, 1990. *Arab Women's Movement.* Cairo: New Woman Research Center.

Abdel Majid Wahid, ed. 1999. *The Annual Arab Strategic Report 1999* [in Arabic]. Cairo: Al Ahram Centre for Political and Strategic Studies.

Abdel Wahab, Leila. 1990. "The Influence of Islamic Movements on the Social Consciousness of Women." In *Religion in the Arab Society,* ed. Abdel Baki El Hermassi. Beirut: Center for Arab Unity.

Al Azhar and Higher Islamic Academy. 1995. *Ma' Houkouk Al Maraa Fi Al Islam* [Supporting the Rights of Women in Islam]. Cairo: Al Azhar, July.

Bannani, Farida. 1998. "Al Nessaweyya: Sawt Masmu'e Fi Al Nikkash Al Dini." [Feminism: A Present Voice in the Religious Debates] In *Zaman Al Nissa' Wa Al Zakira Al Badila* [The Time of Women and The Alternative Memory], ed. Hoda El Sadda. Cairo: Women and Memory Forum.

Baron, Beth. 1994. *The Woman's Awakening In Egypt: Culture, Society, and the Press*. New Haven, Conn.: Yale University Press.

Al Bayoumy Ghanem, Ibrahim. 1999. *Al Awqaf Wa Al Syassa Fi Misr* [The Religious Endowments and Politics in Egypt]. Cairo: Dar Al Shorouk.

Brand, Laurie A. 1998. *Women, the State, and Political Liberalization: Middle Eastern and North African Experiences*. New York: Columbia University Press.

Emara, Mohammad. 1972. *Mohammad Abdou: Al A'amal Al Kamila* [Muhammad Abdou: The Full Works]. Beirut: Al Moassassa Al Arabaiya Li Alnashr.

Al Ghazali, Mohamed. 1989. *Al-Sunna Al-Nabawey ya bayn Ahl Al-Fiqh Wa Ahl Al-Hadith* [The Tradition of the Prophet between Jurisprudence and Hadith Scholars]. Cairo: Dar Al-Shorouk. Al Arabaiya Li Alnashr.

———. 1990. *Kadaya Al-Maraa Bayn Al Taqaleed Al Rakedda Wa Al Wafeda* [The Issues of Women between Sterile Traditions and Alien Currents]. Cairo: Dar Al-Shorouk.

Al-Ghazali, Zainab .1994a. *Nazarat Fi Kitab-illah* [Looking into the Revelation of Allah]. Cairo: Dar Al-Shorouk, 1.

———. 1994b. *Return of the Pharaoh: Memoir in Nasser's Prison*, trans. Mokrane Guezzou. Leicester: The Islamic Foundation.

Al Gohary, Mahmoud M., and Abdel Hakeem Khayaal. 1989. *Al Akhawat Al Muslimat Wa Benaa Al Usra Al Quraneyya* [The Muslim Sisters and the Establishment of the Quranic Family]. Cairo: Dar Al Wafaa.

Haddad, Yvonne. 1998. "Islam and Gender: Dilemmas in the Changing Arab World." In *Islam, Gender and Social Change*, eds. Yvonne Y. Haddad and John Esposito. Oxford: Oxford University Press.

Halim, Abdul, and Abou Shukka, Tahrir. 1995. *Al Maraa Fi 'Asr Al Risala* [The Liberation of Women at the Time of Early Islam].Cairo: Dar Al Qalam.

Hamed Abu Zeid, Nasr. 1993. "Al Maraa: Al Buud Al Ghaiib Fi Al Khitaab Al Dini" [Women: the Abstract Aspect in Religious Discourse]. *Cairo Journal*. No. 123, February [in Arabic].

Hatem, Mervat. 1998. "Secularist and Islamist Discourses on Modernity in Egypt and the Evolution of the Postcolonial Nation-State." In *Islam, Gender and Social Change*, ed. Yvonne Y. Haddad and John Esposito. Oxford: Oxford University Press.

Hijab, Nadia. 1998. "Islam, and Social Change, and the Reality of Arab Women's Lives." In *Islam, Gender and Social Change*, ed. Yvonne Y. Haddad and John Esposito. Oxford: Oxford University Press.

Karam, Azza. 1998. *Women, Islamism and the State: Contemporary Feminisms in Egypt*. London: Macmillan.

Al Masri, Sanaa. 1989. *Khalf Al Hijab* [Behind the Veil]. Cairo: Dar Sinai. [in Arabic]

Mernissi, Fatima. 1994. *Women and Islam: A Historical and Theological Enquiry*. trans. Mary Jo Lakeland. Oxford: Blackwell.

New Woman Research Center. 1994. *Preparatory Research Papers for the ICPD*. Cairo: New Woman Research Centre.

New Woman Research Center Report. 1999. "The Case of Egypt." In *Women in Arab NGOs*, eds. Emily Nafaà, Amina Lemrini, Soha Hendeyya, Fouad Al Sallahy, Maymouna Al Sabbah). Cairo: The Arab Network of NGOs.

Al Qaradawi, Yusuf. 1990. "Introduction." In Aabdul Halim Abou Shukka, *Tahrir AlMaraa Fi Aasr Al Risala* [Liberation of Women at the Time of Early Islam].Cairo: Dar Al-Qalam.

———. 1991. *Awlaweyyat Al Haraka Al Islameyya Fi Al Marala Al Kadema* [The Priorities of the Islamic Movement in the Coming Era]. Beirut: Dar Al Resalah.

———. 1992. *Muslimat Al Ghadd* [Muslim Women of Tomorrow]. Cairo: Dar Al Wafaa.

Resalat Al Islam (formal magazine of Al Azhar). 1952. 4:3 July.

Singermann, Diane. 1995. *Avenues of Participation: Families, Politics and Networks in Urban Quarter of Cairo*. Princeton, N.J.: Princeton University Press.

Singermann, Diane, and Homa Hoodfar. 1996. *Development, Change and Gender in Cairo: A View from the Household*. Indianapolis: Indiana University Press.

Stowasser, Barbara. 1998. "Gender Issues and Contemporary Quran Interpretation." In *Islam, Gender and Social Change*, ed. Yvonne Y. Haddad and John Esposito. Oxford: Oxford University Press.

Women and Memory Forum—1998–1999. *Conference Proceedings*. Cairo: Women and Memory Forum.

APPENDIX

Because the history of both Islam and Christianity is important to understanding the globalization issues in this book, we offer a brief thumbnail sketch of the expansion of both religions over the past 2000 years.

A Brief Summary of Catholic and Muslim Expansion

In many ways, the history of the Muslim and the Christian religions can themselves be considered a story of a kind of ideological and cultural globalization. Christianity has its origins in Judaism. Since then, it has spread to all continents in the world, with particular strength in Europe and Latin America. The Muslim religion originated over six hundred years later, also in the Middle East. It, too, has spread all over the globe, with particular strength in the "Muslim Crescent," which includes North Africa, the Middle East, Central Asia, Pakistan, Bangladesh, India, Indonesia, and other parts of Southeast Asia. The strength and global distribution of those identifying with the two religions today reflects historical patterns of conquest as well as subsequent population demographics. In 1999, Catholics numbered approximately 1.004 billion, concentrated primarily in Latin America (454.1 million) and in Europe (285.7 million), with significant numbers also in Africa (117.2 million), Asia (108.4 million), and North America (70.6 million). In mid-1999, Muslims numbered 1.155 billion and were most highly concentrated in Asia (807 million) and Africa (310.5 million), with significant numbers also in Europe (31.2 million), and fewer in North America (4.4 million) and Latin America (1.6 million) (*World Almanac and Book of Facts 2001*, 692).

Though interconnected by religious contacts and some common cultural values, extensive diversity existed and continues to exist in both the Muslim and the Catholic worlds. Both religions have been established in other societies through syncretism or interplay between the dominant Islamic or Catholic political power of the time, the existing pre-Islamic or pre-Christian religious and communal institutions, local customs, and cultural traditions. This historical and cultural interaction has created different types of Islamic and Catholic societies across time. For instance, the Islamic jurists in their day-to-day administration of justice in the various regions conquered by Muslims had to interact with the practices of new peoples, yielding a law that merges Quranic precepts with local practice. Hence, the evolution of Islamic law, known as the *sharià*, has evolved differently in North Africa than it has in Iraq, resulting in four schools of law among Sunni Muslims, the mainstream of Islam, and other variations among dissenting communities such as the Shià (Bodman 1998). Similarly, Catholic missionaries varied among themselves not only in their own origins and practices, but they invariably incorporated elements of native belief, ritual, folklore, folk heroes, and heroines into their ceremonies and practices. Although officially united under the hierarchical organization of the Roman Catholic Church headed by the Pope, in fact, the practices and beliefs of those who identify themselves as Catholics are extraordinarily diverse.

A BRIEF SURVEY OF CATHOLIC EXPANSION

The history of Catholicism and that of Christianity can be considered the same until 1054, the date when the eastern and the western segments of Christendom split from one another. As mentioned previously, Christianity has its origins in Judaism. Jesus himself was a Jew who lived in what is now Israel under the rule of the Roman Empire. Initially, the Roman imperial officials considered the followers of Jesus nothing more than a Jewish sect. After Jesus' time, the apostles and followers of Jesus spread the monotheistic Christian message throughout the Roman Empire, often being persecuted and killed by those unwilling to have their pagan beliefs and practices challenged. In the early days, this organizing took place in the regional centers of Rome, Jerusalem, Antioch, Alexandria, and Constantinople, where church patriarchs developed liturgy and theology and influenced churches in the surrounding areas. Not until the Edict of Milan in 313 CE did the church obtain legal status under Roman law (Carmody and Carmody 1990, 38). By the time that Constantine came to power as Emperor of Rome, the church was established not only in Italy, Asia Minor, and Greece, but also in North Africa, Gaul, Germany, Spain, and Britain (Straus 1987, 35). Constantine, himself, although he did not convert until his final illness, had a personal predisposition toward Christianity. At the beginning of his reign, he observed all the pagan rituals, but later he gradually placed restrictions on pagan practices and endorsed and displayed Christian symbols. As a ruler, he integrated the Christian religion with the interests of the state in a variety of ways. In 324, he moved the capital of the Empire to Byzantium, intervened in church affairs when he deemed it appropriate, built lavish church structures in Byzantium, Rome, and Jerusalem, granted important privileges to Christian priests, and changed Roman law to make it more in conformity with Christian beliefs (Straus 1987, 50–51).

With the fall of Rome, the Christian popes adapted by changing the mission of the church to that of converting the barbarians to Christianity and building a new Christian society. Much of what had been the western part of the Roman Empire fell into disarray among warring Germanic tribes, not to be reunified until Charlemagne managed to conquer an area stretching from the Pyranees to the Elbe River and from the Atlantic to southern Italy. The Pope, on Christmas Day in Rome in 800 CE, crowned Charlemagne as Emperor of the Romans, "crowned of God," once again consolidating the church and the state in the West. Charlemagne ordered the adoption of the Roman liturgy and canon law throughout his entire kingdom.

In the sixth and seventh centuries, the Franks, Lombards, Angles, Saxons, and Visigoths converted to Christianity. In the seventh and eighth centuries, the Frisian and Hessian Germans became Christian, and in the ninth, tenth, and eleventh centuries, northern Germans, western Slavs, and Russians converted. By the thirteenth and fourteenth centuries, Christianity had become the major religion in the Baltic region (Bokenkotter 1977, 138).

The schism between eastern and the western Christianity began to brew as early as 691, when Emperor Justinian II passed laws that were not in keeping with Roman practice (such as permitting priests to marry) (Carmody and Carmody 1990, 47). Thereafter, eastern and western popes and patriarchs had many disagreements. Pope Sergius rejected Justinian's laws as well as the claim that the eastern patriarch of Constantinople was the equal of the Pope. Perhaps more offensive was the action of Pope Nicholas (858–867) in nullifying the eastern emperor's appointment of Photius as patriarch of Constantinople. A variety of power disputes such as these and others led to the ultimate schism between the East and the West when, in 1054, both sides engaged in a series of mutual excommunications, thereby separating Christendom into two separate branches.

In the last part of the fifteenth century after the Ottoman Turks conquered Constantinople in 1453, the Roman Catholic Church was the preeminent religious institution and the Christian faith as interpreted by Roman popes was the foundation of public and private behavior (Bokenkotter 1977, 204). The church itself, however, was in disarray. The Roman Catholic Church had survived a split within itself in the fourteenth century (The Great Schism), whereby for forty years The Holy

Roman Emperor, England, the Netherlands, Castille, Hungary, Poland, and Portugal stood behind Pope Urban, ensconced in Rome, while France, Scotland, Luxembourg, and Austria followed twenty bishops to elect a new pope, Robert of Geneva, who became Clement VII and established himself in Avignon. After forty years of warring, bickering, and maneuvering, cardinals and churchmen finally met in 1409, declared the two existing popes to be heretics, and elected a new pope (Bokenkotter 1977, 180–184).

In mid-fifteenth century, the schism was over; however, its impact remained. The warring popes had shaken the confidence of many in the church, not only at the level of the papacy but throughout the organization of the church. Church officials crassly sold church offices, often to more than one man. The selling of indulgences and absenteeism were common. The lower clergy were also corrupt, uneducated, superstitious, and without discipline. Into this environment came Martin Luther, a German monk and university scholar, bringing a new view of righteousness and salvation as not something to be attained through good works but, rather, something gratuitously granted by God through Christ, something which the individual can attain through faith. More upsetting and revolutionary than Luther's theology, however, were his attacks on the church's system of indulgences—the selling of salvation for oneself (or for souls in purgatory) in exchange for good works or the purchase of good works. With an escalating crescendo of political and theological activity, the backing of Frederick of Saxony, and the organization of Protestant princes into the Schmalkald League in 1531, by 1555, the split between the Catholic and the Protestant forces was legally recognized. This initially involved only Germany but soon spread throughout Europe. By the end, over half of Europe no longer looked to Rome but had instead converted to one of many varieties of Protestantism.

While the Protestant Reformation was diminishing Roman Catholic influence in Europe during the sixteenth century, Portuguese and Spanish explorers were expanding the influence of Catholicism in Latin America, Africa, and Asia. Church and state were often united on these expeditions as the Spanish and Portuguese monarchies accepted the charge of the Holy See to defend, promote, and maintain the Roman Catholic religion in all lands conquered by their respective colonializing efforts (de la Costa and Schumacher 1978). As early as thirteenth and fourteenth centuries, the Franciscans established missions in China, which were followed by the Jesuits and other Roman missions from the sixteenth to the end of the eighteenth centuries. In 1498, Vasco da Gama sailed around the Cape of Good Hope to arrive in India, bringing with him priests to establish Catholic missions supported by Portuguese kings (Robinson 1915, 68).

Portuguese monks also reached Goa, Ceylon, and Burma as well as Brazil, the Congo, and South Africa in the sixteenth century (Robinson 1915, 145–59, 256–77). The Spanish also sent priests from various Catholic religious orders, the Augustinians, the Franciscans, the Dominicans, and the Jesuits along on their colonizing missions to the Philippines, Central America, and South America in the sixteenth century. The missionaries were charged with converting the conquered subjects to Christianity.

A BRIEF SURVEY OF ISLAMIC EXPANSION

Islam emerged in the early seventh century in the Arab peninsula within a tribal structure emphasizing blood kinship and widely varied customs regarding gender relations that included matrilineal as well as patriarchal marriage and family structures. As argued by Muslim feminists such as Mernissi, Ahmed, Hassan, and Al-Hibri, the intention or desire of Muhammad (Prophet of Islam) and the overall message of the Quran might have been gender egalitarian. Yet, the new Islamic society was the interaction of an ideal with the reality of customs and institutions already deeply and predominantly embedded with patriarchy and class hierarchy. After Mohammed's death, Islam consolidated into an organized state power and expanded into the territories like the Sasanian imperial center. This brought the new Muslim communities in contact with well-established customs of concubinage, veiling, and seclusion for upper-class and elite women. It also further compromised egalitarian ideals and reinforced the adoption of patriarchal practices, thereby shaping the orientation of Islamic tradition (Ahmed 1992; Bodman 1998).

The spread of Islam continued from the Middle East to Inner Asia and from Central Asia, China, and Afghanistan to India and from various parts of India and Arabia to the Malay peninsula and the Indonesian archipelago in the late thirteenth, fourteenth, and fifteenth centuries. While in the Middle East and Indian subcontinent, Islam was established by Arab or Turkish conquests and Muslim regimes were founded by these new elites, in Southeast Asia, traveling merchants and Sufis introduced Islam to existing regimes that often were consolidated by conversion to Islam. Historical distinctions have affected the religious orientation of each Muslim region. For instance, the continuity of native elites in Southeast Asia has given strong expression to the pre-Islamic (Java) component of Islamic civilization in this region (Lapidus 1988, 467).

Under the first two caliphs (successor to the Prophet of Islam), Iraq, Palestine, Damascus, Egypt, and most of Persia were conquered in the 630s and 640s. Under the newly established Islamic state of the Umayyad dynasty, Muslim rule extended to the Atlantic in 691. In 711, Muslim armies reached the borders of Byzantium and entered Transoxiana, conquering Sind, the lower Indus Valley (now the southern part of Pakistan). The last Umayyad fled to Andalusia and founded a kingdom in 756. This Spanish-Umayyad kingdom continued until 1031, witnessing a unique cultural cooperation between Muslims, Christians, and Jews. The only Muslim kingdom in this region that was able to survive until 1492 was that of the Banu Ahmar; the Alhambra was the last work of Arabic art in Spain (Schimmel 1992, 22).

The worldwide diffusion of Islam occurred, for the most part, between the tenth and nineteenth centuries. Following the breakdown of the Arab origin Muslim dynasties of Umayyad and Abbasid, it was mostly the Turkish groups from Central Asia and Iran that formed important Muslim empires in the Near East. The victory of Seljuks in 1071 over the Byzantines opened the way into Anatolia for Muslims and the subsequent developments of Islamic art, the grand mosques, madrassahs, and mausoleums in various cities of what is now Turkey. Following the Mongol onslaught that began in Central Asia in 1220, much of the flourishing Islamic civilization was decimated and the Seljuk Empire disintegrated. Out of the numerous independent principalities that subsequently arose, the family of the Ottomans emerged as leaders and established the Ottoman Empire. Large parts of the Balkans came under Ottoman rule in 1389 (after the battle of Kosova in Yugoslavia) and later Constantinople (Istanbul), conquered in 1453, became the heart of that Empire (Schimmel 1992, 24). Some of the Mongol rulers converted to Islam; Timur (Tamerlane) for instance, reached northwestern India as far as Delhi in 1398 paving the way for the formation of the Mughal Empire, which was founded in 1526 and lasted for more than three centuries. Following an increasing expansion of the British East India Company beginning in 1757 and an abortive military revolt, the British Crown took over most parts of India, ending the last vestiges of the Mughal Empire.

The Ottoman Empire extended its power not only over other parts of the Muslim world but also expanded the influence of Islam farther than before to the West, laying siege to Vienna in 1529. After several centuries of rule by various dynasties from the Shià-Ismaili Fatimid to the Sunnite Kurdish dynasty of Ayyubids and the Kurdish-Turkish mix of Mamluk sultans in Egypt, Syria, and the holy cities of Mecca and Medina, Ottoman troops took them over in 1516. To the east of Ottoman Empire, however, the Persian Safavid dynasty blocked further expansion of the Ottomans by placing a Shiite wedge between the Sunni Ottomans in the West and the emerging, predominantly Sunni Mughal empire in the east (India). This indicates the historical background of the religiopolitical situation in contemporary Middle East, especially Shiite Iran.

Muslim influence was at its height in the late sixteenth century. Although the Islamic empires declined thereafter, Islam has maintained political strongholds in the Middle East and Asia, and its cultural penetration remains in most parts of the old Islamic empires.

REFERENCES

Ahmed, Leila. 1992. *Women and Gender in Islam*. New Haven, Conn.: Yale University Press.
Bodman, Herbert. 1998. "Introduction." In *Women in Muslim Societies: Diversity Within Unity*, eds. H. Bodman and N. Tohidi. Boulder, Col.: Lynne Rienner.
Bokenkotter, Thomas. 1977. *A Concise History of the Catholic Church*. New York: Doubleday.
Carmody, Denise L. and John T. Carmody. 1990. *Roman Catholicism: An Introduction*. New York: MacMillan.
de la Costa, H., and John N. Schumacher. 1978. *Church and State: The Philippine Experience: Loyola Papers 3*. Manila: Loyola School of Theology.
Lapidus, Ira M. 1988. *A History of Islamic Societies*. Cambridge, U.K.: Cambridge University Press.
Robinson, Charles Henry. 1915. *History of Christian Missions*. Edinburgh, Scotland: T&T Clark.
Schimmel, Annemarie. 1992. *Islam: An Introduction*. Albany: State University of New York Press.
Straus, Barrie Ruth. 1987. *The Catholic Church*. New York: Hippocrene Books.
World Almanac and Book of Facts 2001. 2001. Mahwah, N.J.: World Almanac Education Group.

CONTRIBUTORS

JANE H. BAYES, PH.D.

Jane Bayes is a Professor of Political Science and Director of the Institute of Gender, Globalization, and Democracy at California State University, Northridge. She is a co-editor and contributor to *Globalization, Gender, and Democratization* (2001). Other publications which she has authored, edited, or co-edited include *Ideologies and Interest Group Politics: The United States in a Global Economy, Minority Politics and Ideologies in the United States, Women and Public Administration, International Perspectives,* and *Comparable Worth, Pay Equity, and Public Policy.* She is the recipient of the SWAPA Award of the American Society for Public Administration for outstanding research on women. She participated in the Fourth United Nations Congress on Women held in Beijing in 1995 and in the Beijing Plus Five meetings in New York in 2000.

NAJMA CHOWDHURY, PH.D.

Najma Chowdhury is a Professor of Political Science and Chair of the recently established Women's Studies Department at the University of Dhaka in Bangladesh. She is the co-editor, with Professor Barbara Nelson, of the prize-winning volume, *Women and Politics Worldwide,* a comprehensive survey of women and politics in 43 nations. Her research and writing interests focus on women's participation in politics and gender related development issues in her country. She chaired the largest NGO coalition during 1994–95 which undertook extensive mobilization and advocacy, preparatory to the Fourth World Conference on Women. She was also involved with the regional preparatory processes and was an official delegate of the Bangladeshi government to the United Nations Fourth World Conference on Women in Beijing in 1995. She served as a minister in the Caretaker government in Bangladesh during 1996.

HEBA RAUF EZZAT, M. A.

Heba Rauf Ezzat was born in Cairo, Egypt in 1965. She is a wife and the mother of three children. Currently, she is finishing her Ph.D. in political theory at Cairo University with a thesis on "The Concept of Citizenship in Current Anglo-American Liberal Thought." She was a Visiting Researcher at the University of Westminster in the United Kingdom from 1995–96 and at the Oxford Center for Islamic Studies in the United Kingdom in 1998. She is a writer and free-lance journalist who has published many academic articles and studies both in Arabic and English on Islamic political theory, moral philosophy, women's rights and human rights in Islam, and the deconstruction of secularism. She is the author of two books in Arabic: *Women and Politics: An Islamic Perspective* (1995), and *Women, Religion and Ethics* (Debate with Nawal Saadawi) (2001).

YVONNE GALLIGAN, PH.D.

Yvonne Galligan is a Reader in Politics and Director of the Centre for Advancement of Women in Politics at Queens University Belfast, Northern Ireland. She is author of *Women and Politics in Contemporary Ireland* (1999) and is a co-editor and contributor to *Contesting Politics: Women in Ireland, North and South* (2000). She has authored numerous articles and book chapters on women in politics in Ireland. She is vice-chair of a Council of Europe expert group on women in decision-making and has advised the Irish government on implementing the Beijing Commitments and Platform for Action.

AYŞE GÜNEŞ-AYATA, PH.D.

Ayşe Güneş-Ayata is an Associate Dean and Professor of Political Science and Sociology at Middle East Technical University in Ankara, Turkey. In addition to teaching and writing, Professor Ayata has been active in the formal and informal politics of her country. She was a candidate in the 1997 parliamentary elections in Turkey that resulted in the prominence of one of her rivals, the Islamic Welfare Party.

LAURA GUZMÁN STEIN, PH.D.

Laura Guzmán Stein teaches and does research at the Center for Research on Women's Studies University of Costa Rica. As an official delegate to Beijing from Costa Rica, Professor Guzmán-Stein was personally involved in the pre-Beijing regional United Nations Latin American conferences as well as in the official conference in Beijing. She is extremely knowledgeable concerning the politics of the Catholic Church and Catholic organizations in Costa Rica and throughout Latin America, especially as they played themselves out in the pre-Beijing meetings and the official Beijing meeting.

MERHANGUIZ KAR, ATTORNEY

Merhanguiz Kar is a practicing lawyer in Iran who specializes in women's law. She is well known internationally for her writing and speaking. In 2000, both Italy and Canada honored her as International Woman of the Year. Most recently she has been arrested and sentenced to four years in prison in Iran for attending an international meeting in Berlin in 2000 where she criticized the policies and laws of the Islamic Republic of Iran for the ways that they violate women's human rights. She is currently appealing the sentence. Amnesty International has waged a campaign on her behalf.

SUSAN MARIE MAHONEY, PH.D.

As Chair of the M. A. Program in Feminist Spirituality at Immaculate Heart College Center, Susan Marie Maloney, SNJM, Ph.D., initiated the cross-cultural Women Working for Solidarity project which brings together women from diverse spiritualities and backgrounds to overcome violence and racism. Her writings include publications in the *Los Angeles Times* and New Blackfriars (Oxford). As a board member of Women, Development and Earth Foundation on Cebu Island in the Philippines, she does international solidarity work. Currently she is a visiting scholar at California State University, Northridge with the Institute for Gender, Globalization, and Democracy. She is a member of the California Province of the Sisters of the Holy Names of Jesus and Mary (SNJM).

NUALA RYAN

Nuala Ryan is a postgraduate student in the Department of Politics, University College Dublin. She has a particular interest in feminist theology and is involved in a number of discussion groups on the subject. Before turning to academia, Nuala was involved in the business world as company owner and director. She also has a long history of involvement in the Irish feminist movement, serving on the executive of the National Women's Council of Ireland. She is now on the executive board of the European Women's Lobby.

NAYEREH TOHIDI, PH.D.

Nayereh Tohidi is an Associate Professor of Women's Studies at California State University, Northridge and a Research Fellow at the UCLA Center for Near Eastern Studies. Educated in Iran and the United States, Tohidi is the author of numerous articles in both English and Farsi about women in Iran, Azerbaijan, and Central Asia. She has co-edited and contributed to the book *Women in Muslim Societies: Diversity within Unity* and has authored a book on *Feminism, Democracy and Islamism in Iran* (in Persian). She is the recipient of a Harvard University Visiting Lecturer and Research Associate position, a Stanford University Post-Doctoral fellowship, and research grants from Fulbright and the Woodrow Wilson Center. She has consulted for United Nations agencies such as UNICEF and UNDP. She participated in the United Nations World Conferences on Women in Nairobi (1985) and in Beijing (1995).

CELIA VALIENTE, PH.D.

Celia Valiente is lecturer at the Department of Political Science and Sociology of the Universidad Carlos III de Madrid (Spain). Her main research interests are in public policies and social movements in Spain, with a particular focus on gender. Her publications include *Políticas Públicas de Género en Perspectiva Comparada* (Madrid: Universidad Autónoma de Madrid).

INDEX